RECOVERED MEMORIES OF CHILD SEXUAL ABUSE

Publication Number 1098

AMERICAN SERIES
IN
BEHAVIORAL SCIENCE AND LAW

Edited by

RALPH SLOVENKO, B.E., LL.B., M.A., Ph.D.

Professor of Law and Psychiatry
Wayne State University
Law School
Detroit, Michigan

RECOVERED MEMORIES OF CHILD SEXUAL ABUSE

Psychological, Social, and Legal Perspectives on a
Contemporary Mental Health Controversy

Edited by

SHEILA TAUB, J.D.

Charles C Thomas
PUBLISHER • LTD.
SPRINGFIELD • ILLINOIS • U.S.A.

Published and Distributed Throughout the World by
CHARLES C THOMAS • PUBLISHER, LTD.
2600 South First Street
Springfield, Illinois 62704

© *1999 by* CHARLES C THOMAS • PUBLISHER, LTD.

ISBN 0-398-07005-9
ISBN 0-398-07006-7

Library of Congress Catalog Card Number: 99-37927

With THOMAS BOOKS *careful attention is given to all details of manufacturing and design. It is the Publisher's desire to present books that are satisfactory as to their physical qualities and artistic possibilities and appropriate for their particular use.* THOMAS BOOKS *will be true to those laws of quality that assure a good name and good will.*

Printed in the United States of America
TH-R-3

Library of Congress Cataloging-in-Publication Data

Recovered memories of child sexual abuse: psychological, social, and
legal perspectives on a contemporary mental health controversy /
edited by Sheila Taub.
   p.   cm. -- (American series in behavioral science and law)
"Publications number 1098"--Ser. t.p.
Includes bibliographical references and index.
ISBN 0-398-07005-9 (cloth). -- ISBN 0-398-07006-7 (paper)
   1. False memory syndrom. 2.Adult child sexual abuse victims.
3. Recovered memory. I. Taub, Sheila. II. Series.
RC455.2.F35428   1999
616.85'8369--dc21   99-37927
                                                    CIP

CONTRIBUTORS

Pamela Freyd M.S. Ph.D. is the Executive Director of the False Memory Syndrome Foundation and a Research Associate at the Institute for Research in Cognitive Science at the University of Pennsylvania. She received her Doctorate in Education from the University of Pennsylvania in 1981 and has had extensive teaching experience at every level. She has been a principal investigator on two National Science Foundation grants that focused on science education. Under Dr. Freyd's leadership, the False Memory Syndrome Foundation has attracted many distinguished professionals to serve on its Board of Directors and has played a key role in increasing public awareness of the recovered memory phenomenon.

D. Stephen Lindsay Ph.D. is professor of psychology at the University of Victoria in British Columbia. Much of his research since 1985 has focused on memory errors and memory illusions. He is the author or coauthor of more than a dozen journal articles on the recovered-memories controversy. Professor Lindsay codirected (with Professor J. Don Read of the University of Lethbridge) the 1996 NATO-sponsored Advanced Studies Institute on the recovered-memories controversy, which brought together 96 world-renowned experts with a range of perspectives on this topic. Professors Read and Lindsay coedited a book based on the conference, titled *Recollections of Trauma: Scientific Research and Clinical Practice* (1997). Professor Lindsay received his Ph.D. in cognitive psychology in 1987 from Princeton University, where he studied under Marcia K. Johnson.

Anita Lipton B.S. is the coordinator of legal research for the False Memory Syndrome Foundation. She has been tracking all of the legal developments in the area of recovered memories since 1992, the year the Foundation was organized. Although Ms. Lipton is not a lawyer but a teacher of mathematics by training, her work with the Foundation has given her a thorough knowledge of this particular area of the law.

Mark Pendergrast M.L.S. is an independent scholar and investigative journalist whose book, *Victims of Memory: Incest Accusations and Shattered Lives*, has been widely hailed as the most comprehensive treatment of the debate over recovered memories. Pendergrast first became involved in this issue through tragic personal experience—he lost all contact with both of his daughters because of recovered memory therapy. His forthcoming book, *Uncommon Grounds*, is a social and business history of coffee.

David K. Sakheim Ph.D. is a nationally known expert on the treatment of the dissociative disorders and other trauma-related syndromes. He has lectured, consulted, and published widely in this field. He edited *Out of Darkness: Exploring Satanism and Ritual Abuse*, the first book that attempted to present a balanced view of the topic of ritual abuse. Dr. Sakheim has been treating offenders and abuse survivors for over fifteen years. He is currently in private practice in Branford,

Connecticut. Dr. Sakheim graduated from Brown University and obtained his doctorate in clinical psychology from the State University of New York in Albany.

Jonathan Schooler M.S.Ph.D is an associate professor of psychology at the University of Pittsburgh and a research scientist at the University of Pittsburgh's Learning Research and Development Center. He received his B.A. from Hamilton College and his M.S. and Ph.D. from the University of Washington. Professor Schooler has had a long-standing interest in the mechanisms that lead to memory distortions, including the impact of postevent suggestion and the consequences of verbalizing nonverbal memories. In some of his recent work, he has attempted to evaluate the accuracy of what he refers to as "discovered" (rather than "recovered") memories of abuse.

Jerome L. Singer Ph.D is a professor of psychology and child study and director of the Graduate Studies Program in Psychology at Yale University. He maintained a private practice as a clinical psychologist for more than four decades. He obtained his B.A. in psychology from the College of the City of New York and his Ph.D. in psychology from the University of Pennsylvania and did postdoctoral work at the William Alanson White Institute of Psychiatry. Dr. Singer's research interests have included the effect of televised violence on social behavior, creativity and imagination, and conscious and unconscious mental processes. He is the author or coauthor of more than 200 articles and 17 books. He is also the editor of *Repression and Dissociation: Implications for Personality Psychopathology and Health* (1990).

Arthur Taub, M.D., M.S., Ph.D., is the founder and president of the Institute for Pain Research. He is a clinical professor at Yale University School of Medicine. He obtained his medical degree from the Yale University School of Medicine and advanced degrees in biophysics and neurophysiology from the Massachusetts Institute of Technology. Dr. Taub is a neurologist and neuroscientist in private practice in New Haven. His practice includes the diagnosis and treatment of chronic, intractable pain; cognitive neurology; and forensics.

Sheila Taub, J.D., is a professor of law at the Quinnipiac College School of Law in Hamden, Connecticut. She has taught a wide array of courses, including courses in health law, psychiatry and law, and bioethics. She is the author of *Law and Mental Health Professionals: Connecticut* and has also published numerous journal articles in the area of health law. She obtained her undergraduate degree from Brandeis University and her law degree from the Harvard Law School.

PREFACE

This book presents the views of seven scientists, clinicians, and scholars who have studied the controversial issue of recovered memories of sexual abuse from a variety of perspectives. They discuss the history of the recovered memory phenomenon, the social factors that contributed to its development, the issues that face clinicians whose patients report memories of past abuse, the data obtained from scientific studies on memory and memory distortion, and the ways in which the legal system has dealt with claims based on recovered memories of abuse.

The media typically portray the controversy over recovered memories as a battle between two camps, one claiming that all recovered memories are true and the other claiming that all are false. The scientists and clinicians who have contributed chapters to this book paint a more nuanced picture. They all agree that human memory is subject to a great many influences that may affect its accuracy and that a memory, whether recently recovered or always maintained, may be substantially accurate, partially accurate, or wholly inaccurate. At present, there is no way to establish the accuracy of a particular memory in the absence of external corroboration or disproof.

The complexity of memory presents a difficult problem for the courts, which have been called upon to resolve numerous cases, both civil and criminal, that originated with memories of abuse alleged to have been only recently recovered. The introduction by Professor Sheila Taub, editor of this book, discusses how recent changes in the law with respect to scientific and expert testimony may affect the resolution of these issues in the future.

RALPH SLOVENKO
Editor, *American Series in Behavioral Science and Law*

CONTENTS

RECOVERED MEMORIES OF CHILD SEXUAL ABUSE

INTRODUCTION

SHEILA TAUB

This book grew out of a conference that took place in New Haven, Connecticut, on November 14, 1997, titled "Recovered Memories of Child Sexual Abuse: Legal, Scientific and Clinical Issues." Seven of the eight speakers at that conference contributed chapters to this book based largely on their conference presentations, updated where necessary to include later developments.

I became interested in recovered memories of child sexual abuse because of my long-standing interest in how the law deals with novel scientific and medical issues. The subject of recovered memories of abuse presented me with a fascinating case study. A new phenomenon had arisen in the 1980s: adults began suing their parents and others for sexual abuse that had allegedly occurred decades before but had been remembered only recently. The law had responded with unusual rapidity by extending statutes of limitations for lawsuits based on recovered memories, yet scientists and clinicians were sharply divided about the accuracy of these recovered memories. How could all of these things be explained?

After doing extensive research in both the legal and psychological literature for an article on the subject,[1] I conceived the idea of organizing a conference that would bring together nationally known professionals with different views on this highly controversial topic. It was my (somewhat naive) hope that these professionals would find some common ground on which all could agree. I did not anticipate the difficulties I would encounter in recruiting speakers at opposite ends of the spectrum on this incendiary issue. Nevertheless, the eight speakers who made up the final roster provided an excellent overview of the subject from a variety of perspectives. At the end of the day, all of them agreed that the conference had been a worthwhile experience and that a book based on the conference would be a valuable contribution to the debate over recovered memories of abuse.

The conference was sponsored by the Institute for Pain Research, a private charitable foundation organized by Arthur Taub, M.D., Ph.D., a physician who specializes in the treatment of chronic pain. In his introduction, Dr.

---

1. Taub, S. (1996). The legal treatment of recovered memories of child sexual abuse. *Journal of Legal Medicine, 17*, 183-214.

Taub explains the connection between his professional interest in pain and his support for this conference.

In Chapter 1, Pamela Freyd, Executive Director of the False Memory Syndrome Foundation (FMSF), describes the events that led to the formation of the Foundation in 1992. She paints a vivid picture of the consternation of middle-aged and elderly parents who found themselves suddenly accused by their adult children of sexually abusing them in years past. Some of these parents were named defendants in lawsuits made possible by the fact that many states had recently extended their statutes of limitations for claims based on childhood sexual abuse. Although some parents were exonerated by juries, others either were found guilty of the abuse or agreed to settle the claims because they feared that an adverse jury verdict could wipe out their life's savings.

Dr. Freyd summarizes the data obtained from FMSF surveys of accused parents, "retractors" (i.e., former accusers who came to believe their accusations were erroneous), and others. These surveys have yielded invaluable information on the demographics of accusers and accused, the nature of the accusations, and the circumstances under which the accusations came about. The survey data strongly suggest that we are dealing with a phenomenon that began in the mid-1980s, peaked in the early 1990s, and had declined rather sharply by the late 1990s. Dr. Freyd interprets this as being consistent with society going through the various stages of a craze or moral panic. The lack of congruence of the data on recovered memories of abuse with what we know about confirmed child sexual abuse and with what we know about the way memory works also lends support to the theory that many of the "recovered memories" did not reflect actual abuse but were a product of social suggestion.

The FMSF family survey data implicate members of the mental health professions as playing a key role in the development and perpetuation of the recovered memory phenomenon. Many of the accusers had sought therapy for assistance in dealing with relatively mundane problems. Only after undergoing therapy with professionals who viewed childhood sexual trauma as the root cause of all adult problems did they come to believe they had been victims of childhood sexual abuse. The therapy often included techniques, such as hypnosis, that are known to yield "memories" of dubious accuracy.

If what we are dealing with here is in fact a moral panic, where did it come from? What factors in society caused it to arise, suddenly, in the 1980s? Mark Pendergrast, a writer and an accused parent, suggests some answers to these questions in Chapter 2. He compares the search for recovered memories to the search for witches that was prevalent in the 16th and 17th centuries. He notes that the role of "witch," like the role of "incest survivor," conferred certain benefits on the bearer. Pendergrast cites various historical precursors for childhood abuse as a universal explanation for all of women's emotional problems. He sees Freud's use of hypnosis to access repressed memories of childhood sexual experience as similar to what many trauma-search therapists are doing today. He notes that a series of popular books published from the late 1950s to the late 1980s that combined Freud's idea that repressed sexual trauma was at the root of most neuroses with the theory that severe trauma can lead to dissociation and even to multiple personality disorder were required reading for many therapy patients in the 1980s.

Both Freyd and Pendergrast are identified with the position that many, if not most, recovered memories of abuse are artifacts of bad psychotherapy. At the opposite end of the spectrum in the recovered memory debate are those who claim that most recovered memories are accurate representations of historical fact. Many therapists who believe that most recovered memories are substantially accurate now admit, however, that it is possible to create false memories in some individuals under the right conditions. Dr. David Sakheim takes the position, in Chapter 3, that memories of childhood sexual abuse may indeed be repressed and later recovered more or less intact, but that the accuracy of recovered memories may be affected by a host of factors, both intrinsic and extrinsic to the patient. Dr. Sakheim demonstrates how these factors operate through a series of vignettes based on actual cases. He shows that memory is a very complex phenomenon: many trauma memories cannot be neatly categorized as either wholly true or wholly false, and accurate and inaccurate memories may even coexist within the same patient. Dr. Sakheim concludes that patients will be better served by clinicians who appreciate the complexity of memory and its susceptibility to influence by external factors, including the clinician's own beliefs and professional orientation.

In Chapter 4, Dr. Jerome Singer comments on the recovered memory controversy from over four decades of experience as both a clinical and an experimental psychologist. He reviews what is currently known about memory and about repression and dissociation, two concepts that play a central role in the recovered memory debate. Drawing on his own memories of childhood events, he demonstrates the complexity of memory and the difficulty one encounters when one seeks to establish the truth or falsity of memories of early experiences.

Singer reports that as a clinician he had very few patients who reported recovering memories of previously forgotten abuse. He also states that at a 1988 conference on repression and dissociation at Yale University attended by many psychodynamically-oriented clinicians, the subject of recovered memories of child sexual abuse was hardly mentioned. These reports are consistent with the theme sounded by Freyd and Pendergrast, namely, that the intense focus on recovered memories of abuse in the 1980s and early 1990s represented a kind of fad, craze, or moral panic. Dr. Singer notes, however, that many research studies do support the notion of a "repressor personality style." Thus, it is possible that authentic memories of abuse may, in some instances, be repressed and later recovered.

Dr. Singer shows how the findings from his own experimental work involving the stream of consciousness may be relevant to the issue of recovered memories. He takes the position that most recovered memories are neither true nor false but rather are approximations to what occurred in the past. He believes that false memories can also exist, however, and that many of the clinical reports of recovered memories of abuse may be a consequence of therapists' unwitting suggestion and of "patients' desperation to create a new and more meaningful life narrative."

Chapters 5 and 6 were contributed by Drs. Jonathan Schooler and D. Stephen Lindsay, respectively, two experimental psychologists who have done extensive research and published widely on the subject of recovered memories of abuse. Both Schooler and Lindsay believe that some recovered memories may be an accurate reflection of past events but that others are the result of suggestive memory-recovery techniques used by some therapists in attempts to uncover memories of abuse. Both cite laboratory studies that demonstrate the ease with which fictitious memories may be implanted in a significant percentage of research subjects. They note that a sizable proportion of mental health professionals report using techniques in their practice that are similar to (and sometimes much more suggestive than) those used in the laboratory to implant false memories.

One of Dr. Schooler's significant contributions to the recovered memory debate was to locate individuals who had recovered memories of previously forgotten incidents of abuse for which there was strong external corroboration. He describes six such cases in Chapter 5. Schooler points out that several of these cases also demonstrate, however, that individuals can misremember their prior states of forgetting. He discusses the legal implications of this finding.

Schooler and Lindsay agree that researchers have yet to demonstrate the existence of any type of special memory mechanism, such as repression, that is unique to recovered memories of abuse. Both believe that general memory mechanisms can probably account for most cases of accurate recovered memories of abuse, another conclusion that has important legal implications. Schooler also suggests several specific mechanisms that may be at work in the case of some recovered memories of abuse.

Professor Lindsay suggests we think of recovered-memory experiences ("RMEs") as ranging along a continuum from implausible to plausible, with those RMEs at the "implausible" end of the continuum being more likely to reflect illusory memories or false beliefs and those RMEs at the "plausible" end of the continuum being more likely to reflect essentially accurate recollections of long-forgotten abuse. Lindsay offers some tentative criteria for estimating the accuracy of a particular RME.

Lindsay discusses the factors that are likely to produce implausible RMEs and notes that many of these factors are present in what has come to be known as "recovered-memory therapy." He thinks it likely that some individuals are more susceptible to suggestive influence than others. Lindsay also refutes the argument often made by trauma-oriented clinicians that laboratory research, which usually involves the implanting of relatively innocuous memories, has no relevance to the recovery of memories of highly traumatic events such as childhood sexual abuse.

In Chapter 7, Anita Lipton, Coordinator of Legal Research for the False Memory Syndrome Foundation, summarizes the data accumulated by the Foundation's Legal Survey Project, an ongoing, comprehensive study of all materials made available to the Foundation pertaining to lawsuits and legislation that relate to recovered memories of abuse. Lipton analyzed the data contained in 736 American legal cases that were based on recently recovered memories of childhood sexual abuse, of which 633 were civil suits and 103 were criminal actions. She also collated data from malpractice lawsuits brought against mental health care providers, either by former patients or by third parties who were accused of abuse because of allegedly false memories they claim were induced by the therapist's negligence. Lipton presents a statistical breakdown of numerous characteristics of these "repressed memory" claims and discusses some of the legal implications of her findings.

Lipton's statistics indicate that repressed memory claims began to be filed in significant numbers in the mid-1980s, at about the time that many states extended their statutes of limitations for victims of child sexual abuse. The number of new filings of repressed memory claims increased dramatically from 1989 to 1992, reached a peak during the period of 1992-1994, and declined sharply after 1994. Lipton discusses in detail the various state laws that extended the statutes of limitations for lawsuits based on recovered memories of abuse.

Lipton shows how the outcomes of both civil and criminal repressed memory cases have changed over time. Her data indicate that trial judges and juries are growing increasingly skeptical of claims based on recovered memories of abuse. Appellate courts are likewise showing increased skepticism of these claims, with over 70 percent ruling against the plaintiff on the issue of whether to extend the statute of limitations. Several appellate courts have ruled that the theory of memory repression has not been scientifically validated and that testimony based on that theory will therefore be inadmissible in evidence, but a few have reached the opposite conclusion. Lipton points out the weaknesses of the recovered memory evidence presented at the much-publicized trials involving Holly Ramona, Paul Ingram, and George Franklin.

Lipton also presents data on malpractice lawsuits filed against mental health professionals whose patients claimed to have recovered memories of abuse. Although third-party claims (i.e., those brought by persons accused of committing the abuse) must in many jurisdictions overcome the legal hurdle that a therapist is considered to owe no legal duty to anyone but his immediate patient, some of these claims have resulted in plaintiffs' verdicts. Many lawsuits brought by former patients against their therapists for negligently implanting memories of abuse have resulted in out-of-court settlements, some for very large sums of money. Of the small number of jury verdicts in these cases, most favored the plaintiffs.

Although the data collected and analyzed by the False Memory Syndrome Foundation appear to indicate that the recovered memory phenomenon is on the wane, many legal actions against alleged "perpetrators" and against therapists of the accusers are still pending and will be working their way through the courts for some years to come. It is therefore imperative that attorneys and judges understand the scientific issues involved in these cases as well as the legal issues with which they are so closely intertwined. The theory that memories of traumatic events can be lost to one's conscious awareness through a process of "repression," which supposedly differs from the mechanism(s) responsible for the forgetting of nontraumatic events, and can later be returned to consciousness with the details more or less intact by means of various memory recovery techniques, can be and has been subject to scientific testing. The scientific data should be part of the "evidence" in any case based on a claim of recovered memories.

Unlike legal juries, which must return with a definitive verdict in a finite, specified period of time, scientific "juries" often remain out indefinitely, especially on subjects as controversial as this one. Nevertheless, enough data has accumulated (much of it cited in this book) to indicate that allegations of abuse based on memories allegedly repressed for years and only recovered in the course of trauma-oriented psychotherapy should be considered suspect unless there is some objective evidence that the alleged abuse actually occurred.

The testimony of the accuser, who may have undergone hypnosis, sodium amytal interviews, "survivor group" therapy, or other suggestive techniques designed to "recover repressed memories," may be more misleading than enlightening, given the mounting evidence of the ease with which memories for nonexistent events may be implanted in the laboratory. The testimony of the accuser's therapist to the effect that the accuser displays many of the signs and symptoms of someone who was sexually abused in childhood should be admitted only if the therapist can offer reliable scientific evidence that persons with a known history of sexual abuse commonly display these signs and symptoms and that those who have not been so abused rarely do, evidence that does not exist at the present time, to my knowledge.

Testimony of "experts" on the existence or nonexistence of an entity called "repressed memory syndrome" should be subject to the same degree of scrutiny as other kinds of novel scientific evidence, such as DNA-finger-printing or voice-stress analysis. Decades of clinical experience are not a substitute for scientific proof where the stakes are so high for both accuser and accused and where the clinician's insights may be subject to error from a host of factors (see Sakheim, this volume).

In recent years, there has been increasing concern with the proliferation of "junk science" in the courtroom. Juries, sharing the growing scientific illiteracy of the general population, may be inclined to find for plaintiffs who present a picture of having been grievously injured, whether by abuse, by the use of a dangerous product, or by professional negligence, if the plaintiffs' testimony is bolstered by the testimony of one or more "experts" to the effect that the plaintiff was reduced to her present state by some act or agency for which the defendant bears responsibility.

Many judges are ill-equipped to assess the reliability of expert testimony and scientific evidence, having little education or training to prepare them for that task. The manner in which some courts have dealt with recovered memory evidence bears this out. Courts tend to rely on law review articles for the scientific information they need to decide cases (in addition to whatever is presented by counsel and in amicus curiae briefs), but all too often, law review articles present outdated or inaccurate scientific information and a one-sided, politicized view of the issues. Most law review articles from the early 1990s, for example, tended to advocate that courts should be receptive to claims based on recovered memories, some even declaring it antifeminist to question the veracity of recovered memories of abuse. More recent law review articles on the subject tend to accept the notion that at least some recovered memories may be false and that some caution is therefore in order in dealing with these cases.

Courts have displayed much confusion over how to treat evidence pertaining to recovered memories of abuse, in particular, whether it should be classified as "scientific evidence" and subjected to the same scrutiny as other kinds of scientific evidence. Several recent developments in the law of evidence suggest that it should and that courts will be scrutinizing claims based on recovered memories more closely in the future.

For many years, the standard of admissibility for scientific evidence in both state and federal courts was based on a 1923 case (Frye v. United States) involving polygraph evidence, in which the court held that "the thing from which the deduction is made must be sufficiently established to have gained general acceptance in the particular field in which it belongs."[2] Under the *Frye* standard, if a witness qualified as an expert in a particular field and testified that the scientific technique or theory in question had gained general acceptance in that field, the witness's testimony relating to that technique or theory was admissible in evidence, regardless of its content. The finder of fact, usually a jury, decided whether the evidence was worthy of belief and how much credence to give it.

When the Federal Rules of Evidence were enacted in 1974, the continued viability of the *Frye* "general acceptance" test in the federal courts was called into question because the federal rules pertaining to the admission of expert testimony and scientific evidence made no mention of the *Frye* test. In the face of this uncertainty, the lower federal courts reached different conclusions on this issue. Most of them retained the *Frye* test despite criticism that it was vague and excluded valuable scientific evidence that was simply too new to have gained general acceptance. A few federal courts adopted a relevancy criterion based on their interpretation of the Federal Rules of Evidence. Because of this conflict among the federal circuit courts, the United States Supreme Court agreed to decide the issue in the case of *Daubert v. Merrell Dow Pharmaceuticals.*[3]

In *Daubert*, the Supreme Court held, unanimously, that the *Frye* test had been superseded in the federal courts by the Federal Rules of Evidence and that under Rule 702 the trial judge is responsible for ensuring that any scientific testimony or evidence that is admitted is both reliable and relevant. When scientific evidence is proffered, the trial judge must make a preliminary assessment of whether its underlying reasoning or methodology is scientifically valid.

The Supreme Court did not set out a definitive test for the admissibility of scientific evidence in the *Daubert* case but instead listed four factors the trial judge should consider in assessing the evidence: (1) whether the theory or technique in question can be (and has been) tested; (2) whether it has been subjected to peer review and publication; (3) its known or potential error rate and the existence and maintenance of standards controlling its operation; and (4) whether it has attracted widespread acceptance within a relevant scientific community. The Court emphasized that the inquiry is to be a flexible one. Even if relevant, scientific evidence may still be excluded on other grounds. If the judge admits scientific evidence of questionable validity, the Court pointed out, the evidence may still be challenged by cross-examination, presentation of contrary evidence, and careful instruction on the burden of proof.

---

2. Frye v. United States, 293 F. 1013 (D.C. Cir. 1923).

3. Daubert v. Merrell Dow Pharmaceuticals, Inc., 113 S.Ct. 2786 (1993)

The *Daubert* standard is mandatory in all federal courts, but state courts (in which most sexual abuse and recovered memory cases are tried) have the option of applying the *Daubert* standard, the *Frye* standard, or any other standard for the admissibility of scientific evidence or expert testimony. In the years since *Daubert* was decided, some states have explicitly adopted the *Daubert* standard, but others have rejected it, choosing to continue to rely on *Frye*. Even some of the states whose codes of evidence are closely modeled after the federal rules of evidence have chosen not to adopt the *Daubert* standard. One reason for the rejection of *Daubert* in favor of *Frye* is that the *Frye* standard is much easier to administer for judges who are unschooled in science: they need only decide whether the expert witness is qualified to testify by virtue of his training, education, and/or experience in the relevant field. If the witness is deemed qualified, his testimony that a scientific theory or method has achieved general acceptance will generally be admitted, as will evidence based on that theory or method.

With respect to the evidentiary issues in recovered memory cases, the outcome is not necessarily determined by the standard of admissibility of scientific evidence the court chooses to apply. Cases applying either the *Frye* or the *Daubert* standard have come out on both sides of the issue of whether repressed memory syndrome is a valid scientific theory. Both standards are vague enough that it is possible to come out different ways on any given issue, depending on how the trial judge applies the standard. Under *Frye*, the outcome depends on how you define the relevant scientific community: does it include only clinicians who work with trauma patients, for example, or does it also include experimental psychologists who do research on memory? Under *Daubert*, the outcome depends on (1) whether the court believes *Daubert* applies at all, (2) the specific *Daubert* criteria the court chooses to apply and (3) how strictly it applies them.

The *Daubert* decision left many questions about the admissibility of scientific evidence and expert testimony unresolved. A few of those questions have been answered by subsequent Supreme Court decisions. In *General Electric Co. v. Joiner*,[4] the Supreme Court considered the standard to be applied by appellate courts in reviewing trial court rulings on scientific evidence. The Court held that "abuse of discretion" is the appropriate standard, thus giving trial judges a great deal of control over the kind of expert testimony that is admitted or excluded under *Daubert*, as their decisions are unlikely to be reversed on appeal unless they are clearly erroneous.

In the case of *Kumho Tire v. Carmichael*,[5] the Supreme Court considered whether the *Daubert* principle (that the trial judge must rule on the reliability of scientific testimony prior to admitting it into evidence) should apply

---

4. General Electric Co. v. Joiner, 118 S.Ct. 512 (1997).
5. Kumho Tire v. Carmichael, 119 S.Ct. 1167 (1999).

only to scientific testimony or to all expert testimony. (This issue had arisen in some recovered memory cases, in relation to testimony based on the clinical experience of the testifying expert, with varying outcomes.)

The underlying facts in the *Kumho Tire* case were as follows: passengers in a minivan were injured when a tire failed, causing the van to go out of control. The injured passengers sued the tire manufacturer, claiming that the tire had failed because it was defective when it left the hands of the manufacturer. The plaintiffs' expert was well qualified by training and experience to testify on the causes of tire failure, but the trial court rejected his testimony that the tire was inherently defective because, in the court's view, it did not meet the *Daubert* criteria for reliable scientific testimony. There was some evidence that the tire had failed because of excessive wear and tear; there was also evidence that the expert's methodology was not followed by other experts in the field.

The Eleventh Circuit Court of Appeals reversed the decision of the trial court, holding that the tire expert's testimony was nonscientific in nature and that the trial court should therefore not have applied the *Daubert* standard. The Supreme Court granted certiorari to resolve a dispute in the federal courts of appeals concerning the correct standard to apply to nonscientific expert testimony.

The Supreme Court was unanimous in holding that the *Daubert* principle applies to all expert testimony, not just to scientific testimony. In making this determination, the Court said, the trial judge may consider whatever factors might be relevant to the particular kind of testimony being offered. They may, but need not necessarily, include any of the four *Daubert* factors.

Justice Breyer, who wrote the opinion in *Kumho Tire*, pointed out that there is no clear line dividing scientific knowledge from technical or other specialized knowledge and that the various kinds of knowledge are interdependent. The particular questions asked in a *Daubert*-type inquiry will be tied to the facts of the case; some of the four factors specifically mentioned in *Daubert* may be helpful in evaluating the reliability even of experience-based testimony, he wrote.

Even though *Daubert* and *Kumho* are only binding on federal courts, where relatively few recovered memory cases are tried, the trend of making the trial judge the "gatekeeper" of scientific and other expert testimony seems likely to affect more and more state courts in the future. In April, 1999, a federal advisory committee voted to approve changes in the Federal Rules of Evidence pertaining to scientific and other expert testimony that would explicitly incorporate the rulings in *Daubert* and *Kumho Tire*. If these changes go into effect,[6] it seems likely that more state courts will eventually accept the

---

6. Before the changes can go into effect, they must be approved by Congress, a process that is expected to take until December, 2000, at the earliest. Congress could decide to reject the changes approved by the committee or to make further changes.

underlying principle of *Daubert* and *Kumho Tire*, namely, that trial judges must exert greater responsibility to keep junk science out of the courtroom.

A full implementation of the Supreme Court's mandate in *Daubert* and *Kumho Tire* will require judges to become more knowledgeable about the kinds of testimony that should be subjected to criteria of reliability and what those criteria might be. Although some judges have done an excellent job applying the *Daubert* principle, others are clearly not yet up to the task set for them by *Daubert* and expanded by *Kumho Tire*. Many judges will have to be educated in the nature of science and the ways of validating (and attacking) scientific evidence. Some programs for the education of judges already exist on both the federal and state levels. These programs should probably be expanded. The alternative is to have more questionable cases clogging the courts and more legal decisions based on "junk science."

The *Kumho Tire* opinion has important implications for cases involving allegations of recovered memories of sexual abuse, and indeed, for all cases in which expert testimony is offered by mental health professionals based on their clinical experience or other expertise. An expert who makes claims that are in principle capable of empirical testing and validation should be required to show that there is some scientific support for those claims before being permitted to testify. A clinician who testifies, for example, that certain symptoms are strongly suggestive of a history of sexual abuse should not be allowed to rely on clinical intuition as his authority. That is a statement that is capable, in theory at least, of empirical support or refutation. If the research hasn't been done yet, the clinician should not be permitted to make the statement in court.

The degree of validation that is required should depend on the consequences of erroneous judgments. Because our legal system of fact-finding is not perfect, errors are bound to occur. The degree of proof of scientific validity that is required will affect the likelihood of both "false positives" (findings of abuse where none occurred) and "false negatives"(findings of no abuse where abuse in fact occurred). In determining the level of proof that is required in recovered memory cases, and indeed in sex abuse cases generally, society will have to decide, as a matter of policy, how many child abusers should be allowed to go unpunished in order to avoid erroneously labeling an innocent person a child abuser. In cases based on recovered memories of abuse that allegedly took place decades earlier, where objective corroboration of the abuse will often be lacking, the level of proof that clinical expertise in assessing abuse is reliable enough to be admissible in evidence should be high indeed.

If there is no scientific evidence for a special mechanism called "repression" to account for forgotten episodes of abuse, as Schooler and Lindsay suggest, judges should exclude testimony alleging that memories of abuse were repressed. Neither courts nor legislatures should extend statutes of limitations for claims based on recovered memories unless there is some other policy, not dependant on the unproven theory of repression, that would support allowing lawsuits against persons accused of committing abuse many years earlier.

Because of the many scientific weaknesses in the clinical testimony in support of recovered memories of abuse, courts should allow these cases to survive defendants' motions for summary judgment only if strong objective corroboration of both the abuse and the forgetting can be shown at the outset. Trial courts should hold *Daubert*-type, pretrial hearings to decide the strength of the evidence against the accused.

A field that was formerly not very scientific (psychiatry, for example) may have become more scientific with time, as more and more of its assumptions were tested empirically. The testimony of an expert in that field may therefore contain parts that can be scientifically tested and parts that cannot. Testimony of clinicians in recovered memory cases may be of that kind. The parts of an expert's testimony that are capable of being tested under the *Daubert* criteria or other criteria of scientific validity should be put to such scrutiny, even if the expert is testifying in part on the basis of clinical experience. A pretrial, *Daubert*-type hearing is probably advisable any time there is an issue as to whether part or all of an expert's testimony is scientific. Courts should be liberal in allowing experts from related fields to testify at these hearings because courts will need to learn what areas of the proposed expert testimony are susceptible of scientific testing.

Many aspects of memory have been studied scientifically, as the chapters in this volume demonstrate. Clinicians' testimony about their patients' recovered memories should be tested against what is currently known about how memory works, based on laboratory data rather than on clinical intuition. Experts who argue that traumatic memories obey different rules than other memories should have the burden of proof on that issue.

Some have argued that the purpose of trials is not to find the truth (if, indeed, there is such a thing as objective truth) but rather to arrive at a socially acceptable conclusion, and that scientific truth must sometimes be subordinated to social policies, such as the policy that favors believing those who state they were abused in the past, even if objective verification is lacking. I disagree. I do not believe that all truth is relative. Either a woman was raped by her father when she was three years old or she wasn't. For purposes of psychotherapy, it may not be crucial (as some have argued) to establish the truth of historical facts, but for purposes of establishing guilt or innocence, or tort liability, it should be.

Ultimately, society will be best served if verdicts are based on objective truth. The scientific method is the best means we have at the present time of ascertaining objective truth. I therefore applaud the Supreme Court decisions in the *Daubert* and *Kumho Tire* cases and look forward to their full implementation in cases based on recovered memories of abuse, as well as in other cases in which scientific evidence is in dispute.[7] A salutary by-product would be the elevation of standards in the mental health professions. Professional organizations should be actively working to rid their ranks of unscientific practitioners, but if they neglect to do their duty, the courts will have to do it for them.

---

7. See State v. Quattrochi, 1999 WL 284882 (R.I.Super.), in which a court ruled that expert testimony on recovered memories of abuse was inadmissible in a criminal case because the testimony did not satisfy the standards set by the *Daubert* and *Kumho Tire* cases.

INTRODUCTION

Arthur Taub M.D., Ph.D.

I am the President of the Institute for Pain Research (IPR), a small, private, nonprofit corporation that I formed more than two decades ago to promote otherwise unfunded projects in the neurosciences relating to pain. IPR has also sponsored the acquisition of specialized research equipment and of medications and appliances for indigent patients. The conference held in New Haven on November 14, 1997 on recovered memories of child sexual abuse, which formed the basis of this book, was the first conference to be sponsored by IPR. I hope there will be others. IPR's activities are made possible by charitable contributions to the corporation.

What we think of as "memory" is central to the human condition. Memory, both short- and long-term, is the key to the cognitive neuroscientist's concept of the overall function of the brain. The neurologist sees the pain of the devastating loss of memory in brain injury and in Alzheimer's Disease. The neuropharmacologist sees memory wax and wane under the influence of drugs and metabolic change. The psychiatrist and psychologist confront the controlling influence of memory upon thought and behavior. The lawyer and the jurist must assess memory's concordance with fact.

The concept of "recovered memory" of sexual abuse in childhood, as it has developed in recent years, is at a nexus of these issues. The pain of those who experience, correctly or incorrectly as it relates to the facts of the matter, memories of childhood sexual abuse only lately uncovered, and the pain of those who are confronted, often years after the events are said to have occurred, with accusations of sexual abuse, are uniquely poignant.

There is a body of evidence that indicates that early physical traumata influence the experience of pain in adult life. IPR thus fulfilled its mandate to study the pain experience by facilitating the coming together of faculty and attendees with specific, in-depth knowledge, experience, and insight concerning the subject of recovered memories of sexual abuse. I hope the information presented and the views expressed here will serve as a reference point, a waystation, in the journey to clarify what is involved in "recovered memory," and how we, as a society, can come to deal with it.

Chapter 1

ABOUT THE FALSE MEMORY SYNDROME FOUNDATION

PAMELA FREYD

HISTORY

A group of families and professionals affiliated with the University of Pennsylvania in Philadelphia and Johns Hopkins University in Baltimore created the False Memory Syndrome Foundation in 1992 because they saw a need for an organization that could document and study the problem of families that were being shattered when adult children suddenly claimed to have recovered repressed memories of childhood sexual abuse. The Foundation has been a lifeline for devastated families grieving for their lost children. It has also been a catalyst for memory research and for the development of professional guidelines about newly-found memories of sexual abuse. It continues to serve as a clearinghouse for information on the recovered memory phenomenon. Even some of its sharpest critics admit that there was a need for an organization such as the False Memory Syndrome Foundation (FMSF).

Unlike most scientific debates that are contained within university circles, the recovered memory conflict spilled out of academia and inundated the media, the courts, and the lives of families. Political ideology opened the floodgate. In their fervor to call attention to the horrors of child sexual abuse and their eagerness to hold perpetrators accountable for past wrongs, advocates who claimed a special accuracy for "recovered memories" (a claim essentially unchallenged in 1992) succeeded in persuading lawmakers in many states to extend the statutes of limitation that govern lawsuits based on recovered memories of child sexual abuse. The FMS Foundation stepped onto the flood plain and asked for the evidence to support these new claims about memory. The Foundation suggested that zeal to solve the problem of child sexual abuse had created another problem: potential false memories. Some wrongly criticized the Foundation as opposing the efforts to end child abuse. Psychiatrist Judith Herman, who noted in her influential 1992 book *Trauma and Recovery* that "The systematic study of psychological trauma . . .

depends on the support of a political movement,"[1] accurately described the Foundation's role when she said that: "they are trying to impose a scientific agenda on a political debate."[2] That is precisely what the Foundation has tried to do.

Since its inception, the FMS Foundation has documented the "recovered repressed memory" phenomenon by collecting professional articles, books, statements, newspaper and magazine articles, television and radio programs, and advertisements of all types. Foundation staff and researchers have requested and collected stories of families and former patients by asking them questions in a systematic manner. In addition, the Foundation has conducted four surveys: (1) a 1993 survey of 550 families in which abuse accusations were made; (2) a 1994 survey of 40 accusers who subsequently retracted their accusations ("retractors"); (3) an ongoing survey of legal cases, starting in 1993; and (4) a 1997 survey update of 2,056 families. The information obtained from these surveys has enabled the Foundation to gain some understanding of both the participants in and the social context of the false memory phenomenon. This chapter will provide an overview of the FMSF's activities and what they have revealed.

STARTING THE FMS FOUNDATION

Families who contact the Foundation are generally devastated and in a state of shock. They don't understand what caused their children to rewrite their personal histories and to change from showing love to being alienated from their families. The change can be seen in some "before" and "after" letters that are reprinted below. The first letter, written by a son to his father, is the kind of letter we hope every dad might get:

> Dear Dad,
> Just a note to thank you for taking such good care of me and my friend during our much too short stay. My friend is impressed and a bit envious of the loving relationship and open lines of communication that you and I share. . . I love you and I am glad you are my dad.
>
> Love, "D"

Imagine that same father's distress when just a few months later, out of the blue, he received the following letter:

---

1. Herman, J.L. (1992). *Trauma and Recovery*. New York: Basic Books. P. 9.

2. Herman, J.L., quoted in Hollingsworth, J. (1994, September 4). Recovered memory cases spark psychology debate. *Tampa Tribune*. P. 7.

I am writing this letter for two reasons: (i.) to attain closure for myself regarding my relationship with you and (ii.) in the hope that you will seek help before you hurt anyone else the way you hurt me.

I have spent 37 years of my life denying and minimizing the torture that was my childhood and adolescence. I genuinely hope this letter causes you to seek help–you are very sick man. I do not wish to hear from you unless you are willing to admit the things you did to me and to seek help for your sickness.

"D"

The author of this letter, a man in his mid-30s, had rewritten his past, offering no opportunity for dialogue but only an ultimatum: confess and enter therapy or there will be no contact.

A pre-therapy letter to a mother read as follows:

Thank you for your love and support. I love who you are, not just as a mom but as you. I am so grateful to have you in my life and in the lives of my children. I don't know if they'll ever put your name in a history book, but in my life you're not only one of the greatest women but one of the greatest people. You've taught me so much about just being a good person.

Love, "S"

Imagine the mother's confusion and hurt when she received this letter, a few months later, from her daughter who was now in therapy:

At this time and for an indefinite period of time, I do not wish to have contact of any sort between us. I find it too painful because I believe you are being false. I have also decided my well-being is more important to my family than the gifts and letters you send the kids. Please discontinue. . . I give up the hope I had for a relationship with you.

Families who received similar letters gathered to help each other endure their grief. Although society normally supports families when they lose their children, it does not do so for families accused of sexual abuse; they are considered guilty until proven innocent.

Families had another concern: they worried that they would be sued. In the late 1980s and early 1990s, the notion that a person could "get strong by suing" became popular. Indeed, *The Courage to Heal*, sometimes called the "Bible" of the survivor movement, contained a section on suing parents that featured a list of lawyers who would take such suits.[3] Many families received letters from lawyers similar to the one below:

Dear Mr. and Mrs. "R",

Please be advised that this law firm represents your daughter. She has consulted with me regarding the effects she is suffering from severe childhood trauma resulting from the abuse inflicted by you. The trauma described is unspeakable.

---

3. Bass, E. & Davis, L. (1988). *The Courage to Heal.* New York: Harper Collins.

As a result of this trauma, without relating all of the details in this letter, she has been unable to hold a full-time job. Without filing a Court action, Ms. "R" has authorized me to make the following demand letter for settlement:
• You assume responsibility for Ms. "R's" medical and therapeutic expenses including any hospitalization for the remainder of her life.
• Reimbursement to Ms. "R: for therapy and hospitalization expenses incurred during 1990 and 1991, in the estimated amount of $10,000.
• Payment of $250,000 to help, in some small way, to compensate her for the disabilities, pain, suffering, humiliation and severe lifetime trauma that she has suffered and is expected to suffer.
• A life insurance policy to be taken out on your lives with Ms. "R" to be named as beneficiary to ensure that the settlement be paid.
If I do not hear from you in 10 days, I will assume that you do not intend to enter into settlement and will advise Ms. "R" regarding the appropriate judicial relief. Rest assured, however, that if you do not settle this matter, in any lawsuit, Ms. "R" will be requesting substantially higher sums and her attorney's fees. As a lawyer, I have dealt with many of these cases, and the facts that have been related to me and which will be related to a jury, warrant the imposition of substantial punitive and compensatory damages.

Your daughter's lawyer

Some families were sued and lost their homes and life savings. Others succumbed to extortion demands. As recently as a few years ago, teachers, therapists, doctors, clergy, and others were often fired from their jobs on the basis of an unproven accusation of child sexual abuse. Although families who contact the Foundation are mostly elderly and retired, some people who were employed in positions dependent on public confidence believed they could not afford to risk the accusation becoming public. They would have found it almost impossible and certainly expensive to defend themselves against accusations made twenty to forty years after the fact, when evidence was gone, witnesses were dead, and memories had faded. Some families therefore succumbed to extortion demands because they believed they could not afford the personal or financial cost of a lawsuit. Others ignored the demands and suffered extreme anxiety, living in fear of what would happen next.

One thing is certain: after a family or individual has been accused of sexual abuse, life is never the same. The stigma of the accusation, true or false, sticks like tar. For example, in 1995, the television program Dateline asked 502 people, "If someone has been charged and acquitted of child abuse, would you still be suspicious of them?" Seventy-seven percent responded *yes*, they would be suspicious; another 12 percent were not sure.[4] Only 11 percent said they would not be suspicious.

---

4. Phillips, S. (Producer). (1995, November 8). *Dateline "Innocence Lost," Question of the Week.* New York: NBC.

The sticking power of sex abuse accusations—even if false—was demonstrated in July 1998 in the reviews of a one-hour PBS documentary of the life of Cardinal Bernardin.[5] Although only six minutes of the program were devoted to the sexual abuse allegation against him and its later retraction, many reviews of the program mentioned the accusation, and some even made the accusation the main topic of the review.[6]

Families thus had many personal reasons for joining together, but the FMS Foundation is not a family support group. Many of the parents, professionals in their own right, wanted to address the issues of memory that their children claimed supported their accusations. As the original group of families and professionals considered the structure that the organization might take, they felt that it would be important to enlist the help of members of the scientific and clinical communities who had a proven track record of research involving memory and suggestibility. With the help of world-renowned memory and hypnosis researchers Emily and Martin Orne, the families contacted researchers and clinicians, approaching only senior members of their respective fields in order that no careers would be harmed by the passionate debate that was growing within the therapeutic community over the validity of recovered repressed memories.

As word of the fledgling organization spread, interested professionals began to contact the Foundation. Some of them joined the FMSF Scientific and Professional Advisory Board. It soon became clear that an important strength of the Advisory Board was the diversity of opinion on topics that relate to the FMS controversy, among them being hypnosis and repression. At the same time, the members of the Advisory Board are united in adhering to the fundamental notion that extraordinary claims require extraordinary evidence. They all believe that external corroboration is necessary in order to establish the truth of a memory. They are also united in their concern that patients and families may suffer harm when therapists use techniques that increase the risk of suggesting memories of events that never occurred.

---

5. PBS "Bernardin" July 2, 1998.

6. Caldwell, D.K. (1998, June 27). Cardinal virtues. *Dallas Morning News*, p. 6G; Blake, J. (1998, June 27). Media with a message: Television. *The Atlanta Constitution*, p. 2C; A Hollow Look at a Hallowed Man Cardinal Joseph Bernardin was reversed, but docu doesn't explain why. (1998, June 30). *Hollywood Reporter*, p. _; Reel, B. (1998, July 1). Documentary on Cardinal Comes Close to the Mark. *Newsday*, p. A43; Stammer, L.B. (1998, July 1). Friends Recall Cardinal's Remarkable Life. *Los Angeles Times*, p. F10; Finnigan, D. (1998, July 1). Bernardin: The Life and Legacy of Cardinal Joseph Bernardin. *Daily Variety*, p. 15; Goodman, W. (1998, July 2). Anchored by Church Teachings, Driven by Vatican Change. *New York Times*, p. E5; Mink, E. (1998, July 02). Bernardin Shines Light on a Moral Beacon. *New York Daily News*, p. 104; Bole, W. (1998, July 3). PBS to air story of Bernardin's life. *News and Observer*, p. F2; Brennan, P. (1998 July 05). PBS's Portrait of a Cardinal; For Him, a Moment of Near-Disgrace Gave Way to Days of Grace. *Washington Post*, p. Y07.

The forty-nine members of the Scientific and Professional Advisory Board are people to whom the Foundation turns for information and advice. They do not represent the Foundation, nor do statements issued by the Foundation necessarily represent the thinking of the advisory board. The caliber of the Scientific and Professional Advisory Board is reflected in the impact that the FMS Foundation has had in the media and the scientific community.

ACTIVITIES OF THE FOUNDATION

The day-to-day running of the Foundation is the responsibility of the Executive Director, who reports to the seven-member Board of Directors. The Foundation is funded by the dues and contributions of the people who contact it. As a charitable corporation organized pursuant to section 501(c)(3) of the Internal Revenue Code, the FMSF does not lobby. The FMSF goals are:
   • to seek the reasons for the spread of FMS, which is so devastating to families,
   • to work for ways to prevent it,
   • to aid those who have been affected by it and to reconcile them with their families.

From the time the FMSF was founded (in 1992) to the spring of 1997, approximately 18,000 families who were struggling with accusations based on recovered memories contacted the Foundation. Calls and letters came from all 50 states, Guam, Puerto Rico, Australia, Canada, Chile, Denmark, England, Germany, Israel, Japan, Mexico, the Netherlands, Norway, Philippines, Sweden, South Africa, and New Zealand. Organizations similar to FMSF have been formed in Australia, England, the Netherlands, and New Zealand.

The Foundation has also received calls for help from thousands of families reporting that they have been falsely accused of abusing a minor child in situations that do not involve the recovery of repressed memories. Requests for information or advice have come from professionals and students, from people who say that they are questioning their own memories or therapy experiences, and from retractors (i.e., people who now believe that the abuse memories they recovered in therapy are not true memories).

One of the Foundation's first activities was to try to identify the professional and cultural forces that might be contributing to the families' problems. The evidence was ubiquitous and the Foundation immediately brought it to professional attention. Some of the evidence came from professionals' own writings and statements; some came from popular books, magazine articles, movies, and television programs. By writing letters to professionals about these particular statements or writings and through articles in the FMSF Newsletter, the Foundation focused attention on some of the misguided beliefs that were the bedrock of the recovered memory problem.

The Foundation has never claimed to know whether the abuse allegations that are reported to it are true or false. The patterns seen in the reports are a cause for concern, however, because it is frequently reported that psychotherapists have used suggestive memory enhancement techniques. The Foundation has stated that claims of abuse should be taken very seriously and that good therapy practice requires that a careful diagnosis be made before treatment is started. Because patients seeking help for mental anguish may present cognitive distortions, prudence would dictate that a therapist make a good faith effort to find some independent corroboration of the alleged abuse before making a diagnosis and exercise caution before making a forensic judgment that will affect the lives of others.

BELIEF ABOUT MEMORY IN THE POPULAR CULTURE

Professionals

A critical characteristic of the reports received by the Foundation is that the accused families never had an opportunity to defend themselves. They were told that unless they confessed, they would be cut off from all contact with the accusers. Families were routinely told that they were "in denial." Denial of sex abuse was seen as proof that sexual abuse took place. It still is by some.

> Denial of sexual abuse is one of the 150 Possible Adult Symptoms of Childhood Sexual Interference.[7]

A lack of abuse memories was seen as no impediment to claiming survivor status. A book published by the "Hazelden" Foundation has the following title: Can I Trust My Memory? A Handbook for Survivors With Partial or No Memories of Childhood Sexual Abuse.[8]

A respected clinician made the following comment:

---

7. Littauer, F., & Littauer, F. (1988). *Freeing your mind from memories that bind.* Nashville, TN: Thomas Nelson.

8. Spear, J. (1992). *Can I trust my memory? A handbook for survivors with partial or no memories of childhood sexual abuse.* Center City, MN: Hazelden Foundation.

Those with access to memory usually wish to forget, repress, or minimize what they know. Those with absent, hazy, or fragmented memory are usually desperate to remember, until memory returns.[9]

The Foundation is frequently asked how a person could "know" that he or she is a survivor of abuse if there is no memory of abuse.

Some professionals have encouraged people to confront the person they thought *might* be the abuser, even if they were not sure that they had been abused:

> Once you make the decision to go ahead, the actual disclosure is an empowering experience. Telling the people in your family how you were hurt is the most expedient form of healing....Avoid being tentative about your repressed memories. Do not just tell them; express them as truth. If months or years down the road, you find you are mistaken about details, you can always apologize and set the record straight.....You cannot wait until you are doubt-free to disclose to your family. This may never happen. . . .[10]

Some professionals who believe in the accuracy of recovered repressed memories assume that 50 percent of their patients will not remember sexual abuse and incest and that the therapist's job is to draw out such memories.[11] One therapist writing for the Tompkins County New York Mental Health Association wrote about using "forceps" to help recover memories:[12]

> Many abuse victims are heading into therapy not realizing at first that underneath their daily difficulties and hang-ups lies a buried memory of sexual abuse. Trained therapists can often spot the signs indicating an incestuous past....In childhood, a forceps delivery gets the child unstuck so that life can begin. When working with sexual abuse survivors [who have no memory] using a directive and forceful psychotherapeutic tool may help shorten a client's recovery process by months or years.

Books

Many of the seminal ideas of the recovered memory movement had appeared in a few popular books of the past several decades. For example, in 1957, *The Three Faces of Eve* introduced the world to multiple personality

---

9. Courtois, C. (1992). The memory retrieval process in incest survivor therapy. *Journal of Child Sexual Abuse, 1(1)*, 15-29, at 15.

10. Fredrickson, R. (1992). Repressed memories: *A journey to recovery from sexual abuse.* New York: Simon & Schuster. pp. 203-204.

11. Maltz, W. (1990, December.). Adult survivors of incest: How to help them overcome the trauma. *Medical aspects of human sexuality.* pp. 42- 47.

12. Bobrow, M. (Spring 1993). Helping sexually abused clients to remember: The use of forceps in psychotherapy. *States of mind,* publication of the Tompkins County, New York, Mental Health Association.

disorder.[13] Sixteen years later, *Sybil* popularized the idea that MPD was caused by child abuse that was so horrific that all memories of it were repressed.[14] *Michelle Remembers* introduced the notion of intergenerational satanic ritual abuse and torture in time for those ideas to be picked up in the McMartin day care case in the mid-1980s.[15] By the end of the 1980s, belief in recovered repressed memories was firmly embedded in our literature and movies. Most bookstores now featured a new section: recovery books. By 1992, the recovery section shelves were filled with incest recovery stories that incorporated all of the above beliefs.

Television

People make sense of their lives by the things they see around them and the stories they hear. In order to learn about popular beliefs and attitudes, we need only turn on a television set to see what stories are being told. Virtually every home in the country has television, which has been the dominant influence on the opinions and lives of people since its birth fifty years ago. As the influence of television has grown, however, the distinction between news and entertainment has diminished. This is most obvious in the daytime talk shows. By 1995, about 150 daytime talk shows were available to viewers on a weekly basis.[16] Driven by ratings, shows compete by featuring outrageous, bizarre, and weird guests interspersed with serious, credible people. Keeping them separate can be a challenge. The popularity of recovered repressed memories as a topic for these shows was captured in a 1994 Don Addis cartoon showing a talk show host and her guest seated before a camera. The caption read: "Not a single repressed memory of abuse! I didn't know there were any of you left."

Stories of satanic ritual abuse and incest were a staple of the "talks." Roseanne Barr told viewers on a "Sally Jesse Raphael" program in October, 1991 that she remembered her mother molesting her while she was changing her diaper, and Sally gave that virtually impossible claim credibility by telling the world she believed it.[17] A month later on "Oprah," Roseanne said: "When someone asks you, 'Were you sexually abused as a child?' there's only two answers. One of them is, 'Yes,' and one of them is, 'I don't know.'" To this, Oprah provided unconditional positive support rather than

---

13. Thigpen, C.H., & Cleckley, H.M. (1957). *The three faces of Eve.* New York: McGraw-Hill.

14. Schreiber, F.R. (1973). *Sybil.* New York: Warner.

15. Smith, M., & Pazder, L. (1980). *Michelle remembers,* New York: Pocket Books.

16. Heaton, J.A., & Wilson, N.L. (1995). *Tuning in trouble: Talk tv's destructive impact on mental health.* San Francisco: Jossey-Bass.

17. Goldstein, E., & Farmer, K. (1993). *True stories of false memories.* Boca Raton: Upton Books. p. 211.

pointing out the absurdity or, at the very least, the political nature of Roseanne's comment.[18] Geraldo Rivera is infamous for fueling the spread of the satanic ritual abuse panic, and programs that romanticize multiple personality disorder continue to this day.[19] Poking fun at the authority the television talk shows have assumed in our culture, a 1995 *New Yorker* cartoon by Richter pictures a man listening to his lawyer say: "Your case has been turned down by Oprah, but we're appealing to Sally Jesse Raphael."

Advertisements and Checklists

Some proponents of recovered repressed memories advertised widely. One such advertisement stated: "Remembering incest and childhood sexual abuse is the first step to healing...We can help you remember and heal."[20] For the reader of this airline magazine advertisement who might be unsure as to whether the message applied to her, a checklist of symptoms was provided. The reader who suffered from any of the following was advised to visit a treatment center where people can get help in recovering their memories:

• MOOD SWINGS • PANIC DISORDERS • SUBSTANCE ABUSE •RAGE • FLASHBACKS • DEPRESSION • HOPELESSNESS • ANXIETY • PARANOIA • LOW SELF ESTEEM • RELAPSE • RELATIONSHIP PROBLEMS • SEXUAL FEAR • SEXUAL COMPULSION • SELF MUTILATION • BORDERLINE PERSONALITY • IRRITABLE BOWEL • MIGRAINE • P.M.S. • POST TRAUMATIC STRESS • BULIMIA • ANOREXIA • A.C.O.A. • OBESITY • MULTIPLE PERSONALITY • HALLUCINATIONS • RELIGIOUS ADDICTIONS • PARENTING PROBLEMS • SUICIDAL FEELINGS.

The implicit message of such a checklist is that people who suffer from a migraine headache or an irritable bowel or low self-esteem or any of the other listed symptoms probably have a problem that they don't even know they have, and that they will not get better until they remember what happened. Are there any people alive who have not at some time experienced some of these "symptoms?"

A telephone call to the 800 number given in this advertisement informed the caller that she would be flown from anywhere in the country for a four week stay at no cost to the caller. If the caller's insurance did not cover the full stay, the voice on the telephone said, the treatment center would cover the balance. In the early 1990s, private mental hospitals and treatment cen-

---

18. Ibid., 210.

19. Victor, J.S. (1993). *Satanic Panic: the Creation of a Contemporary Legend.* Chicago: Open Court. p. 83.

20. Advertisement for ASCA Treatment Centers in Bellflower, CA. (1992, Summer). *Hemisphere,* the United Airlines Magazine. p. _.

ters had more beds than patients, and aggressive recruitment captured many an unwary patient.

Treatment centers often advertised the specifics of their programs for recovering memories. On the pages of *The Professional Counselor* (December, 1992, p. 54), ASCA Co-Dependency Centers advertised an "Intensive Memory Retrieval Program for Incest Survivors and MPD. . ." The ad mentioned specific techniques such as body work, psychodrama, and narco-analysis. In other ads, ASCA have also mentioned dream analysis, rage work, and play therapy–all said to aid in the recovery process. In *Treating Abuse Today* (vol. 4, no. 3, p. 11), the Masters and Johnson Sexual Trauma and Dissociative Disorders Programs advertised the "Use of hypnosis and guided imagery to facilitate abreaction and memory retrieval." The FMS Foundation has worked hard to call attention to the danger of suggestion in using these techniques in the misguided effort to recover historically accurate memories.

Checklists seemed to be everywhere in 1992 and 1993. Carol Tavris gave the public its first major warning about their use in 1993 in an article in The New York Times Book Review.[21] She endured a firestorm of complaint letters from readers who adamantly believed in the efficacy of checklists and the truth of "recovered repressed memories." A few years later, one psychologist compiled a list of over 900 different symptoms that had been claimed in books and advertisements to be evidence of past abuse.[22] When he reviewed the professional literature, however, he found that not one of the 900 symptoms reliably proved an abuse history. There is no checklist of signs or symptoms that prove a history of past sexual abuse. By 1998, fortunate-

---

21. Tavris, C. (1993, January 3). Beware the incest-survivor machine. *The New York Times Book Review.* p. 1.

22. London, R.W. (1995, March.) Therapeutic treatment of patients with repressed memories. *The Independent Practitioner.* pp. 64-67, at 64.

ly, many professional organizations had issued statements urging caution in inferring past abuse from symptoms on checklists.[23]

By 1998, professional organizations had also warned about the misuse of hypnosis and other techniques that are sometimes used in the misguided belief that they can recover accurate memories, but such warnings did not exist when the Foundation was formed. Professional organizations have now warned that the truth of a memory can only be assured through external corroboration. Such statements represent a strong advance that will help to slow down the "recovered repressed memory" phenomenon, but as yet, these same organizations provide no mechanisms for holding their members accountable for engaging in practices likely to induce false memories. That gap has contributed to the surge in legal activity focussing on the scientific status of "recovered repressed memories" in recent years.

FAMILY SURVEY AND UPDATE

While the Foundation was learning about the trends and beliefs relating to "recovered repressed memories" that had spread throughout the culture, it wanted to learn, as well, about the families who were calling or writing to request help and information. If the abuse accusations were indeed false,

---

23. American Medical Association Council on Scientific Affairs. (1985, April). Scientific Status of Refreshing Recollection by the Use of Hypnosis. Chicago, IL: Author; American Psychiatric Association. (1993, December). Statement on Memories of Sexual Abuse. Washington, D.C.: Author; American Medical Association Council on Scientific Affairs. (1994, May). Memories of Childhood Sexual Abuse. Chicago, IL: Author; Australian Psychological Society Limited. (1994, October). Guidelines Relating to the Reporting of Recovered Memories. Sydney, Australia: Author; British Psychological Society. (1995, January). Recovered Memories: The report of the working party of the British Psychological Society. Leicester, U.K.:Author; American Society of Clinical Hypnosis. (1995, February). Clinical Hypnosis and Memory: Guidelines for Clinicians and for Forensic Hypnosis. Des Plaines, IL: Author; Michigan Psychological Association. (1995, September-October). Recovered Memories of Sexual Abuse: MPA Position Paper. *Michigan Psychologist*, p. ; American Psychological Association. (1995, August). Questions and Answers about Memories of Childhood Abuse. Washington, D.C.: Author; National Council on the Practice of Clinical Social Work. (1996, June). Evaluation and Treatment of Adults with the possibility of Recovered Memories of Childhood Sexual Abuse. Washington, D.C.: National Association of Social Workers; Canadian Psychological Association. (1996, August). Guidelines for Psychologists Addressing Recovered Memories. Ottawa, ON: Author; British Association for Counselling. (1997). False Memory Syndrome: A Statement. Warwickshire, U.K.: Author; Netherlands Institute for Study of Criminality and Law Enforcement. (1997). Recovered Crimes: Sexual Abuse Reported to the Police after Therapy: Advice to the Minister of Justice. Leiden, The Netherlands: Author; Royal College of Psychiatrists. (1997, June). Reported Recovered Memories of Child Sexual Abuse. *Psychiatric Bulletin, 21*, 663-665; Scientific Advisory Board of the False Memory Syndrome Foundation. (1998, May). Statement. Philadelphia, PA: Author; Roth, S. and Friedman, M.J. (1998, June). Childhood Trauma Remembered: A report on the current scientific knowledge base and its applications. Northbrook, IL: The International Society for Traumatic Stress Studies.

two obvious hypotheses were that (1) there was something about these families that made them vulnerable to false accusations, or (2) there was some pathology in the accuser that made him or her more likely to develop false memories. The data we collected did not support either of these hypotheses.

Beginning in September 1992, FMSF sent a 20-page Family Survey to approximately 900 accused families who had taken the initiative to contact the Foundation. (These families are not a random sample of all families accused of sexual abuse, as those who contact the FMSF are not necessary representative of all such families.) The survey questionnaires were sent in several batches, with the last batch mailed in September 1993. Five hundred and ten questionnaires (56%) were returned and coded.

In January 1997, 3,510 one-page surveys were mailed to families who were members of the Foundation in order to update some of the questions on the Family Survey. These 3510 families included the 900 that had been contacted in 1992. Families were considered "members" if they had paid dues or indicated that they wished to join but could not afford to do so. By March 25, 1997, 2,111 surveys had been returned (60.14%). Fifty-five surveys were not included in the analysis because they involved allegations by a minor or because they were unsigned or illegible.

When Were Families Accused?

One observation from the Family Survey and Update is that the FMS phenomenon is relatively recent. The graph below shows a marked increase from 1988 to 1992 in the number of families per year who learned that they had been accused of decades-old sexual abuse. This rise was followed by an equally sharp decrease from 1992 to 1996. Such a sudden rise and fall seems to support the notion that some change in practice or some change in the culture, or both, had taken place, because the alleged incidents of abuse were supposed to have occurred over the course of several decades. In other words, it was probable that what was being observed was an epidemic of accusations occurring in the present rather than an epidemic of abuse that had taken place many decades earlier.

One possible interpretation of these data is that the problem of FMS has been moving through the identified stages of a craze or moral panic.[24] The first stage is characterized by the perception of a threat by a few people who then try to make the public aware of the threat. (In the case of the false memory phenomenon, this stage might be considered to have occurred in the '60s and '70s with the publication of books about MPD and SRA.) In the next phase, awareness of the perceived threat explodes and many people join in

---

24. Penrose, L.S. (1952). *Objective study of crowd behavior.* London: H.K. Lewis.

Table 1-1
YEAR IN WHICH FAMILIES LEARNED OF ACCUSATION

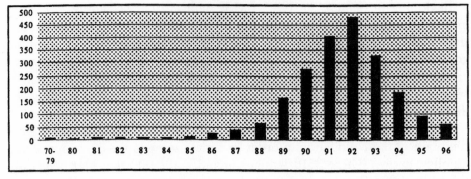

(Family Survey Update)

1996(N=60);	1991(N=407);	1986(N=27);	1981(N=7);
1995(N=92);	1990(N=227);	1985(N=14);	1980(N=2);
1994(N=188)	1989(N=167);	1984(N=8);	1970->1979(N=6).
1993(N=331);	1988(N=68),	1983(N=12),	
1992(N=482);	1987(N=40);	1982(N=7);	

the concern. (In this phase of the false memory phenomenon, MPD was entered into the psychiatric *Diagnostic and Statistical Manual III* (in 1980), the International Society for the Study of Multiple Personality and Dissociation was formed and MPD and SRA hit the talk shows in a major way.) In the later stages of a craze or moral panic, increasing numbers of people grow skeptical about the threat and come to consider that it was exaggerated. As resistance spreads, there may be social controversy. (This would appear to be the stage in which the FMS Foundation was formed.) Finally, the concern diminishes until it is maintained only by marginal groups. In the case of FMS, the number of accusations may be waning because this craze has reached a downward phase. People may have become immune to the threat because of all the information in the media about the false memory controversy.

Another possible interpretation of this data is that therapists are now much more cautious about advising patients to confront their parents with accusations of abuse. The guidelines recently issued by professional organizations, noted earlier, have very likely caused many therapists to reconsider their past practices in this regard.

Yet another possible explanation for the apparent decline in the number of accusations is that parents who have been accused in recent years did not need to contact the FMS Foundation for information, and thereby give up their anonymity, because the public was more educated about the problem as a result of the efforts of many professionals and the publicity given to the subject in the media. Perhaps all of the above factors have contributed to the observed decline in the number of abuse accusations reported annually to FMSF.

What Are Families Accused of Doing?

Approximately one-third of the families that contacted the Foundation said they didn't know what, specifically, they were being accused of. Perhaps the accusers didn't know, or perhaps they chose not to tell. Many parents received calls or letters that said, "You know what you did!" The accuser then refused all further contact with the parents.

For those families who were informed of the specifics of the accusation, the Family Survey indicates that more than half of the accusations were of a nature that would be expected to leave some physical evidence. These accusations included rape, murder, satanic ritual abuse, intercourse, sodomy, and insertion of many different types of foreign objects into vaginas and anuses. Accusations of oral sex, digital sex, masturbation, exposure, fondling, or molesting were less frequent. Given the violent nature of so many of the acts that were alleged, it is significant that neither the accusers nor their therapists sought any external corroboration through examination of childhood school or medical records. Families reported that when they offered such information, both therapists and accusers routinely refused it.

According to the Family Survey data, the alleged abuse was usually said to have been ongoing and repeated over a long period of time, the average duration of the alleged abuse being seven years. Reports in which the alleged victim claimed to have been abused from the age of three years to sixteen years were not unusual. The alleged victims claimed their memories were repressed an average of 28 years, with the period of repression ranging from 4 years to 53 years.

Research on memory indicates that traumatic events are generally remembered. In a survey of the literature on the subject, Lindsay and Read (1995) noted that "studies of memory for traumatic events offer little support for the idea that adults with extensive histories of extreme [child sexual abuse] often forget those histories yet could recover memories under appropriate conditions.[25] Indeed, the evidence reviewed in this section suggests that this is a rare phenomenon, such that most practitioners would encounter few such cases." It is difficult to reconcile the claims of memory repression with claims of the severity of reported events and the frequency of the reported

---

25. Lindsay, D.S., & Read, J.D. (1995). Memory work and recovered memories of childhood sexual abuse: Scientific evidence and public, professional, and personal issues. *Psychology, Public Policy, and the Law 1(4)*, 846-908, 861.

events given what is known from research on memory about the likelihood of remembering.

Did the Accusation Involve Satanic Ritual Abuse?

The responses given in the Family Survey Update to the question of whether the accusation involved a claim of satanic ritual abuse were as follows: Yes = 18.40 percent; No = 64.74 percent; Don't know = 16.86 percent (N=2,056). Eighteen percent of the families reported accusations of activities associated with an intergenerational satanic cult, including elaborate ceremonies and ritual slaughter of babies or animals. The data from the Retractor Survey, however, indicate that almost 50 percent of that group of accusers had held the belief that their parents were involved in intergenerational satanic cult activities. This difference, 18 percent versus 50 percent, may reflect differences in the populations studied in the Family and Retractor surveys or it may reflect the fact that many families were never told of the satanic ritual abuse (SRA) accusations even though their accusers harbored a belief that such activities had taken place.

Three major reports now demonstrate a lack of evidence for an intergenerational satanic conspiracy.[26] Because so much information has appeared in the media about the lack of any scientific and investigative evidence for the existence of satanic ritual abuse, we predicted that we might see a decrease in the rate of SRA accusations over time in reports to the Foundation. As indicated in Table 1-2, the percentage of new accusations that involve claims of SRA has been generally decreasing, although in a few years (1989, 1992, and 1994) there was a small rise relative to the preceding year. This ongoing decrease adds another piece of evidence that the accusations were a reflection of a social belief system or moral panic that is now in the downward phase.

At What Age Did the Alleged Abuse Start?

As shown in Table 1-3, below, data from the Family Survey show that approximately 68% of the accusers believed they remembered abuse that occurred before they reached the age of 4 years.

These data are thought-provoking because memory research has repeatedly documented that early childhood memories are frequently quite unreli-

---

26. Lanning, K. (1992). Investigators guide to allegations of 'ritual' child abuse. Behavioral Science Unit, FBI, Quantico, VA; LaFontain, J.S. (1994). The extent and nature of organized and ritual abuse. Department of Health, HMSO; Goodman, G., Quin, J., Bottoms, B.L., & Shaver, P.R. Characteristics and sources of allegations of ritualistic child abuse. Report to the National Center on Child Abuse and Neglect.

Table 1-2
PERCENT OF SRA ACCUSATIONS BY YEAR ACCUSED WERE INFORMED

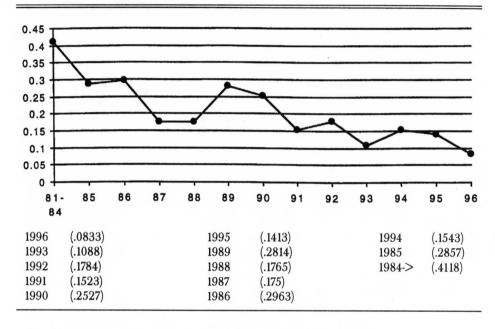

1996	(.0833)	1995	(.1413)	1994	(.1543)
1993	(.1088)	1989	(.2814)	1985	(.2857)
1992	(.1784)	1988	(.1765)	1984->	(.4118)
1991	(.1523)	1987	(.175)		
1990	(.2527)	1986	(.2963)		

Table 1-3
AGE AT WHICH ABUSE ALLEGEDLY STARTED

age	N	%
0-2	N=149	34.97
2-4	N=142	33.33
4-6	N=71	16.67
6-9	N=40	9.38
9-13	N=18	4.23
13-17	N=6	1.41

What do we know about the accusers?

Gender of Accuser
Male 8.43%   Female 91.57%

Did the accusations involve "repressed" memories?
Yes 92.62%   No 1.41%   Don't know 5.98%

From Family Survey Update N=2,056___

Circumstaces of the accusations

Was the accuser in therapy when accusations were made:
Yes 91.82%   No 2.71%   Don't know 05.47%

(From Family Survey Update N=2,056)

able. Children do not form autobiographical memories of events during their first few years of life. Memory researchers consider that this period of childhood amnesia, as it is usually called, results from the normal development of memory processes.[27] The formation of memories requires a degree of biological, conceptual, and linguistic development that is simply not present in the very young child. Furthermore, memory is a constructive process. There are no magic drugs or therapy techniques that can guarantee the accurate replay of past events. Memories are not videotapes but rather are active reconstructions influenced by current perceptions, interpretations and feelings. It is extremely difficult to reconcile the Family Survey data on the age at which the abuse allegedly started with what is known about the scientific processes of memory and about childhood amnesia.

The violent nature of so many of the alleged abuses, the very young age in which the alleged abuses are believed to have started, the multiple incidents of alleged abuse, the extended time periods over which the alleged abuses are said to have taken place, and the accusations of satanic conspiracies for which there is no credible evidence all require explanation. Given the lack of any corroboration for the acts of abuse of which the families are accused, the spread of a social belief system or moral panic seems a highly probable explanation for the accusations.

Who Is Accused?

A characteristic of both formal and informal family reports to FMSF is the changing nature over time of both the alleged abuse and the alleged perpetrators. As the horrible "memories" grow, fathers and mothers often replace neighbors and dead grandfathers as the primary perpetrators. In 51 percent of the reports in the Family Survey, only fathers were accused, although this may have come about after others were considered and dropped. While mothers are accused of being the only abuser in 6.5 percent of reports, in over 36 percent, the mothers are accused of active participation with their spouse in the abuse. This means that in 42 percent of reports, mothers are accused of active abuse. (Some mothers are accused of inserting umbrella handles or Barbie dolls into the vaginas of infants while changing their diapers.) It is difficult to reconcile the high percentage of mothers accused of active sexual abuse of their daughters with the evidence that women rarely abuse very young children, especially female children.[28] In addition, almost all the remaining mothers have been accused of "emotional neglect" and of

---

27. Usher, J.A., & Neisser, U. (1993). Childhood amnesia and the beginnings of memory for early life events. *Journal of Experimental Psychology: General, 122,* 155-165.

28. Finkelhor, D. (1994). Current information on the scope and nature of child sexual abuse. *The Future of Children, 4* 31-53.

"not protecting" the alleged victim. Some mothers have been sued for "not protecting" their children from abuse said to have taken place many years ago.

Another unusual aspect of the reports to the Foundation is that very few siblings were accused of perpetrating the abuse. Current research shows that sibling incest is far more prevalent than father-daughter incest, the ratio of the former to the latter being 13:1.[29] In the FMSF data, however, fathers were accused of abuse five times more often than were siblings. The survey data with regard to lawsuits are even more strange. Less than 4 percent of the repressed memory legal cases being tracked by the Foundation were brought only against siblings. The FMSF survey data, which appear to reverse many of the patterns seen in the statistics on documented child sexual abuse, may be another indication of the social nature of the FMS phenomenon.

If abuse cuts across class and racial divisions, as many have claimed, the absence of racial minority groups among the accused families that have contacted the Foundation needs to be explained. Moreover, the families that contact the FMSF seem to reflect a particularly well-educated segment of our society. The Family Survey data indicate that 28.2 percent have completed a 4-year college program and approximately 30 percent of the fathers have education beyond college. Given the fact that the accused are mostly in the 50 to 80 year age range, this seems a high educational attainment. Family Survey data indicate that over 71 percent of the parents are still married to their first spouse. Given the rate of divorce in our country, this appears high. About 70 percent of the families described themselves as active in their religion. Those who said that they were very active were more likely to be accused of involvement in satanic ritual cult conspiracies.

The FMSF data about the people who are accused raise many questions. Why are more fathers than siblings accused? Why are almost no minority groups represented? How can it be that such a high percentage of mothers are accused? Anyone who seeks to explain these anomalies must consider the possibility that the accusations are a result of social influence rather than historical fact.

A study that compared the results of polygraph ("lie-detector") tests in persons accused of sexual abuse on the basis of "recovered repressed memories" with those of persons accused of sexual abuse by alleged victims who claimed always to have remembered the abuse found that in the group of 46 alleged offenders in which repressed memory was involved only 2 (4%) of the subjects were found to be deceptive, whereas in the group of 300 alleged offenders whose accusers said they had always remembered the abuse 234

---

29. Levitt, E.E., & Pinnell, C.M. (1995). Some additional light on the childhood abuse-psychopathology axis. *The International Journal of Clinical and Experimental Hypnosis.* Vol. XLIII, no. 2, 145-162.

(78%) were classified as deceptive.[30] This is a striking difference and adds to the peculiar statistical characterization of FMS families. One possible interpretation of these results is that the polygraph test did function as an effective lie-detector and the vast majority of persons in the group that was accused on the basis of recovered repressed memories had not in fact committed the abuse, whereas a majority of those in the other group had committed the abuse.

What Do We Know About the Accusers?

The data from the Family Survey Update (N=2,056) indicate that most of the accusers are female (Male = 8.43%; Female = 91.57%). A large majority of the accusations were based on "recovered repressed memories." (In reply to the question, "Did the accusations involve "repressed" memories?" respondents' answers were: Yes = 92.62%; No = 1.41%; and Don't know = 5.98%.) About half of the accusers are in their 30s and most are between 25 and 45 years of age. The accusers are predominately Caucasian. Analysis of the Family Survey indicates that the accusers are as highly educated as their fathers, with almost 30 percent of them having postcollege education. Again, this data is difficult to reconcile with the fact that child sexual abuse reportedly cuts across class and racial divisions. It does, however, match well with data on the population that seeks out psychotherapy. The likelihood of using psychotherapy has been found to be higher for females than males, higher for those with at least 16 years of education, and higher for Caucasians than those of other races, 90.5 percent of psychotherapy users being white.[31]

In trying to understand why someone would make such a horrible accusation if it were not true, we first hypothesized that the accusers had some sort of pathology that would have been evident during their development.[32] This did not appear to be confirmed in the reports from the parents. In the Family Survey (N=494), the percentage of accusers who had some history of psychiatric or psychological treatment at various times was about 7.7 percent in childhood, 18.2 percent in adolescence and 23.9 percent in college. This is puzzling. On the one hand, if 68 percent of the accusers had been as horrifically abused before the age of four as they believe, one might expect that

---

30. Abrams, S. (1995, Summer). False memory syndrome vs. total repression. *J. Psychiatry and Law*, 283-293.

31. Olfson, M., & Pincus, H.A. (1994). Outpatient psychotherapy in the United States, I: Volume, costs and user characteristics. *American Journal of Psychiatry, 151:9*, 1281-1294.

32. Wakefield, H., & Underwager, R. (1992). Recovered memories of alleged sexual abuse: Lawsuits against parents. *Behavioral Sciences and the Law, 10,* 483-507.

more than 7.7 percent would have shown some signs of problems near the time that the abuse took place that would have required treatment. Problems in school, in relationships, or in physical symptoms are not in evidence, however.

Accusers claimed that they had "dissociated" during the abuse and that that was the reason they had no memory of it. While the scientific evidence for repression has fallen short, the psychiatric profession does recognize the existence of dissociative disorders. According to Daniel Schacter, however, it seems unlikely that people would be symptom-free for 20 or 30 years after a traumatic stress that was sufficient to produce dissociation and then suddenly start showing symptoms. Says Schacter, "If people become skilled enough at dissociation to develop total amnesia for traumatic experiences, it would imply the existence of a dissociative disorder—a serious matter. If they have engaged in extensive dissociation, then patients who recover previously forgotten memories involving years of horrific abuse should also have a documented history of severe pathology that indicates a long-standing dissociative disorder."[33]

On the other hand, if the accusers had not been abused, one might also expect them to have shown pathology during their childhood that could help explain their vulnerability for adult changed personalities and behavior. But it was in their adult years that most sought therapy for the first time. While there is some evidence that a small percentage of the accusers have serious mental illness, most sought therapy for coping with life events such as depression, anxiety about relationships, weight control problems, job loss, and divorce. The evidence seems to indicate that these life-problems were reinterpreted by the therapists as being problems caused by repressed memories of sexual abuse. The Family Survey is based on reports from parents, but the reports from retractors reinforce this point. It is difficult to reconcile accusers' current claims with the fact that most of the high-achieving accusers apparently lived for decades with no symptoms that required professional attention.

The FMSF data raise many questions about the demographics and health of accusers. A social explanation seems highly probable. A legal suit brought in King County Superior Court of Washington by a retractor against her therapist and settled in the spring of 1995 in favor of the retractor illustrates this point. Evidence was introduced in court that at the beginning of therapy the patient had tested in the normal range on a standard personality test but that her test results were well beyond normal limits after therapy

---

33. Schacter, D.L. (1996). *Searching for memory: The brain, the mind and the past.* NY: Basic Books. p. 262.

began and hypnosis was used. The patient did appear to have suffered severe trauma, but the trauma seems to have been the result of the therapy.[34]

Circumstances of the Accusations

Although it is entirely possible that someone could develop false memories in any setting, therapy is a constant in the reports to the Foundation. When asked, "Was the accuser in therapy when accusations were made?" the answers of those who responded to the Family Survey Update were: Yes = 91.82 percent; No = 2.71 percent; and Don't know = 05.47 percent (N=2,056). Retractors' and accused family members' descriptions of the progress of the therapy raise serious concerns for many in the professional community. In report after report, the therapy seemed to take the same path. Patients entered therapy searching for help with a current problem and the therapist reinterpreted it as a symptom of a problem dating from childhood. The therapists seem to have directed the course of therapy based on the following assumptions: that a huge proportion of people have been sexually abused, that child sexual abuse results in psychopathology when the victims reach adulthood, and that there are signs or symptoms by which the therapist can identify a person who has been abused. The patient's report that he or she has no memory of being abused is assumed to indicate that the abuse was so bad that the patient "repressed" the memory or had traumatic amnesia at the time of the abuse.

The therapist assumes that, in order to get better, the patient must remember the abuse. Therapists may tell patients that even if they don't have a memory of being abused, they needn't assume that they were not abused, because some abuse survivors never get memories.[35] Therapists also assume that they have the ability to help patients recover their "repressed" memories. They believe they can do this, first, by "providing a safe place" for the patient to recall childhood traumas. The means used to call up repressed memories may include the formal induction of hypnosis; the use of guided imagery, relaxation techniques, sodium amytal, or dream interpretation; the provision of suggestive books such as *The Courage to Heal and Secret Survivors*; or the requirement that the patient attend group therapy sessions in which people share abuse stories.[36]

After the psychotherapy, patients come to believe they are abuse victims; they redefine their identity. They perform psychological surgery, a "paren-

---

34. Legal News (Case of Laura Deck). (1995, June). FMSF Newsletter.

35. Bass, E., & Davis, L. (1988). The Courage to Heal. New York: Harper Collins.

36. Blume, E.S. (1985). *Secret survivors: Uncovering incest and its aftereffects in women.* New York: Ballantine Books.

tectomy," and detach from their parents and any other people who do not validate and support the new abuse belief.[37] This behavior is shockingly similar to that of people who enter cults.

The FMSF data about the families and the accusations raise many questions, especially in light of statements from some professionals claiming that only a small percentage of FMSF parents could be telling the truth.[38] Since the formation of the FMS Foundation in 1992, all of the assumptions of these therapy practices have come under serious challenge because they are risky and unsupported by scientific theory or evidence. The assumptions and practices fall far short of the standards of care that have been outlined in the ethics codes for the practice of psychiatry and psychology. That these practices have taken place is incontrovertible: many therapists have written books that state their theoretical assumptions and describe the therapy practices that have been of concern; therapy records that have been introduced as evidence in court cases provide documentation that some therapists engage in these practices; and television documentaries such as CNN Special Reports (1993) and the 1994 four-hour PBS Frontline documentary "Divided Memories" provide visual evidence of these practices. Many professionals continue to dismiss the FMS problem as caused by the practices of only a few therapists, but research indicates otherwise; these assumptions and practices have been widespread in the therapeutic community.[39]

The problem of FMS is real, it is dangerous, it is widespread and it is tragic. Yet, as of this time, no major American mental health association has taken strong action to prevent or discourage its members from engaging in these dangerous practices. Until they do, the problem will increasingly be dealt with by the legal system. Since its formation, the FMS Foundation has been tracking legal developments related to the false memory problem, first examining suits brought against families based only on "recovered repressed" memory evidence and then, several years later, looking at lawsuits brought by former patients against therapists for misuse of memory recovery techniques. What the Foundation has learned is presented in Chapter 7.

---

37. Briere, J. (1989). *Therapy for adults molested as children: Beyond survival.* New York: Springer.

38. See, for example, Gangelhoff, B. June 12, 1994. A mental health dilemma; Searching for truths in memories. *Houston Post.* "Using what she says is a proven standard for measuring false allegations of child sexual abuse, [Judith] Herman estimates that, at best, only 10 percent of the FMS parents could possibly be telling the truth."

39. Poole, D.A., Lindsay, D.S., Memon, A., & Bull, R. (1995). Psychotherapy and the recovery of memories of childhood sexual abuse: U.S. and British practitioners' beliefs, practices, and experiences. *Journal of Consulting and Clinical Psychology, 653(3),* 426-437.

Chapter 2

FROM MESMER TO MEMORIES: A HISTORICAL, SCIENTIFIC LOOK AT THE RECOVERED MEMORIES CONTROVERSY

In the next few pages, I will attempt to provide a brief historical overview that puts the modern hunt for repressed memories into context. I will note some of the more significant events that occurred in the last 400 years or so, from the hunt for witches in the 16th and 17th centuries to the publication, in 1988, of *The Courage to Heal*, a book that has had an enormous and detrimental effect.[1] By encouraging women to act *as if* they have memories of abuse, even if they don't have them yet, and suggesting that many people were abused throughout their childhoods even if they don't remember it, the book has contributed greatly to the epidemic of recovered memories of abuse that began in the 1980s.

During the 16th and 17th centuries, most of Europe engaged in a frantic search for evil witches, a process which bore an alarming resemblance to the modern hunt for pedophiles—except, of course, that there really *are* pedophiles, which makes the epidemic search for repressed memories more confusing. To the clerics, philosophers, and lawyers of the 1500s, however, there was also no doubt that witches existed and exerted a malevolent force everywhere. For the most part, those accused of being witches were older women who were believed to possess extraordinary powers. They were thought to have formed an underground international organization and to practice hideous rituals involving bestiality, murder, rape, and other atrocities.[2]

The zealous clerics and judges who ferreted out these evil witches had help from numerous manuals that described the symptoms of witchcraft in

---

1. Bass, E., & Davis, L. (1988). *The courage to heal.* New York: Harper Collins.

2. Trevor-Roper, H.R. (1969). The European witch-craze of the sixteenth and seventeenth centuries and other essays. New York: Harper & Row; Spanos, N. P., and Gottlieb, J. (1979). Demonic possession, mesmerism, and hysteria: A social psychological perspective on their historical interrelations. *Journal of Abnormal Psychology*, 88(5), 527-546; Mackay, C. (1841, 1932). *Extraordinary popular delusions and the madness of crowds.* London: Richard Bentley (L.C. Page & Co. reprint).

great detail. The first and most famous, the *Malleus Maleficarum*, or *Hammer of Witches*, written by Heinrich Kramer and James Sprenger, was published in 1486.[3] It is a remarkable document that, like its modern equivalent, *The Courage to Heal*, offers an internally logical and quite convincing way to identify the root cause of any human problem. In the 15th century, however, it was witchcraft rather than repressed memories of sexual abuse that wreaked havoc in people's lives. It was clear to the clerics that the terrible events described were true–they were, after all, independently repeated, with the same details, all over Europe and even in America, by people who had never met one another. How could they have reported these events if they were not true?

Some, but not all, of the confessions made during the Witch Craze were extracted by torture. Many "witches" confessed to the most ridiculous charges. For every victim whose story popped out under duress, there were two or three who genuinely believed they were witches. They had developed very coherent, detailed memories of the orgies in which they had taken part, the babies they had roasted and eaten. Young girls would describe in gory detail how they had been deflowered by the Devil, though examination proved them to be virgins.

Exactly why social movements such as the Witch Craze occur is a difficult question to answer, but it appears that periods of general social unrest provide a standard backdrop for such events. When life is too confusing, a scapegoat helps, whether it be a witch, a Jew, a Communist, or a purported pedophile. In this case, women were the primary victims: they were accused of witchcraft, confessed, and were burned at the stake.

In 1972, Phyllis Chesler made the following observation in her book, *Women and Madness*: "No longer are women sacrificed as voluntary or involuntary witches. They are, instead, taught to sacrifice themselves for newly named heresies."[4] The history of medicine and psychology in Western civilization has been, in large part, a fulfillment of that dictum–women (and men, too, though in fewer numbers) have been taught to sacrifice themselves on the altar of the latest theory or fad.[5]

Demonology, a parallel phenomenon to the belief in witches, predated the two centuries of the Witch Craze and lasted well beyond it–to this day, in fact. Because she shared the same cultural frame of reference as the priest, the demoniac usually truly believed that she was possessed and would involuntarily exhibit all of the expected characteristics. In addition, there were

---

3. Kramer, H., & J. Sprenger (1486, 1971). *Malleus maleficarum*, translated and introduction by M. Summers. New York: Dover.

4. Chesler, P. (1972). *Women and madness*. Garden City, New York: Doubleday. p. 34.

5. Shorter, E. (1992). *From paralysis to fatigue: A history of psychosomatic illness in the modern era*. New York: Free Press.

benefits that went along with the role, particularly for women who normally had little societal power. They received a great deal of sympathetic attention, they had the power to identify witches or predict the future, and they enjoyed a lightened work load as well as a dramatic self-importance.[6]

With the arrival of the "Enlightenment" and the dawn of the "scientific" age, demons and witches became less popular. The cloak of "expert" was transferred from the cleric to the physician and, eventually, the therapist. The symptoms and treatment, however, didn't change all that much. Now women were called "hysterics," a pejorative word deriving from the Greek word for the uterus. The idea was that a "floating womb" accounted for most problems.[7]

In 1702, a London physician named John Purcell described "vapours, otherwise called hysterick fits." Sufferers exhibited the following symptoms: "First they feel a heaviness upon their breast, a grumbling in their belly, they belch up, and sometimes vomit . . . They have a difficulty in breathing and think they feel something that comes up into their throat which is ready to choke them; they struggle, cry out, make odd and inarticulate sounds or mutterings; they perceive a swimming in their heads, a dimness comes over their eyes; they turn pale, are scarce able to stand; their pulse is weak, they shut their eyes, fall down and remain senseless for some time." This describes, for the most part, a classic panic attack.[8]

In the 1750s, Edinburgh physiologist Robert Whytt discovered the nervous system; female patients now were diagnosed with "nervous disorders." As a cynical commentator wrote in 1786: "Before the publication of [Whytt's] book, people of fashion had not the least idea that they had nerves. But a fashionable apothecary [general practitioner] of my acquaintance, having cast his eye over the book...[began telling them], 'Madam, you are nervous.'"[9]

In the late 1700s, Franz Anton Mesmer invented the "science" of animal magnetism, posited on the belief that humans have a "subtle fluid" whose unequal distribution can be realigned by a magnetizer who makes "passes" over patients. Mesmer moved to Paris in 1778, where he became increas-

---

6. Spanos, N. P., & Gottlieb, J. (1979). Demonic possession, mesmerism, and hysteria: a social psychological perspective on their historical interrelations. *Journal of Abnormal Psychology, 88*(5), 527-546; Bourguignon, E. (1976). *Possession.* San Francisco: Chandler & Sharp.

7. Shorter, E. (1992). *From paralysis to fatigue: A history of psychosomatic illness in the modern era.* New York: Free Press; Merskey, H. (1979). *The analysis of hysteria.* London: Bailliere Tindall; Merskey, H. (1995). *The analysis of hysteria: Understanding conversion and dissociation.* (2d ed.). London: Royal College of Psychiatrists.

8. Shorter, E. (1992). *From paralysis to fatigue: A history of psychosomatic illness in the modern era.* New York: Free Press. p. 6; American Psychiatric Association. (1994). *Diagnostic and statistical manual of mental disorders* (4th ed.). Washington, D.C.: Author. p. 395.

9. Shorter, E. (1992). *From paralysis to fatigue: a history of psychosomatic illness in the modern era.* New York: Free Press. p. 24.

ingly convinced that the power of animal magnetism resided within himself. He emphasized the need to establish "rapport" with his patients, eliciting an almost mystical bond between the powerful male magnetizer and his weak female patient. He termed this relationship "magnetic reciprocity." Mesmer's flashy therapy—he wore purple robes and held court in a dimly lit room full of mirrors, stained glass, gentle music, and the scent of orange blossoms, while he waved his magnetizing rod and stared deeply into his patients' eyes—attracted young women who had vague abdominal complaints and other troubles. Mesmer believed that only when his patients reached a "crisis," characterized by convulsive contortions, would their fluids properly realign themselves. Not surprisingly, his young women obliged by performing as expected, after which, emotionally and physically spent, they experienced at least temporary symptom remission.[10]

Mesmer was eventually discredited and subsequent practitioners dropped much of his mumbo-jumbo, realizing that they could put patients into a hypnotic trance without magnets. In 1843, James Braid popularized the term "hypnosis." He eventually came to believe, correctly, that hypnosis worked through the suggestibility of the client. He thought that by having the hypnotic subject concentrate on one idea to the exclusion of all else (for example, "my arm cannot bend"), the idea would become true. Other hypnotists believed they could cure a new disease called "catalepsy," in which women froze into weird positions and couldn't move. In fact, these physicians both *created* and *cured* catalepsy by hypnotic suggestion.[11]

Around the same time, in the 1840s, "spinal irritation" became all the rage. A doctor could diagnose it by probing a woman's spine. One astute physician objected in 1849. He wrote: "Attracting the patient's chief attention and filling her head with the fear that some disease exists in that situation [the spine], greatly misleads the practitioner."[12]

Like the current crop of patients with "multiple personality disorder" or "dissociative identity disorder" (the new official diagnosis), the cataleptics proved to be intriguing patients who often displayed supernatural powers of vision or touch. The condition purportedly heightened these senses. One woman could hear only through her stomach, while many cataleptics

---

10. Shorter, E. (1992). *From paralysis to fatigue: a history of psychosomatic illness in the modern era.* New York: Free Press; Baker, R. A. (1990). *They call it hypnosis.* Buffalo, NY: Prometheus Books; Ellenberger, H. F. (1970). *The discovery of the unconscious: The history and evolution of dynamic psychiatry.* New York: Basic Books; *Extraordinary popular delusions and the madness of crowds.* London: Richard Bentley (L.C. Page & Co. reprint). pp. 304-345.

11. Shorter, E. (1992). *From paralysis to fatigue: A history of psychosomatic illness in the modern era.* New York: Free Press. pp.130-146.

12. Shorter, E. (1992). *From paralysis to fatigue: A history of psychosomatic illness in the modern era.* New York: Free Press. pp. 25-39

claimed that they could see their own insides. French magnetizer Charles Despine created and treated numerous cataleptic patients in the early 1800s through hypnosis. Despine's prize pupil was a 21-year-old seamstress named Micheline Viollet. At first, she did not reveal expected symptoms such as "ecstasy" (a sort of rapturous trance) and somnambulism. When Despine told her that "they surely will one day appear," Micheline obligingly developed the required symptoms. If anyone she disliked so much as looked at her, she would instantly become immobile. Like many such patients, Micheline went on to become a "healer" in her own right. The literature of the age is full of women who converted easily from patient to practitioner, having found a vocation in life.[13] (Similarly, many former patients who have recovered "memories" of abuse have gone on, in modern times, to become recovered memory therapists.)

When catalepsy and spinal irritation passed out of favor, they were replaced by "reflex theory." According to this new dogma, nervous connections running along the spine regulated *all* bodily organs, including the brain, independent of human will. One organ could therefore affect a far-distant organ. Suddenly, the long-suffering uterus returned to the fore. The organs of generation were implicated in numerous troubles, ranging from paralysis to fits. Doctors often diagnosed women by pressing on their ovaries and inducing convulsions. The awful solution? Remove the offending parts, excise the ovaries![14]

In the latter half of the 1800s, the theory of the "reflex arc" came into full flower. According to this theory, a problem in one organ of the body could be the result of disease in a distant, seemingly unrelated, organ. Faced with "paralysis of the tongue," doctors deduced its cause: a constipated colon. Similarly, an entire school of German ophthalmologists diagnosed diseases of the eye as stemming from uterine troubles. In a final flourishing of the theory, both European and American doctors concluded that the mucous lining of the nose was neurologically connected to the genitals. Consequently, a nosebleed might supplant menstruation, while chronic masturbation could be cured by nasal operations.[15]

In the progression from witches and demons to animal magnetism and diagnoses of hysteria, irritable spine, catalepsy, and reflex arcs, nothing had materially changed other than the role that the patients were expected to play. Many of the symptoms—dizziness, a choking sensation, vague pains,

---

13. Shorter, E. (1992). *From paralysis to fatigue: A history of psychosomatic illness in the modern era.* New York: Free Press. pp. 130-146.

14. Masson, J. M. (1986). *A dark science: Women, sexuality and psychiatry in the nineteenth century.* New York: Farrar, Straus & Giroux. pp. 45-54, 128-138; Shorter, E. (1992). *From paralysis to fatigue: A history of psychosomatic illness in the modern era.* New York: Free Press. pp.81-86.

15. Shorter, E. (1992). *From paralysis to fatigue: A history of psychosomatic illness in the modern era.* New York: Free Press. pp. 40-68.

panic attacks, and feelings of depersonalization–remained the same, although blaspheming against God, speaking in a demonic voice, or defining oneself as possessed became less popular. In many ways, however, as the late Nicholas Spanos pointed out, those labeled as "hysterics" shared many characteristics with demoniacs: "They tended to be unhappy women who were socialized into viewing themselves as weak and passive, dissatisfied with their lives, socially and economically powerless, and without access to means of voicing their dissatisfactions or improving their lot outside of adopting the role of a sick person."[16]

In the 1870s and 1880s, Jean-Martin Charcot created a veritable psychiatric circus at his Salpêtrière, a combination poorhouse, home for the aged, and asylum for insane women. Charcot was a great neurological systematizer who became fascinated by "hysteria." It happened that women with mental disorders were housed alongside epileptics. When some of these women, who had no apparent organic problems, began to imitate the epileptic fits, Charcot initially labeled them "hystero-epileptics." Many of Charcot's (and, later, Freud's) patients may have actually suffered from real, undiagnosed neurological disorders such as temporal lobe epilepsy, organic brain damage, tuberculous meningitis, encephalitis, Tourette's syndrome, multiple sclerosis, or syphilis. By ignoring their real ailments and focusing on "hysteria," Charcot effectively blamed the patients for the disorder.[17]

On the other hand, it is probable that many of Charcot's cases were indeed psychosomatic. Charcot came to rely increasingly on hypnosis. Unfortunately, he himself *induced* and *encouraged* his patients' problematic behavior rather than helping to alleviate it. In other words, many of his "hysterics" were iatrogenically influenced to believe in a mythical disease and to act out its appropriate symptoms. (It is also possible that some of Charcot's patients were faking in order to secure insurance payments. "Railway brain" was a recently-named ailment in claims against train companies of the time.)[18]

Several of the historical movements I have just traced combined in the extraordinary career of Sigmund Freud. In 1885, Freud came to study under Charcot for a few months. The experience catalyzed Freud, diverting him from neuropathology to psychopathology. In a letter to his fiancée, Freud wrote that Charcot was a genius who was "uprooting my aims and opinions," giving him a "new idea of perfection." While some critics complained of

---

16. Spanos, N. P., and Gottlieb, J. (1979). Demonic possession, mesmerism, and hysteria: A social psychological perspective on their historical interrelations. *Journal of Abnormal Psychology, 88*(5), 542.

17. Webster, R. (1995). *Why freud was wrong: Sin, science and psychoanalysis.* London: HarperCollins; New York: Basic Books. pp. 71-167.

18. Shorter, E. (1992). *From paralysis to fatigue: A history of psychosomatic illness in the modern era.* New York: Free Press. pp. 166-200.

Charcot's showmanship, the young Austrian physician clearly loved it. "My brain is sated, as if I had spent an evening at the theatre."[19]

Freud followed in the grand tradition of physicians who identified the precise symptoms they expected to find, then proceeded to induce them. Freud believed in much of the quackery that had preceded him, including the notion that excessive masturbation caused neurosis, that there was a nasal reflex arc, and that hysteria could be provoked by pressing on the ovaries, which he termed "stimulation of the hysterogenic zone." Freud believed in a variety of hands-on therapies, one of which played a significant role in early recovered memory cases (to be discussed below).[20]

Writing to his best friend, Wilhelm Fliess, in 1895, Freud said, "I have invented a strange therapy of my own: I search for sensitive areas, press on them, and thus provoke fits of shaking which free her [the patient]."[21] That same year, Freud treated a 27-year-old named Emma Eckstein, who came from a prominent socialist family and was active in the Viennese women's movement. Like many "hysterical" or "neurasthenic" patients of the era, she came to Freud with vague complaints, including stomach aches and menstrual problems. He deduced that she suffered from excessive masturbation that could be cured by operating on her nose. He prevailed on Fliess, a well-respected Berlin ear-nose-and-throat specialist, to perform the operation. At first, Fliess had used cocaine on his patients' noses, which provided temporary relief (and a pleasant buzz, no doubt). Then he had cauterized their noses, but that too failed to do the trick. Finally, he decided that removal of a portion of the left middle turbinate bone would permanently cure female sexual afflictions. Freud concurred, and the unfortunate Emma Eckstein believed them.[22]

Fliess bungled the operation, sewing a large piece of gauze into Eckstein's nose. She nearly died of a massive hemorrhage as a result. Freud managed to rationalize the entire affair, assuring Fliess that it was "one of those accidents that happen to the most fortunate and circumspect of surgeons." In the end, Freud even managed to blame Emma Eckstein. Her bleeding was all

---

19. Freud, S. (1953-1974). *Standard edition of the complete psychological works of Sigmund Freud*, translated by J. Strachey. 24 volumes. London: Hogarth Pr. Vol. 3, p. 9-10.

20. Pendergrast, Mark (1995, 1996). *Victims of memory: sex abuse accusations and shattered lives*. (2d ed.). Hinesburg, VT: Upper Access. pp. 411-423; Crews, F. (1995). *The memory wars: Freud's legacy in dispute*. New York: New York Review; Crews, F. (1993, November 18). The unknown Freud. *New York Review of Books*, 55-66; Esterson, A. (1993). *Seductive mirage: An exploration of the work of Sigmund Freud*. Chicago: Open Court; Webster, R. (1995). *Why Freud was wrong: Sin, science and psychoanalysis*. London: Harper Collins; N.Y.: Basic Books.

21. Freud, S. (1985). *The Complete letters of Sigmund Freud to Wilhelm Fliess, 1887-1904*, translated and edited by J. M. Masson. Cambridge, MA: Belknap Press. p. 120.

22. Masson, J. M. (1984, 1992). *The assault on truth: Freud's suppression of the seduction theory*. New York: Harper Perrenial. pp. 55-106.

caused by hysteria! Incredibly, Eckstein remained true to Freud, even becoming a psychotherapist later herself.

Emma Eckstein was one of the first patients upon whom Freud practiced another form of questionable therapy that became the cornerstone for his psychological theories. He concluded that her problems stemmed not only from masturbation (known as "self-abuse" in those days), but from a repressed memory of sexual abuse when she was eight. He prompted her to recall a visit to a confectioner's during which the shopkeeper had grabbed her genitals through her clothing. This memory was mild, however, compared to those he eventually elicited from Eckstein in 1897: "I obtained a scene [i.e., a "memory"] about the circumcision of a girl. The cutting of a piece of the labia minora (which is still shorter today), sucking up the blood, following which the child was given a piece of the skin to eat." Like many modern physicians who are "experts" in child sexual abuse, Freud had found physical "evidence" to corroborate this memory.[23]

Taking his lead from Charcot, Freud had begun hypnotizing patients late in 1887, primarily using direct suggestion in an attempt to ameliorate their symptoms. Until then, he had relied primarily on various forms of ablutions ("hydrotherapy"), mild electrical stimulation, massage, and the "rest cure."[24]

Soon, Freud also started to use hypnosis to access what he suspected were repressed memories. In 1895, in uneasy collaboration with Joseph Breuer, Freud published *Studies in Hysteria*, in which he elaborated his theory that unconscious repressed memories caused hysteria, obsession, and other neurotic symptoms. "The patient only gets free from the hysterical symptom by reproducing the pathogenic impressions that caused it and by giving utterance to them with an expression of affect, and thus the therapeutic task *consists solely in inducing him to do so*," Freud wrote.[25] The following year, he elaborated on this theory in three essays, making it clear that he considered *repressed memories of childhood sexual abuse* to be the root cause of all hysterical symptoms.

Until the end of 1895, Freud relied at least partially on hypnosis to delve into his patients' unconscious. Frustrated by his inability to hypnotize some subjects—and by the outright unwillingness of others—Freud had already invented a new "pressure procedure" in which his patients lay down, closed their eyes, and allowed Freud to press on their foreheads or squeeze their heads between his hands. They were then to report whatever images or

23. Freud, S. (1985). *The complete letters of Sigmund Freud to Wilhelm Fliess, 1887-1904*, translated and edited by J. M. Masson. Cambridge, MA: Belknap Press. p. 227.

24. Freud, S. (1953-1974). *Standard edition of the complete psychological works of Sigmund Freud*, translated by J. Strachey. 24 volumes. London: Hogarth Press. Vol. 2, pp. xi-xiii, 110-111.

25. Freud, S. (1953-1974). *Standard edition of the complete psychological works of Sigmund Freud*, translated by J. Strachey. 24 volumes. London: Hogarth Press. Vol. 2, pp. 283.

words popped into their heads. When he insisted that his patients report unusual thoughts, they finally obliged him, though it often took two or three head squeezes. "I derived from this analysis a literally unqualified reliance on my technique," Freud wrote with satisfaction. In the quotes that follow from Freud, bear in mind that when he speaks of an "analytic procedure" or "pressure," he is referring to this literal pressure of his hands on his patients' heads.[26]

Before arriving at the crucial traumatic childhood scene, Freud believed that he had to go slowly, establishing rapport and gaining patients' confidence. Then, through "repeated, indeed continuous, use of this procedure of pressure on the forehead," he delved for memories like an archeologist digging ever deeper. "We force our way into the internal strata, overcoming resistances all the time; we get to know the themes accumulated in one of these strata and the threads running through it." Finally, after pursuing numerous side paths, he could "penetrate by a main path straight to the nucleus of the pathogenic organization... Now the patient helps us energetically.... Resistance is for the most part broken."[27]

By February of 1896, Freud explicitly blamed hysteria on *"precocious experience of sexual relations with actual excitement of the genitals, resulting from sexual abuse."* His 13 cases were "without exception of a severe kind" that could be classed as "grave sexual injuries; some of them were positively revolting." Freud believed that he had discovered the "source of the Nile," as he put it, explaining all hysteria. Within a few years, however, he abandoned this so-called "seduction theory."[28]

Did Freud indeed uncover horrifying repressed memories of paternal incest, or did he merely provide a template for the modern brand of memory seekers? We can get a clue from Freud's arrogance. "We must not believe what they say [when they deny having memories], we must always assume, and tell them, too, that they have kept something back.... We must insist on this, we must repeat the pressure and represent ourselves as infallible, till at last we are really told something."

"We must not be led astray by initial denials. If we keep firmly to what we have inferred, we shall in the end conquer every resistance by emphasizing the unshakable nature of our convictions." It is instructive to read Freud's 1896 description of how he unearthed repressed memories: "The

26. Freud, S. (1953-1974). *Standard edition of the complete psychological works of Sigmund Freud*, translated by J. Strachey. 24 volumes. London: Hogarth Press. Vol. 2, pp. xi-xiii, 153-154, 267-271.

27. Freud, S. (1953-1974). *Standard edition of the complete psychological works of Sigmund Freud*, translated by J. Strachey. 24 volumes. London: Hogarth Press. Vol. 2, pp. 272, 294-295.

28. Freud, S. (1953-1974). *Standard edition of the complete psychological works of Sigmund Freud*, translated by J. Strachey. 24 volumes. London: Hogarth Press Vol. 2, p. 276; vol. 3, p. 152, 164, 180, 208-215; Freud, S. (1985). *The complete letters of Sigmund Freud to Wilhelm Fliess, 1887-1904*, translated and edited by J. M. Masson. Cambridge, MA: Belknap Press. p. 226.

fact is that these patients never repeat these stories spontaneously, nor do they ever in the course of a treatment suddenly present the physician with the complete recollection of a scene of this kind. One only succeeds in awakening the psychical trace of a precocious sexual event under the most energetic pressure of the analytic procedure, and against an enormous resistance. Moreover, the memory must be extracted from them piece by piece, and while it is being awakened in their consciousness they become the prey to an emotion which it would be hard to counterfeit."[29]

"Before they come for analysis the patients know nothing about these scenes," Freud proudly noted. "They are indignant as a rule if we warn them that such scenes are going to emerge. Only the strongest compulsion of the treatment can induce them to embark on a reproduction of them." Once they finally produced a suitable memory, they often tried to deny it. "Something has occurred to me now, but you obviously put it into my head," they would say, or "I know what you expect me to answer," or "Something has occurred to me now, it's true, but it seems to me as if I'd put it up deliberately." To these protestations, Freud turned a deaf ear. "In all such cases, I remain unshakably firm." Often, the doctor was even more blunt. "The principal point is that I should guess the secret and tell it to the patient straight out."[30]

While Freud abandoned his seduction theory, he never admitted that he had forced incest memories on his clients. Instead, he claimed that they had spontaneously produced such fantasies. Thus was the Oedipal Complex born. As a result, for many years patients who had always recalled childhood sexual abuse were frequently told by their therapists that they had merely fantasized it. In the meantime, over the years, the idea of repressed memories kept resurfacing, with the "birth trauma" memories of Otto Rank, Sandor Ferenczi's mental excavations of the 1930s, "narco-analysis" using so-called "truth serum" barbiturates, drug abreactions of World War II veterans, etc.[31]

During the same period, Pierre Janet created his theory of dissociation, hypothesizing that those who have undergone extensive trauma forget it entirely by taking their attention away. While we all "dissociate" sometimes–thinking about one thing so much we forget where we are driving or who we called on the phone–the idea of "massive dissociation," in which people completely forget extensive abuse, is questionable. The late 1800s

---

29. Freud, S. (1953-1974). *Standard edition of the complete psychological works of Sigmund Freud*, translated by J. Strachey. 24 volumes. London: Hogarth Press. Vol. 2, pp. 279, 281; vol. 3, p. 153, 269.

30. Freud, S. (1953-1974). *Standard edition of the complete psychological works of Sigmund Freud*, translated by J. Strachey. 24 volumes. London: Hogarth Press. Vol. 2, pp. 280-281; vol. 3, p. 195, 204.

31. Pendergrast, Mark. (1995, 1996). *Victims of memory: sex abuse accusations and shattered lives*. (2d ed.). Hinesburg, VT: Upper Access. p. 497.

were, in some ways, remarkably similar to the late 1900s, with old values in shambles and a fascination with hypnosis, psychology, and psychic powers.[32]

Let us now jump to America in the 1970s. During the late '60s, psychology had gone pop, with encounter groups and the like, and by the '70s, the country was poised for an onslaught of diverse therapies. Social workers joined clinical psychologists as licensed therapists. During the '70s, people sought all manner of therapy, including Synanon, est, Silva Mind Control, transcendental meditation, primal scream, co-counseling, rebirthing, direct analysis, gestalt, and transactional analysis. What all of these approaches had in common was the notion that people repressed by modern technology had to get in touch with their *feelings* in order to feel better.

Psychologist Arthur Janov provided the prototype for the current trauma therapist with his wildly popular 1970 book, *The Primal Scream.* Janov's patients were told that they must recall repressed memories of trauma at the hands of their parents, and that only in reliving them—and screaming bloody murder—would they be healed. The therapist didn't have to worry about a particular symptom list because "*all* neuroses stem from the same specific cause." Once cured by the Primal Scream(s), a patient would lead "a tensionless, defense-free life in which one is completely his own self and experiences deep feeling and internal unity."[33]

The process by which Janov elicited his screams would be familiar to any brainwashing expert. For three weeks, patients must not work or attend school. During the first week, they must stay in a hotel room without TV, radio, or any other distraction. The night before their first session, they should not sleep. "The isolation and sleeplessness are important techniques which often bring patients close to a Primal," Janov noted. "Lack of sleep helps crumble defenses." Noting with satisfaction that patients arrive already suffering, the therapist instructed them to lie spread-eagle on a couch "in as defenseless a physical position as possible." Patients were then encouraged to "sink into the feeling" of childhood. After a "chipping away process" of several hours—during which Janov urged "Feel that! Stay with it!"—they finally arrived at their Primal Scene and screamed something like, "Daddy, be nice!", "Mommy, help!" or "I hate you, I hate you!" At the end of the day, the patient returned to his hotel room. "He still may not watch television or go to the movies," wrote Janov. "He really does not want to because he is consumed with himself."[34]

---

32. Pendergrast, Mark. (1995, 1996). *Victims of memory: Sex abuse accusations and shattered lives.* (2d ed.). Hinesburg, VT: Upper Access. pp. 180, 424-425, 432-435.

33. Janov, A. (1970). *The primal scream: Primal therapy, the cure for neurosis.* New York: Dell. pp. 20-30.

34. Janov, A. (1970). *The primal scream: Primal therapy, the cure for neurosis.* New York: Dell. pp. 79-85.

Meanwhile, the notion of multiple personalities, first posited in a limited way by Pierre Janet but popularized by American psychologist Morton Prince in the early part of this century, had been revived in the 1950s by Eve's three faces—which eventually grew to 22 personalities.[35] But it was *Sybil*, published in 1973 and made into a popular movie in 1977, that really spawned the modern crop of multiples and provided the cornerstone for an assumed background of sexual abuse. Sybil came to Dr. Cornelia Wilbur as a severe anorexic and soon revealed a second side of herself named Peggy. Over time, 16 different entities emerged, all having "split" from the original because of horrendous sexual and physical abuse.[36] The identification of Sybil as an MPD has recently been debunked by Dr. Herbert Spiegel, who was her substitute therapist at the time. "When Sybil came to therapy with me," Spiegel says, "and we were discussing some phase of her life, she asked me, 'Do you want me to be Peggy, or can I just tell you?' That took me aback, and I asked her what she meant. 'Well, when I'm with Dr. Wilbur, she wants me to be Peggy.' I told her that if it made her more comfortable to be Peggy, that was fine, but otherwise it wasn't necessary. She seemed relieved and chose not to assume different personalities when she was with me."[37]

With the publication in 1980 of *Michelle Remembers*, by Michelle Smith and her psychiatrist, Lawrence Pazder, the element of satanic ritual abuse was added, along with the possibility of demonic possession.[38] Also in 1980, psychiatrist Ralph Allison published *Minds in Many Pieces*, in which he described an exorcism of one of his multiple personality patients.[39] The same year, the third edition of the *Diagnostic and Statistical Manual of Mental Disorders* (DSM-III), published by the American Psychiatric Association, first recognized multiple personality disorder as a bonafide psychiatric disorder. Because American insurance companies will pay only for mental illnesses sanctioned by the DSM, multiple personalities suddenly became lucrative and acceptable in the United States and Canada. The 1980s witnessed a veritable explosion of MPD and ritual abuse cases in North America, though many of them were diagnosed by a small cadre of "specialists."[40]

35. Prince, M. (1905, 1908, 1957). *The dissociation of a personality: a biographic study in abnormal psychology.* New York: Meridian Books; Thigpen, C. H. and H. M. Cleckley (1957). *The three faces of Eve.* New York: McGraw-Hill.

36. Schreiber, F. R. (1973). *Sybil.* New York: Warner.

37. Pendergrast, Mark (1995, 1996). *Victims of memory: Sex abuse accusations and shattered lives.* (2d ed.). Hinesburg, VT: Upper Access. pp. 153-154.

38. Smith, M., & L. Pazder. (1980). *Michelle remembers.* New York: Pocket Books.

39. Allison, R. (1980). *Minds in many pieces: The making of a very special doctor.* New York: Rawson, Wade.

40. Pendergrast, Mark (1995, 1996). *Victims of memory: Sex abuse accusations and shattered lives.* (2d ed.). Hinesburg, VT: Upper Access. pp. 62-63, 151-188.

At the same time that a plethora of questionable therapies became popular, a newly energized feminist movement allowed many women who had been victims of real incest to come forward for the first time publicly, in the late 1970s and early 1980s. Thus, in 1974, Ellen Bass, a young feminist creative writing instructor, received a crumpled half-sheet of paper from a shy student, detailing sexual abuse. Very little of this early material about incest mentioned repressed memories, though Freud had made the concept of repression a theoretical given. Most of the women who were finally speaking out had never had any trouble remembering that they had been abused. It was all too real for them. Their problem was being *unable to forget it.*[41] Even the title of the 1983 anthology edited by Ellen Bass, called *I Never Told Anyone*, implied that although the victims of incest had remained silent all these years, they had never forgotten. By then, however, the idea of repressed memories was becoming somewhat popular. "My healing began with my simultaneous decision to accept myself as a lesbian and to enter therapy," wrote Yarrow Morgan in the Bass anthology. In therapy, she recovered forgotten memories of abuse by her mother and father while she was still in her crib.[42] In 1988, Ellen Bass and one of her creative writing colleagues, who had recovered memories of abuse by her grandfather, published *The Courage to Heal*,[43] which has sold over a million copies and is almost invariably involved in cases of recovered memories of abuse.

In conclusion, based on both the historical events described above and on the scientific evidence for and against recovered memories of abuse (discussed at length in *Victims of Memory*), there has never been a shred of proof for the existence of widespread intergenerational ritual abuse cults, with their accompanying load of murder, cannibalism, and the like. The best "evidence" is the same as that offered for witches—the "victims" all tell similar stories.[44] It is now abundantly clear that most (and perhaps all) multiple personalities—whether renamed DID or not—are artifacts of therapy or books, produced by expectation and cuing in suggestible, vulnerable, attention-

---

41. Pendergrast, Mark (1995, 1996). *Victims of memory: Sex abuse accusations and shattered lives.* (2d ed.). Hinesburg, VT: Upper Access. pp. 27-69.

42. Bass, E., & L. Thornton, (eds.). (1983). *I never told anyone: Writings by women survivors of child sexual abuse.* New York: Harper & Row. pp. 86-87, 103-105.

43. Bass, E., & Davis, L. (1988, 1994). *The courage to heal: A guide for women survivors of child sexual abuse.* (3rd ed.). New York: Harper Perennial.

44. Pendergrast, Mark (1995, 1996). *Victims of memory: Sex abuse accusations and shattered lives.* (2d ed.). Hinesburg, VT: Upper Access. pp. 188-189; Victor, J. S. (1993). *Satanic panic: The creation of a contemporary legend.* Chicago: Open Court; Lanning, K. V. (1992). *Investigator's guide to allegations of "ritual" child abuse.* Quantico, VA: FBI Academy.

seeking clients.[45] MPD undeniably exists, but only after the condition and belief has been induced in a vulnerable person. It is gratifying that two notorious MPD gurus—Bennett Braun and Judith Peterson—have recently found themselves in the news, recognized for the harm they have done to their clients. Braun settled a lawsuit against him by a former patient for $10.5 million and is about to lose his medical license.[46] Peterson, sued by numerous former clients, has settled for undisclosed sums.[47]

The theory of massive repression or massive dissociation—in which years of prolonged traumatic events are completely forgotten, only to be recalled later—has virtually no concrete scientific support.[48] As psychologist Endel Tulving puts it, "One of the most widely held, but wrong, beliefs that people have about memory is that 'memories' exist, somewhere in the brain like books exist in a library, and that remembering is equivalent to somehow retrieving them. The whole concept of repression is built on this misconception."[49] Instead, it is now clear, thanks in large part to the experiments of Elizabeth Loftus and others, that memory is continually subject to distortion, suggestion, and reconstruction—particularly under the influence of hypnosis.[50]

Hypnosis or drugs should *never* be used for memory retrieval purposes, although such suggestive methodologies can be useful for smoking cessation or other instances in which clients give informed consent and know that they will be subject to suggestion. Nor should other leading methods be used, such as guided imagery, dream analysis, or misinterpretation of "body memories" or panic attacks. A word of caution, however. If a therapist *believes* in the possibility of massive repression, he or she is likely to *cue* the patient. The

---

45. Pendergrast, Mark (1995, 1996). *Victims of memory: Sex abuse accusations and shattered lives.* (2d ed.). Hinesburg, VT: Upper Access. pp. 151-188; Merskey, H. (1992). The manufacture of personalities: The production of multiple personality disorder. *British Journal of Psychiatry, 160,* 327-340; Merskey, H. (1995). *The analysis of hysteria: Understanding conversion and dissociation.* (2d ed.). London: Royal College of Psychiatrists; Piper, A., Jr. (1997). *Hoax and reality: The bizarre world of multiple personality disorder.* Northvale, NJ: Jason Aronson.

46. Associated Press. (1998, August 14.). Illinois to discipline psychiatrist accused of brainwashing patient. *Beacon Journal* (Akron). p. A4.

47. Another malpractice suit is settled (Carl v. Peterson, Spring Shadows Glen Psychiatric Hosp., et al., U.S. Dist. Ct., Southern Dist., Texas, Case No. H-95-661). (1996, September.). *FMS Foundation Newsletter,* Vol. 5, No. 8.

48. Pope, H. G., Jr. (1996). *Psychology astray: Fallacies in studies of "repressed memory" and childhood trauma.* Boca Raton, FL: Upton Books.

49. Pendergrast, Mark (1995, 1996). *Victims of memory: Sex abuse accusations and shattered lives.* (2d ed.). Hinesburg, VT: Upper Access. p. 74.

50. Loftus, E., & Ketcham, K. (1991). *Witness for the defense: The accused, the eyewitness, and the expert who puts memory on trial.* New York: St. Martin's; Loftus, E., & Ketcham. (1994). *The myth of repressed memory: False memories and allegations of sexual abuse.* New York: St. Martin's; Schacter, D. (1996). *Searching for memory: The brain, the mind, and the past.* New York: Basic Books; *Memory distortion: How minds, brains, and societies reconstruct the past.* (1995). Edited by D. L. Schacter. Cambridge, MA: Harvard University Press.

danger of *inadvertent cuing* cannot be stressed enough.[51] Those who believe that all memories are probably true if they arise without forceful, obviously suggestive methods are treading dangerous ground.

Some recent scientific studies have been touted as supporting the possibility of memory repression. There are some intriguing PET scans and other studies that indicate hippocampal shrinkage in those who have undergone documented, prolonged trauma, but such studies have little bearing on so-called recovered memory. In general, people recall severe trauma *better* than other events.[52]

After years of research into this issue, I have yet to find even one convincing case of massive repression or massive dissociation. To be convinced of the validity of a case, I would want to interview the accuser and the accused and to see any physical evidence, such as medical records or diaries. The so-called "corroboration" that has been accepted by various surveys is frequently flawed—e.g., another sibling retrieving memories after the first led the way, or other questionable anecdotal evidence, such as the mother saying, "I always knew he spent too much time tucking you into bed." Even confessions by those accused do not necessarily constitute corroboration, as the witches of long ago, and the well-known current case of Paul Ingram have made clear.[53]

There is no way definitively to disprove the theory of massive repression or massive dissociation, since one cannot prove a negative. But if massive repression routinely occurred, why is it only in the past decade that recalling years of abuse has become a wholesale American pastime? Some might answer that uncovering such memories requires a skilled therapist to elicit the proper abreaction. Yet consider Arthur Janov's primal screamers of the early 1970s, all of whom were encouraged to relive buried trauma memories. Of all the cases related in Janov's book, only one involved incest memories.[54] Why? Clearly, Janov didn't *expect* or *need* sexual abuse as an etiology. Any old trauma would do, so that's what his patients produced. If there were truly so many repressed incest memories, they most certainly would have swamped primal scream sessions.

---

51. Frank, J. D. (1961, 1973). *Persuasion and healing: A comparative study of psychotherapy.* Baltimore, MD: Johns Hopkins University Press. pp. 219, 335.

52. Schacter, D. (1996). *Searching for memory: The brain, the mind, and the past.* New York: Basic Books; Pendergrast, Mark. (1995, 1996). *Victims of memory: Sex abuse accusations and shattered lives.* (2d ed.). Hinesburg, VT: Upper Access. pp. 105-110.

53. Wright, L. (1994). *Remembering satan: A case of recovered memory and the shattering of an American family.* New York: Knopf.

54. Janov, A. (1970). *The primal scream: Primal therapy, the cure for neurosis.* New York: Dell.

I have found a few cases in which people were sexually abused for a limited period of time, forgot that the events occurred, and then recalled them much later. Most of these cases have firm corroborating evidence, although there is always the question of whether people "really forgot" the abuse or not.[55]   Nonetheless, it should come as no surprise that people can forget events and then recall them later. None of these cases, however, involved "massive repression." Extraordinary claims such as those based on the theory of massive repression require extraordinary proof—and that is extraordinarily absent to this date.

---

55. Pendergrast, Mark. (1995, 1996). *Victims of memory: Sex abuse accusations and shattered lives.* (2d ed.). Hinesburg, VT: Upper Access. pp. 89-91, 277-278.

Chapter 3

CLINICAL ASPECTS OF RECOVERED
MEMORY

David K. Sakheim

The veracity of recovered memories of traumatic events has been hotly debated in the clinical and research literature. Unfortunately, most of the contributions have been aimed at proving either that supposedly recovered memories are invalid or that trauma can cause dissociative phenomena and that lost or blocked material can later be accurately uncovered.[1, 2] Instead of allying with either side of this polarized debate, I will describe some clinical examples of "memory" that I have encountered in my practice and supervision experiences in order to show that "recovered memories of trauma" are very complex phenomena that can include both true and false elements and that are influenced by many other important factors. I will use case histories to illustrate the ways in which memory processes may be affected by the patient, the therapist, the alleged perpetrator, important support systems, insurance companies, lawyers, the courts, societal factors and the parties' expectations. In this way, I hope to encourage a different, more integrated, approach to our understanding of this area. The case vignettes have been written to demonstrate a variety of clinical phenomena and for that reason, the facts have been altered as little as possible. I have changed only

1. Loftus, E. (1993). The reality of repressed memories. *American Psychologist, 48,* 518-537; Yapko, M. D. (1994). *Suggestions of abuse: True and false memories of childhood sexual trauma.* New York: Simon and Schuster; Richardson, J.T., Best, J., & Bromley, D.G. (1991). *The satanism scare.* New York: Aldine De Gruyter; Boyd, A. (1991). *Blasphemous rumors: Is satanic ritual abuse fact or fantasy?* London: Fount; Pendergrast, M. (1995). *Victims of memory: Incest accusations and shattered lives.* Hinesburg, VT: Upper Access.

2. Terr, L. (1994). *Unchained memories: True stories of traumatic memories, lost and found.* New York: Basic Books; Van der Kolk, B. (1990). Trauma and memory. In M. Fass & D. Brown (Eds.), *Creative mastery in hypnosis and hypnoanalysis: A festschrift for Erika Fromm.* Hillsdale, N.J.: Erlbaum; Herman, J. (1992). *Trauma and recovery: The aftermath of violence–from domestic abuse to political terror.* New York: Basic Books; Fredrickson, R. (1992). *Repressed memories: A journey to recovery from sexual abuse.* New York: Simon & Schuster; Gould, C. (1992). Diagnosis and treatment of ritually abused children. In D.K. Sakheim & S.E. Devine (Eds.), *Out of darkness: Exploring satanism and ritual abuse.* Lexington, MA: Lexington Books. pp. 207-248.

those aspects that could identify the specific individuals involved and I have combined some minor details for the sake of brevity.

The debate about trauma memories has been more of a polarized political struggle than a scientific dialogue. Researchers and clinicians take sides in the battle and even refuse to present on "scientific" panels if the other side is represented. (The present conference was no exception. Because FMS members were present, many clinicians and researchers refused to attend or present.) Thus, most panels, seminars, books and lectures tend to advance only one side of this issue. This turns each group of professionals into "spin doctors" rather than real doctors, into "preachers to the converted" rather than true scientists.

COMPLEXITY OF MEMORY

In a previous paper I described the case of a young woman who had grown up in an extremely violent home, having been abused by both parents and her older brother.[3] All three had admitted the abuse and her brother had been convicted for other violent rapes that he had committed later in life. This patient had recovered other memories of abuse that had been forgotten for years. She was able to validate many of these with external corroboration as well. Because of the extensive abuse, this patient had developed a severe trauma-related syndrome; part of this reactive coping style included a dissociative disorder. For example, as a child, during regular, violent sexual assaults, she would "leave her body" and "go into" a beautiful picture that hung on the wall of her room. By going into a trance state she was able to feel that she was away from the violence and in the peacefulness of the picture.

During her treatment, this patient experienced a series of flashbacks that she could not resolve. These involved images of a priest, dressed in satanic garb, stabbing a newborn baby. The patient was flooded with many feelings about this "memory" and at times wondered whether she had been one of the people in the scene, either the priest who did the killing, the woman who gave birth to the baby, or even the baby who was killed. At times, when she experienced the flashbacks, she felt that she was none of these people, but somehow had been a witness to this terrible scene.

Unlike other "memories" that she eventually was able to sort out, this one remained vague and unclear, and she finally gave up trying to understand it.

---

3. Sakheim, D.K. (1996). Clinical aspects of sadistic ritual abuse. In W.J. Ray & L.K. Michelson (Eds.), *Handbook of dissociation: theoretical, empirical, and research perspectives.* New York: Plenum Press.

She accidentally discovered the answer, however, when she was in her parent's attic on one of her quests for validation of other memories. She saw the picture that she had described hanging on the wall with some of her mother's other pornographic and sadistic material. She suddenly remembered that her brother had raped her in the attic (an unusual place for either of them to be) and that she had tried to escape using her dissociative strategy of going into the nearest picture on the wall. The picture in the attic was not like the serene landscape that hung in her room, but rather this violent image of the satanic ritual. The patient's flashbacks now made more sense to her. She took down the picture and brought it into therapy to show me how close it had been to her "memory."

I have not presented this example to show that all memories of satanic rituals are generated in this fashion or to discount the possible veracity of any other recovered memories. (In fact, this patient had validated many of her previous memories and is probably one of the best examples that I have seen of someone who has blocked and then found trauma memories.) I offer this example to demonstrate some of the complexity that can be present in this work. Was this a "false memory"? Although it clearly was false in some respects, this patient was being abused at the time of this incident (only not exactly in the ways she first thought), she had developed the dissociative defenses through previous exposure to violence, and she was actually quite traumatized by experiencing herself in the "satanic" picture. To describe this solely as a "false memory" would certainly not do it justice. Yet it would be incorrect to say that her memory was "true," especially because saying so could have important implications (if the person being accused were on trial, for example). To try to classify this as either a "true" or a "false" memory would therefore miss the importance and complexity of what was involved. Such simplistic thinking both creates a potential for false accusations and stifles the therapy process.

OVERVIEW OF CLINICAL AND RESEARCH ISSUES

Several chapters in this volume detail the research and clinical work that demonstrate how memory is stored as well as how it can be influenced and distorted. There is no question that a memory is a very complex composite of facts, pre-existing constructs, the emotional significance of the events in question, later formulations by the individual and others, and a variety of factors that can influence or change it over time.[4] It is unfortunate that the primary focus of recent discussions about memory in our field (as well as in the media) has tended to be on whether a memory is "real" or "false." Even in the scientific literature, discussions tend to focus on whether or not a recovered memory can occur.[5]

Many studies have now been done and more are underway that show that some percentage of people who have been abused lose memory for all or part of the trauma for some period of time.[6] According to various studies, from 20-80 percent of incest survivors report temporary memory losses.[7] Similar findings have been reported in other types of populations that experienced extreme events. For example, 20-65 percent of murderers reported having forgotten some or all of the events that they experienced and then later having obtained a more complete memory.[8] In the Williams study of known trauma cases, 38 percent of the subjects had no memory for a validated trauma 17 years earlier.[9]

Most clinicians and researchers agree that (1) at least some percentage of abused patients can block memory for a traumatic event and later reconstruct it; and (2) some percentage of patients can also create distortions in recovered memories of trauma. They may disagree about the frequency of each type of situation, but that is a question that current research may help to clarify. Instead of debating whether or not "true" and "false" memories can occur, it would be far more useful to study the conditions that give rise to true and false memories and the various defensive functions that each can serve.

Daniel Brown has provided a helpful review of the research and clinical findings to date.[10] He concluded that people who experience trauma generally have superior recall of the main events but some forgetting of details.

---

4. Brown, D. (1995). Pseudomemories: The standard of science and the standard of care in trauma treatment. *American Journal of Clinical Hypnosis, 37:3*, pp. 1-24; Hammond, D.C., Garver, R.B., Mutter, C.B., Crasilneck, H.B., Frischholz, E., Gravitz, M.A., Hibler, N.S., Olson, J., Scheflin, A., Spiegel, H., & Wester, W. (1995). *Clinical hypnosis and memory: Guidelines for clinicians and for forensic hypnosis.* New York: American Society of Clinical Hypnosis Press.

5. Loftus, E. (1993). The reality of repressed memories. *American Psychologist, 48*, 518-537; Terr, L. (1994). *Unchained memories: True stories of traumatic memories, lost and found.* New York: Basic Books.

6. Briere, J., & Conte, J. (1993). Self-reported amnesia for abuse in adults molested in childhood. *Journal of Traumatic Stress, 6*, 21-31; Williams, L.M. (1992). Adult memories of childhood abuse: Preliminary findings from a longitudinal study. *Advisor, 5*, 19-20.

7. Brown, D. (1995). Pseudomemories: The standard of science and the standard of care in trauma treatment. *American Journal of Clinical Hypnosis, 37:3*, pp. 1-24.

8. Brown, D. (1995). Pseudomemories: The standard of science and the standard of care in trauma treatment. *American Journal of Clinical Hypnosis, 37:3*, pp. 1-24.

9. Williams, L.M. (1992). Adult memories of childhood abuse: Preliminary findings from a longitudinal study. *Advisor, 5*, 19-20.

10. Brown, D. (1995). Pseudomemories: The standard of science and the standard of care in trauma treatment. *American Journal of Clinical Hypnosis, 37:3*, pp. 1-24.

The greater the impact of the event or the more personally significant it is, the better remembered it is likely to be. He noted the evidence that memories are sometimes lost and later recovered, but he also recognized that false memories can and do occur. He concluded that false memories are more likely to occur in the small subgroup (3-5%) of the population that is most dissociative and in younger individuals who are trying to remember, when social coercion is employed by a trusted person or when the memories in question have little significance. Among other factors that he found contributed to memory distortions in clinical situations were the patient's emotional arousal at the time of the traumatic event, trance influences in the memory recovery process (especially when the patient was highly hypnotizable, whether or not formal hypnotic procedures were utilized), the techniques used by the therapist (such as leading or suggestive questions), and the therapist's own preexisting beliefs and biases or overidentification.

Brown urged therapists who work with recovered memories to exercise caution about the premature acceptance of a patient's certainty of the truth or falsity of a recovered memory, the potential dangers when the patient comes with intense symptoms for which there is as yet no adequate explanation, and the potential power of outside groups, such as support groups, to push a patient to become prematurely certain about unclear or vague feelings and images.

It would be helpful to know how each of the following factors can affect the outcome of the memory recovery process in a therapeutic context: the patient's internal defensive needs, the patient's external situation, the therapist's techniques and preexisting belief system, the therapist's internal processes and external situation, the patient's family of origin and current support system, and the society in which the memory recovery process takes place. In this chapter, I will attempt to give examples of the operation of each of these factors, in the hope that later research will begin to examine them more rigorously.

IMPACT OF THE FALSE MEMORY SYNDROME FOUNDATION

Until fairly recently, many clinicians working with trauma memories assumed, incorrectly, that anything remembered under hypnosis was true. They ignored the work of researchers such as Orne and Lawrence and Perry, who showed that subjects who had been hypnotized had more true and false memories than nonhypnotized subjects, could not differentiate between the true and false elements of memories obtained under hypnosis, and indeed become convinced of the accuracy of both false and true details that are recalled under hypnosis.[11, 12] In the past decade, however, many competent therapists have become aware of the potentially problematic nature of memories obtained under hypnosis.

Early on, most trauma therapists were dealing with severely traumatized patients where there was no question that the abuse had occurred. The patients were children with scars from burns, cuts, or broken bones and long histories of hospitalizations for abuse; soldiers who had just returned from combat in Vietnam; or victims of rape and other kinds of assault and violence who were being treated for posttraumatic stress disorder (PTSD). The therapist's sole focus was on trying to help the patient to recover the ability to function. If every detail about the story of what had occurred was not exact, it made little difference to anyone. Therapy was geared toward teaching these patients that they were not crazy, but rather, had symptoms that were predictable results of their traumatic experiences.

The new trauma model replaced the prior mode of dealing with such patients by assigning them labels, such as "schizophrenia" or a variety of personality disorders, which had tended to translate into "crazy," "bad," and "hopeless," in effect stigmatizing and blaming the victim. The patients' symptoms were now seen as understandable, given the awful and overwhelming circumstances with which they had had to learn to cope. This created hope for recovery, as patients came to understand how they had coped in a traumatic situation and, now that they were out of that situation, how they could learn new ways to cope as well as unlearn some of the ways that were no longer useful.

The occasional puzzling case, such as the veteran who, when pursuing disability benefits for PTSD, turned out never to have been in the service, was brushed off as bizarre but unusual. Such cases seemed to be from another realm, and few in the field had the time or money to explore them further. Most trauma victims had clear histories, and when patients didn't come with corroborating evidence, it usually seemed unnecessary to try to obtain it. Clinicians were usually working on limited budgets and were seeing patients for significantly reduced fees in veterans' centers and poorly funded clinics, so time available to do what seemed like unnecessary exploration was extremely limited. These clinicians were also fighting a climate of disbelief that had predated much of the trauma work, in which childhood sexual abuse had been written off as fantasy and combat trauma was viewed as a problem only if it stirred up preexisting pathology. The trauma therapists were working hard to prove to those in the field that trauma could be real and could have devastating effects even on healthy people. Thus, the polit-

---

11. Orne, M. (1979). The use and misuse of hypnosis in court. *International Journal of Clinical and Experimental Hypnosis, 27*, 311-341.

12. Lawrence, J.R., & Perry, C. (1988). *Hypnosis, will and memory.* New York: Guilford Press.

ical climate was not conducive to attending to patients who appeared to be exaggerating or creating distorted descriptions of traumatic events.

As long as trauma work was confined to therapists' offices, it mattered little to the participants whether such errors occurred, although they clearly did not represent the best therapeutic practice. However, once the field of trauma therapy left the privacy of the therapy office and entered the courtroom and the media, the veracity of trauma memories became much more salient and important, and "memories" and accusations began to be examined much more thoroughly. This was compounded by the fact that some therapists had advised patients who disclosed abuse memories to end all contact with their families, and some patients had gone public with their stories. Accused parents began to fight back. Some parents sued or worked to discredit therapists involved in trauma work. The veracity of all the details of the abuse accusations took on much greater significance to everyone involved. Whether the perpetrator of the abuse was a father or a neighbor or, indeed, whether the abuse had ever occurred at all, may not have seemed so important to ascertain in the past, but suddenly it became very important because the alleged perpetrator could be sued or put in jail, or lose his reputation. He or she could also turn around and sue the therapist involved in the patient's treatment. Unfortunately, what should have been a process geared toward learning the truth became a war between opposing factions. War is never conducive to honesty, complexity, vulnerability, or clarity, but, ironically, the battles may have ultimately pushed the field to learn more than anyone had thought it necessary to know about memory, and in the process, greatly improved our ability to help future patients.

Early on, the political goal of convincing professionals and the public that sexual abuse is a real social problem allowed many patients and clinicians to ignore the victims of false accusations. For example, years ago, an advocate for a group that represented sexual abuse survivors berated me for inviting representatives of the False Memory Syndrome Foundation, along with survivors, researchers, and therapists, to a conference on what was then understood about recovered memories. She said: "It doesn't matter if a few people get falsely accused. The vast majority of allegations are true and allowing in that viewpoint will only hurt survivors' credibility and add respectability to the FMS movement." Someone who was otherwise a very caring person had allowed politics and the furthering of a particular point of view to take priority over the welfare of individuals. Sadly, I think that most of the players in this struggle have at times been guilty of that.

The one good outcome of this controversy, as I noted above, is that the average therapist in the trauma field is now learning basic, important information about trauma and memory, including the following: one cannot diagnose sexual abuse from a symptom checklist, many kinds of abuse and trauma besides sexual abuse can create problems for people, and memory distortions can play a role in the world of highly hypnotizable individuals.[13] The continuing debate and intense media coverage has forced more research and a deeper examination of the issues involved.

CASES ILLUSTRATING PROBLEMS THAT CAN EMERGE IN MEMORY WORK: FACTORS THAT CAN AFFECT RECOVERED MEMORIES IN A CLINICAL SETTING

The research and debate in this area has been enlightening, but I believe that individual patients can teach us the most. The material that a patient brings to therapy is influenced by the patient's internal views, values, and defensive processes as well as important external factors in the patient's life. This is also true for the therapist. Both internal processes, such as the therapist's personal experiences and countertransference reactions, and external factors, such as the therapist's theoretical orientation or professional affiliations, can influence the memory recovery process. The patient's family of origin and current support system can influence the process, and the changing social climates under which the memory recovery takes place certainly

Table 3-1
FACTORS THAT CAN AFFECT RECOVERED MEMORIES IN A
CLINICAL SETTING

I. Patient factors
    A. Internal Defenses
    B. External Influences
II. Therapist factors
    A. Internal Defenses
    B. External Influences
    C. Beliefs/Orientation
III. Perpetrator factors
    A. Internal Defenses
    B. External Influences
IV. Family of Origin factors
V. Current Family/Support System factors
VI. Societal factors
    A. Institutions
    B. Values

---

13. Ganaway, G. (1989). Historical truth versus narrative truth: Clarifying the role of exogenous trauma in the etiology of MPD and its variants. *Dissociation, 2*, 205-220.

will affect both whether the process occurs at all and its outcome. Table 3-1 lists the factors that can affect the memory recovery process.

I. Patient Factors

Some of the internal defensive processes that can distort recovered memories in a clinical setting have been described well by Ganaway, Greaves, and Sakheim.[14] Examples are given below.

A. Internal Defenses

A patient can report trauma when it is not true, deny it when it is true, or accurately describe that it did or did not happen. In fact, all of these can occur within the same session or about different aspects of the same description. This can make it difficult for a therapist to know the full implications of what is being presented. Clinicians see patients being affected in many ways by trauma, the most usual having to do with ways that the individual needs to distance herself from the overwhelming feelings and impulses that emerge. This picture is further complicated by the fact that individuals can also have reason to distort, imagine, or even lie about traumatic experiences, and it is not always possible to tell what is happening from clinical contact alone.

In most cases, patients are trying to communicate about and integrate significant experiences and feelings through which they have lived in order to be able to move on with their lives. Because severe trauma can create a fragmenting of experience, and the recovery process can involve knowledge, awareness, and feelings coming back in a piecemeal fashion, it is often tempting to try to put these pieces together prematurely. This usually does a disservice to the patient, who needs to be able gradually to integrate these elements, along with any corroborating information that is available, in order to best know the truth about his or her experiences. Clinicians and patients need to be able to tolerate the ambiguity that is usually a necessary part of this process.

---

14. Ganaway, G. (1989). Historical truth versus narrative truth: Clarifying the role of exogenous trauma in the etiology of MPD and its variants. *Dissociation, 2,* 205-220; Greaves, G. (1992). Alternative hypotheses regarding claims of satanic cult activity: A critical analysis. In D.K. Sakheim & S.E. Devine (Eds.), *Out of darkness: Exploring satanism and ritual abuse.* Lexington, MA: Lexington Books. pp. 45-92; Sakheim, D.K. (1996). Clinical aspects of sadistic ritual abuse. In W.J. Ray & L.K. Michelson (Eds.), *Handbook of dissociation.* New York: Plenum Press.

1. Accurate Recall of Actual Experiences

One often reads newspaper articles about cases of severe, ongoing child abuse where authorities were repeatedly called in to investigate and, time after time, concluded that no abuse was occurring, until finally the child was found dead or severely injured. Similarly, patients who come to therapists and report severe abuse are sometimes disbelieved, and are thought to be delusional or exaggerating. I once interviewed a patient who had been in many hospitals for PTSD symptoms but who had been repeatedly diagnosed as schizophrenic or with a delusional disorder because the abuse that she had reported had seemed too bizarre and extreme: she reported having been kidnaped, kept prisoner, and raped by her personal physician. This patient had eventually learned to carry newspaper clippings describing the physician's arrest and conviction so that her treatment providers would believe her. Because of the unlikely circumstances she was describing and because she presented in an odd fashion, I probably also would have come to the same conclusion as her previous therapists, had I not seen her corroborating material. (I later came to understand that her unusual presentation was in part related to her fear of doctors that followed from the abuse by her doctor.)

I have been consulted on a case in which a woman had her three children removed from her home because she had tried to kill them. She admitted doing this, and stated that at the time she believed that they would be better off dead than living in what she believed to be a very cruel world. Her children initially had blocked memories of her attempt to kill them and are only having them emerge now that they are out of the home and in psychotherapy. The memories that have been returning appear to be quite accurate and have been validated by the mother, who is now in therapy herself and who is trying to understand her own actions. This case is another good example of validated recovered memories.

Prior to the attempted murder, this mother had been reported for child abuse many times by neighbors and others and yet no petition had ever been filed to the Connecticut Department of Children and Families (DCF) and no protective action had ever been taken in regard to the children because the mother had several family members who occupied official positions in the community (including a cousin who was the mayor) that enabled them to squelch any such reports. Would the therapists have believed the children's "memories" if the mother had not gotten caught in the attempted murder and had denied the accuracy of their memories? If the children had told their therapists that their mother had been reported on multiple occasions, but the town was in on a conspiracy of silence that included the mayor and the police, would the therapists have believed it? The therapists would be unlikely to seek either validating or disconfirming data, but would be likely to believe or disbelieve the story based on a preexisting notion of how such stories come to be. We should learn from scenarios such as this one that even "far-fetched stories" can sometimes be true, and that often we cannot know the truth or falsehood of what is presented without external corroboration.

Recently, a psychologist told me that 35 years ago he had diagnosed a patient as delusional after she spoke about having been abused by a priest because "everyone knew that priests would never do something like that." She had been hospitalized and unsuccessfully treated (with drugs and shock treatment) for many years, during which time she continued to insist that the abuse had occurred. The psychologist was feeling very guilty about this treatment, having rethought the case in light of some of the recent revelations about abuses by members of the clergy. One hopes that therapists will not repeat these types of treatment errors in the future.

Our discussions of true and false memories must not be allowed to blind us to the reality that child abuse is pervasive in our society. This is not an idle fear. As the FMSF has become more vocal, I have heard clinicians and others dismiss allegations of child abuse as "false memory" or as "made up," without proper investigation. It would be terribly sad if we used the fact that false memories can occur to discredit abuse reports or to decrease our felt responsibility to address the problem of child abuse on a societal level.

We must also realize that there is a great deal we still don't know about memory, especially trauma memory. Some "experts" have stated, for example, that adults cannot remember events that occurred before age two, and such rules of thumb about memory are sometimes cited to prove that a patient's recall must be false. I had a case that appears to be an exception to this rule. My patient had an 18-month-old daughter sleeping in bed with her when her boyfriend came home drunk and hit the baby and then proceeded to beat up the mother. The mother left this man's home the following day and moved to another state. She and her daughter never saw him again. The mother wanted to start her life over there and since she also believed that her daughter would not recall these events as an adult, they were never discussed. Her daughter is now grown up and recently went into psychotherapy for a variety of problems. She came home one day and described the events of that evening in great detail to her mother. The daughter was wondering if this was a real memory, and according to her mother, it was accurate down to the description of the bedspread, floor tiles and appearance of the boyfriend. Of course, this is a story told by the mother and could contain errors or distortions. Whether or not it is completely accurate, it suggests that we should do a lot more research on trauma memories before we make such certain pronouncements about them.

2. Denial

Severe trauma typically leads to a need for distance for the person who experienced it. The trauma can be minimized, distorted, seem unreal or insignificant or as if it is happening to someone else, or, in extreme cases, be denied altogether. It seems unnecessary to supply clinical examples here because the literatures on combat trauma, prisoner of war trauma, the holocaust, rape, child abuse, and natural disasters are all replete with such examples. Dissociation, repression, and denial are only a few of the mechanisms involved. This type of distortion has been well documented and reviewed elsewhere.[15] Denial-based defenses are probably the most common reactions to trauma seen in clinical settings.

3. Metaphoric Communication

Some patients discuss their experiences in metaphor when the experience itself is too painful or when their internal defensive structure makes a more direct discussion impossible. A therapist's failure to understand this can lead to years of misdiagnosis and mistreatment, as it did for one woman I saw who initially described her childhood using the metaphor of a nuclear explosion. She did not say it was like a war, or it was as if there had been a nuclear blast. She talked about the devastation after the bomb was dropped. She described walking through the post nuclear landscape and of being the only survivor of the bomb. She was a very sensitive and poetic individual who spoke in powerful images. Because I knew that no nuclear bomb had fallen on her part of the world, I listened to her words and tried to translate them into a language of experiences. I listened to the themes and feelings involved and tried to apply them to what I knew of her life. That was very important to her healing. Had I treated her words as delusion alone, I would have missed her experience and deprived her of feeling understood, as had happened in the past. On the other hand, had I believed her words and responded as if she were speaking literal truth, I would not have helped her either.

---

15. See Davis, R., & Freidman, L. (1985). Emotional aftermath of crime and violence. In C. Figley (Ed.), *Trauma and its wake: The study and treatment of post traumatic stress disorder.* New York: Brunner/Mazel. p. 90; Browne, A., & Finkelhor, D. (1986). Impact of child sexual abuse: A review of the literature. *Psychiatric Bulletin, 99,* 66-77; Bryer, J., Nelson, B., & Miller, J. (1987). Childhood sexual and physical abuse as factors in adult psychiatric illness. *American Journal of Psychiatry, 144,* 1426-1430; Herman, J. (1992). *Trauma and recovery: The aftermath of violence - from domestic abuse to political terror.* New York: Basic Books; Sakheim, D.K., & Devine, S.E. (1995). Trauma related syndromes. In C.A. Ross & A. Pam (Eds.), *Pseudoscience in biological psychiatry: Blaming the victim's body.* New York: John Wiley and Sons. pp. 255-272.

Sometimes therapists do not know whether a patient is speaking metaphorically and instead of deferring judgment, try to conclude immediately whether the statements are true or not. Statements considered to be untrue are treated as delusions. Sometimes, as in this case, the truth is more complex. This woman needed to speak about nuclear war for over a year before she could begin to discuss the seemingly more mundane trauma in her childhood, which had felt like nuclear devastation to her. She probably was able to share much more about the truth of her childhood with her images of nuclear war than she would have with the "truth." Through her use of this metaphor, she was saying, "I lived through such loneliness and isolation that it was like the aftermath of a nuclear explosion where everyone else had died." In certain respects, her words were more evocative and communicative about the experienced horror of her early years than the "truth" would have been.

4. Screen Memories

Sometimes an abuse incident is so overwhelming that it is distorted in a person's memory because the true memory would bring up too many overwhelming feelings. I saw a woman who insisted that she had been sexually abused by a monster. She had turned her father's image into a monster to protect their relationship. This type of "memory" arises when the perpetrator needs to be replaced with someone who can more easily be seen in that role, as when a father is replaced by a neighbor. Usually, as therapy progresses and the "memory" is processed, the patient is able to get to the truth of it, as she gradually handles the feelings involved. This phenomenon clearly has potential implications for courtroom testimony, however, and shows why external corroboration is so important in a legal case. It also speaks to why a therapist must not jump to a conclusion about what happened in a particular situation. Even when there is clear reason to suspect abuse, the details may evolve over time in ways that are initially not suspected.

5. Trance Phenomena in the Creation or Retrieval of Memories

Some patients have an extreme ability to dissociate, a defense that may be life-saving during severe trauma but that can lead to distortions in the processing or retrieval of the memory. This "hypnotic" defense allows individuals to distort what is occurring in order to survive it. The patient is able to use his hypnotic ability to distance himself from the trauma. He may feel that parts of his body are numb or don't belong to him, that he is out of his body all together (for example, that he is watching the experience from the ceiling or even further away) or that it is happening to someone else, or he may have no recall of the event at all. It is no wonder then, that upon later recall, there can be distortions in memory.

The patient may use his ability to dissociate when pursuing recall in therapy. If the therapy is handled improperly, the patient can then incorporate new hypnotic elements that feel very real. I had one very dissociative patient, for example, who, while recalling a childhood experience of being drugged, had an alter hallucinate that a bookcase in my office melted to the floor, whereupon the plant on top of the bookcase fell down, spilling dirt all over. The only way I was able to convince her that it had not happened was by later showing her that the plant on top of the bookcase was fake and therefore could not have spilled dirt on the floor. This same patient once visualized flying on a cloud as part of finding a "safe place." She later had an alter who was absolutely convinced that she had flown.

I have seen many examples of therapists who, in the course of hypnotizing such highly dissociative patients, inadvertently created "memories" that the patient came to believe were true because of the vividness of the sensations experienced under hypnosis. For patients with such extreme hypnotic abilities, this can happen even without formal hypnosis, because the patients often go in and out of trance states on their own. Especially for this subpopulation, it is obviously extremely critical to have external corroboration of any memories that get described if it is important to validate any of the details.

This is not to say that the memories are totally fabricated or that they do not contain important traumatic elements. On the contrary, it has always been my experience that some kind of trauma had occurred that had caused this defense to be used in such an extreme fashion. Sometimes the distortions are part of the traumatic experience itself and sometimes they can be part of other defenses that are going on in response to trauma. The patient described earlier who imagined herself in the satanic picture is a good example of how such a distortion can occur when other traumatic events are taking place.

6. Shame-Based Defenses

Sometimes distortion in reporting or memory can occur as a result of shame. I saw a woman who had developed many personalities as a result of severe child abuse. She had also developed self injurious behaviors as a means of self-soothing, something that is not unusual for severe trauma survivors.[16] One of her alters would regularly inflict cuts on her body whenever she was feeling overwhelmed. On one such occasion, the process got out of control and she severely damaged her groin area, requiring her to seek medical attention. She was so embarrassed and ashamed that she made up a story of having been raped by a man who had followed her home. She imagined the event so clearly and with such detail that the other alters believed it had actually happened. Later, one of the other alters went to the police and helped to produce a sketch of the attacker, who, of course, was never found. It wasn't until many years later that the alter who had made up the rape story admitted what had occurred. This was devastating for the other alters, in part because it made them question all of their memories and perceptions (probably rightly so). Interestingly, many of this patient's other memories had been externally validated. This is another case of a false memory in a patient with a real abuse history that had caused her to develop a dissociative disorder and a pattern of self-injury. The combination of the two, along with the shame that she felt, had led to the need for the creation of this "false" memory. Again, to view it as only a "false memory" would miss a lot of important and clinically useful, true information.

The profound sense of shame that many childhood trauma survivors feel can lead to other kinds of memory distortions, the most typical being a minimization of the traumatic event. Patients feel that hurtful events perpetrated against them do not count in the same way that they would if they happened to someone else. Reported memories may therefore leave out or minimize important aspects of what took place. I have seen patients, for example, who spoke about how badly they felt about a parent being angry or upset; they initially omitted the fact that they had been beaten because it didn't seem relevant or important.

7. Delusional Material

Most therapists, especially those who work in inpatient settings, have seen many patients whose beliefs that they were being injured or persecuted resulted from a psychotic process and did not reflect reality. The "persecution" can sometimes involve sexual or other forms of abuse. Such delusional beliefs are usually fairly easy to detect clinically, as when the patient suffers from a schizophrenic disorder. A pure paranoid disorder may be harder to detect, as the "persecution" can follow fairly logically from the initial, distorted, premise. It is therefore very important to obtain corroborating evidence for the initial premise.

---

16. See Briere, J. (June, 1993). *Tension reduction behaviors*. Paper Presented to Fifth Regional Conference on Abuse and Multiple Personality. Washington, D.C.; Sakheim, D.K. (November, 1990). *Multiple personality disorder as a PTSD syndrome*. Paper presented to Conference on Disorders of Extreme Stress, Hartford, Connecticut.

8. Exaggerated Memories

Some patients need to exaggerate their memories, the most common reason being to communicate the intense feelings that lie behind them. This can happen because the therapist has become numbed to more usual descriptions of certain kinds of events. This is happening more and more as therapists hear descriptions of horrendous abuse and become hardened to the less severe family pathologies. In abuse treatment programs even recollections of incest may evoke little empathy or interest from the staff because they have heard the story too often.

The patient may also exaggerate memories of abuse because she cannot now remember what a certain event was actually like for her as a child. A young woman I saw described having been forced to abort and then eat her baby. As treatment progressed, it became apparent that this had never happened. This patient had lived with an alcoholic father whose behavior while intoxicated had caused her great shame and humiliation. He had admitted fondling her on one occasion. She had always known about this, but had never felt that it was enough to account for her feelings and problems, as it seemed like a fairly mild trauma. Media coverage of abuse issues that focused on rape and incest furthered her sense that what she recalled about her life was not very significant. The only thing she could imagine that would account for her strong feelings of shame was something along the lines of infanticide and/or cannibalism. "Trying on" these images and struggling with them helped her to see how intense her feelings had been and still were. The false scenario helped her to have more empathy for herself as a child.

It would not have been useful to treat this merely as an issue of "truth" or "falsehood." Treating the "memories" as true could have led her down a very dangerous road; treating them as "false" would have deprived her of the creative way that her mind was trying to teach her about an aspect of her experience that she needed to better understand. It helped her tremendously to learn that she could have such intense feelings about her father's drinking and about being molested. To communicate the intensity of the child's experience may sometimes require the use of such extremely powerful images.

9. Conscious Lying

A young woman in a partial hospitalization program was claiming to have MPD as a result of a severe trauma history. She was looking for financial assistance with occupational training when I met her. As we reviewed her work history, she told me about having been trained as a nurse at a local university. As I happened to know that this school did not have a nursing program, I confronted her about her lying. She then began to disclose the range of lies she had been telling. She told me she had learned to lie in her family, where lying was not only tolerated but was an accepted norm. She began to see that many of her lies contained elements of important truths. For example, she had really wanted to be a nurse and had seen no way to make this happen. She wanted people to see her that way, rather than as a mental patient, and so she lied about being a nurse. Once she was given the opportunity to obtain some of her goals in a more honest fashion and was given the respect that she had wanted, she actually began nurse's training. She had also lied about her diagnosis and exaggerated her trauma history. Much of this had started in previous treatment where the only attention she received was for being a bright MPD patient. As more was revealed about her family upbringing, it became clearer why she had come to see lying as a valid means of getting what she needed; it had seemed the only way to obtain important and valid goals.

10. Patient-Therapist Intimacy

Unless one has witnessed or participated in an abreactive therapy session, it is difficult to understand the level of intimacy that is involved. Usually, the patient is talking about events that were extremely painful and is doing so while reexperiencing at least some of the intensity of the feelings that accompanied the events. The therapist typically guides the patient through this process, often in a very empathic fashion that may involve moving closer to the patient, offering a tissue, holding a hand, putting a hand on the patient's shoulder, or even giving a hug. For some patients, this may be the closest that they get to another human being. Although the process is helpful for many, it can offer an addictive form of secondary gain to others. I saw one patient, for example, who began to tell more and more elaborate and gruesome stories of violent abuse. Only after the stories began to get quite bizarre and the sessions took on a very scripted format did I began to realize that she was "hooked" on the process. Because we had by then developed a good relationship, we were able to deal with this. She was then able to work on her real feelings of isolation and loneliness as well as her fears of being close to people (notably, fears that had developed because of an extremely emotionally abusive and unpredictable childhood with two disturbed parents). Interestingly, as I reviewed this patient's records to write this chapter, I noticed that she had told me in our very first meeting that she had loved to make up elaborate bedtime stories for her daughter and that one of the major factors that led her to start therapy was losing the only closeness she had ever felt with another person when her daughter became independent and suddenly no longer wanted to hear the stories. Unfortunately, it took me quite a while to catch on to what was behind the "memories;" until then we spent a lot of time pursuing and processing her elaborate "memories" of abuse.

The memory recovery process is a very rewarding one for both the patient and the therapist. It brings two people together, makes them both feel very special, close and courageous, and it feels like very important and powerful work. The process itself can create intimacy in the relationship regardless of whether the memories turn out to be real or false. At times, however, as in the above case, issues of secondary gain will need to be addressed.

11. Other, as Yet Unknown, Phenomena

There are other, as yet uncategorized, types of memory distortions that can occur. For example, the brother of one of my patients confided to his sister that he had gone to see a therapist who specialized in combat PTSD and that he was being helped to unfold a history of combat trauma in Vietnam. This individual had never been in the service, but he had been severely abused by his mother. He had experienced sexual abuse as well as physical abuse that was so out of control that he could not bring himself to share it with anyone. His mother, who was psychotic and at times violent, had bitten him badly enough to leave scars on his arms. She had tortured him and his sister on many occasions. Her behavior had been humiliating and emasculating. He confided to his sister that he found it easier to talk about war trauma than about what had really occurred. Interestingly, his therapy appears to be helping him, even though it involves working with "false memories." It may be the degree to which the material and feelings discussed are close to the actual ones that makes the process useful. My guess is that he will ultimately need to tell the truth in order to really get well, but it is an empirical question worth investigating as to whether working with false memories can prove helpful in any respects. There are, for example, many reports of patients who have obtained dramatic symptom reduction while working on past life trauma or alien abductions. There is clearly a need for more research in this area.

B. External Factors
1. Patient Belief Systems

I have seen numerous patients who came to treatment because they experienced difficulties in relationships or suffered from depression or anxiety. Often they had only vague memories of their childhood. Many of them had tried a variety of support groups. Such groups can be extremely helpful, but some can be quite problematic. Some groups, for example, assume that everyone is an incest survivor and teach that the primary problem to overcome is denial. I have heard patients in such groups say that they are "waiting for the memories." Some patients have been told that the reason they don't have memories must be because the abuse was "preverbal," and that even though they may never have actual clear memories of abuse, that doesn't mean that nothing happened. Members in these groups call themselves "survivors" even if they have no memory of having survived something significant. As the patient develops important relationships within the group, it can become extremely difficult to buck its teachings, especially if the patient is otherwise very isolated. If the patient were to realize that she were not an incest survivor, she would no longer be welcomed in some of these settings. This is especially true if she had initially had "memories" and then later decided that these were inaccurate or "false." As long as support is contingent on only one way of making sense of memory, patients will continue to be inhibited from discovering their own important truths.

2. Malingering for Secondary Gain/Differential Reinforcement of Abuse Claims

I was asked to consult on the case of a woman in a state hospital who was claiming to be a ritual abuse survivor. This hospital's psychiatric unit was notoriously understaffed and underfunded, but as this was at a time when interest in ritual abuse was at its highest, this patient suddenly found herself with a psychiatrist who met with her individually, a psychologist who met with her on a daily basis (often for hours at a time), two social workers to help her with discharge arrangements and with "safety issues," and a number of other staff members who took an interest in her. One even invited the patient to live with her until she could find a place of her own to stay after her discharge from the hospital. I came to believe that this patient was malingering for a variety of reasons, but I saw other, more clear, examples of malingering for secondary gain after she left the unit. Some patients who had been wondering if they had sexual abuse histories began to wonder if they had been ritually abused. Some even began having nightmares and flashbacks about ritual abuse. One could argue that the first patient's presence had merely triggered real ritual abuse memories for these other patients. A simpler explanation is that when mental health professionals differentially reinforce and show interest in certain problems over others, those problems are more likely to be presented.

Unfortunately, many clinicians have lost interest in hearing about a merely problematic family environment, and, like the TV shock shows, need more and more horror to keep their interest alive. This puts patients in a very untenable position. They can either lie to get some help or they can suffer alone with their pain. Patients don't always have to lie, because clinicians sometimes help patients to reinterpret mundane facts as having more significance than they really have. One patient came to me for a consultation because she recalled her parents burning candles in their living room. She had always remembered having been molested by her father, but when her therapist heard about the candles, he was sure that he had a satanic ritual abuse case and sought consultation. This patient would have benefitted if her therapist had heeded the old adage, "If you hear hoofbeats, think of horses, not zebras."

3. Incorporated Memories

As a consultant to a partial hospitalization women's trauma program, I saw a number of women who incorporated other people's memories into their own. While it is possible for one person's memories to act as a trigger for, or a reminder of, an authentic memory, or even to give a patient "permission" to discuss a certain area, it became clear to me that some patients in this program were absorbing experiences that were described by others into their own "memories." This seemed especially likely to occur in those patients who were both very empathic and very dissociative. They seemed to experience vividly what was being described and then later to become confused as to whether it was their own memory.

A few patients in this program studied books, attended group sessions, and interviewed other patients on the unit, apparently to learn how to portray a trauma survivor in order to reap the secondary gains associated with that status. Most of the patients who appeared to incorporate other patents' memories had documented trauma histories of their own, however, and were not attempting to get secondary gain. These patients had difficulty differentiating boundaries between themselves and others. One woman explained that after hearing someone else in the program vividly describe a traumatic experience, it became hard for her to tell whose it was. This woman's hypnotic abilities combined with her own (documented) abuse history had made all subsequent experiences confusing to sort out. Many of her own past experiences had come to feel very unreal and distant, or even as if they belonged to someone else. Thus, other people's memories could feel more real to her than her own.

Other patients who incorporated someone else's memory later realized that the feelings described by the other person resonated with their own experiences. For someone who has difficulty putting words to his own experience, hearing another person tell a compelling story that contains the same feelings can be very confusing as well as very seductive emotionally. To categorize this kind of experience as a "false memory" would miss the fact that it is based on a real trauma history, a real dissociative disorder, and a real identification with the material being presented. There may be false elements involved, but there is also an underlying truth that it is important to address.

4. Misperception Based on Trickery or Confusion

Some abusers deliberately try to trick their victims in order to silence them or to make any later descriptions by the victim less credible. One repeat child molester described to me how he would sometimes dress up as different well-known characters (Santa Claus, for example) so that the child would not be taken seriously by anyone he tried to tell about the abuse. This same individual also described how he had pretended to kill a "baby" that was really just a doll in order to terrorize his victims into never telling anyone what he had done to them. Patients have told me about abusers who would describe horrible images during the abuse. Some perpetrators were said to use hypnosis in an attempt to induce a memory loss for the abuse or to control the victim's later behavior with posthypnotic suggestions. These kinds of experiences can create a lot of confusion for the child victim. It can be very difficult to sort out, years later, what was real, what was described by the adult, and what was only imagined. Some of the victims of the molester who pretended to be killing a baby may now believe that that is what they saw, having no way of knowing that the "baby" was only a doll. In addition, because they probably experienced it as a terrifying event at the time, telling them now that it was only a trick or "false memory" would most likely not be enough to help them heal from such a horrifying experience.

5. Torture or Drug-Induced Distortions

I have seen patients who were given drugs while being abused or who were tortured to the point where they passed out. These kinds of experiences are certainly not conducive to the development of completely accurate later recall, especially if the drugs given were hallucinogenic. One patient who had been orphaned as a toddler by drug addicted parents was raised on the streets of New York by her brothers, who were using and dealing heroine. They thought they were being good to her by injecting her with it from an early age. Needless to say, her early memories are pretty confusing. Other patients have admitted to me that they gave their children drugs or alcohol to keep them quiet. Their children surely have very confusing memories of such times.

Some patients have described their minds playing tricks on them while they were severely injured. It is not unusual for a veteran who has had a battle injury to describe being delusional from the pain and fear. For example, some see angels or have other dissociative experiences to distance themselves from the trauma. This can then create distortions in memory for what actually took place.

It is not an easy process to sort out memories formed under such circumstances. Focusing on truth or falsehood alone is not helpful to the process. It may be impossible to ever fully know what took place. The very unclear nature of these memories is part of the trauma from which these patients need to heal. Being deprived of clear memories can be a very difficult thing to live with.

6. Subtle Secondary Gain

The members of a patient's support group, her spouse or friends may respond with a lot of support for the idea that the patient was abused. These individuals may put pressure on the patient to pursue that explanation for her symptoms. This can influence the process of making sense out of feelings and memories, especially for someone who is in the group that Brown described as the 3-5 percent of the population who are the most hypnotizable.[17] This can also work in the opposite direction if the patient's environment is very unsupportive of the idea that she was abused, a not unusual situation, because the family of origin often strongly denies the allegations (whether they are true or false). If the patient has trouble trusting her own internal reality, such outside pressures can create either a certainty or a doubt that should not be there. As Brown points out, most of the problems with memory distortions appear to come from this 3-5 percent of highly hypnotizable individuals.[18] It is very important, when working with such patients, not to lead or influence them and to be prepared to deal with the other outside influences that can occur. Before doing memory recovery work, a therapist would do well to assess whether the patient is a member of this subgroup.

II. Therapist Factors

Therapists have influenced the memory recovery process in both directions. For many years they denied the existence of sexual abuse and in so

---

17. Brown, D. (1995). Pseudomemories: The standard of science and the standard of care in trauma treatment. *American Journal of Clinical Hypnosis, 37:3*, pp. 1-24.

18. Id.

doing did a major disservice to their patients.[19] Recently, however, many therapists have clearly erred in the other direction in assuming that certain symptoms implied a sexual abuse history and pushing this interpretation on their patients. Both approaches were a reflection of their time and both have created problems for patients. The recent tendency to over-diagnose sexual abuse is in part a reaction to the previous denial of its existence. As it became clear that the problems of many patients, especially those who had experienced trauma, could not be explained by either a psychoanalytic model or a biological model, many therapists began to look to a trauma model to explain psychiatric symptoms. The trauma model can be very useful in many cases, but it should not be used in isolation.

The field of psychiatry has been influenced mainly by professionals with either a biological or psychoanalytical orientation. Not enough has been learned, therefore, about the ways that trauma can affect people. For example, the diagnostic manual of psychiatric disorders (DSM-IV) still does not have a specific diagnostic category for someone who was repeatedly sexually abused as a child, despite the fact that both research and clinical work have shown that such an individual will often experience problems in many different areas on reaching adulthood.[20] These may include disturbances in relationships and the use of general distancing defenses. Hypnotic distancing defenses are often used to push away intrusive feelings and reactions that stem from the traumatic experiences. The person may experience visual, auditory, tactile, taste, and somatic "memories" of the experience as bits and pieces of it return in fragmentary form. The abuse can also cause physical and physiological consequences, a variety of cognitive disruptions, and, sometimes, aggressive or sociopathic reactions. Depression, problems with shame, self-esteem, and difficulties with self-soothing are extremely common, and it is not unusual to see disturbances in a person's spirituality as well. Thus, it is quite common for a person who has experienced repeated trauma to qualify for many DSM-IV (symptom-based) diagnoses (e.g., depressive disorders, anxiety disorders, dissociative disorders, somatic disorders, sexual dysfunction disorders, sleep disorders, eating disorders, brief reactive psychotic disorders, as well as many of the personality disorders and V-codes, such as "Marital Problems"), and yet none of these diagnoses communicate anything about the abuse itself. This may change with DSM-V, as a trauma-based category of "Disorders of Extreme Stress" is being considered for inclusion therein.

---

19. Masson, J.M. (1984). *The assault on truth: Freud's suppression of the seduction theory.* Toronto: Farrar, Straus and Giroux.

20. See Sakheim, D.K., & Devine, S.E. (1995). Trauma related syndromes. In C.A. Ross & A. Pam (Eds.), *Pseudoscience in biological psychiatry: Blaming the victim's body.* New York: John Wiley and Sons. pp. 255-272.

The ignoring of trauma as an important etiological factor in diagnostic and treatment approaches led to a split in the mental health field. Clinicians who worked with returning Vietnam veterans and with severely abused children and adults found the existing constructs to be quite limited. For example, the prevailing view that only a person with preexisting pathology would suffer trauma from combat seemed patently absurd to anyone who worked with veterans returning from a year in the DMZ (demilitarized zone). Similarly, the idea that early childhood stages of development determined all of adult adjustment or that psychiatric symptoms had a largely biological basis seemed bizarre to clinicians working with concentration camp survivors or prisoners of war.

Therapists who worked with trauma populations therefore became somewhat separated from the mainstream. For this new group of trauma therapists, many of the long-standing traditions of the field got lost, at times, in their rebellion against the field's lack of consideration for the importance of an individual's reactions to trauma. Trauma clinicians sometimes overdiagnosed trauma syndromes, lacking feedback from peers who could offer other ideas, just as nontrauma clinicians sometimes underdiagnosed trauma reactions because they lacked input from their trauma-oriented colleagues. This only furthered the split between the two sides and the lack of communication between them.

A clinician's biases in regard to the importance of trauma as an etiologic factor can affect both his view of the patient's "memories" and what matters the patient will pursue in therapy. For example, some clinicians faced with a patient alleging ritual abuse would not ask for elaboration; they would assume distortion and work accordingly. Other clinicians, who assume ritual abuse is possible, might focus on the "memories" and try to find how they have affected the individual's life. Thus, it is important to look at therapist factors as well as patient factors to understand how memories arise and are either pursued or suppressed in treatment. Although therapists can in this way influence a patient's memories, the vast majority of patient memories are not so easily amenable to simple therapeutic influences. If they were so malleable, psychotherapy could be a simple process of creating happy or positive recovered memories for patients.

A. Internal Defenses and Beliefs
1. Therapists' Preexisting Beliefs About Abuse

A therapist's beliefs about the veracity of recovered memories will play a major role in how he or she deals with them in treatment. I have seen therapists who believe that any hypnotically-recovered memory is true, and who therefore pursue abreactive work with the "remembered" material and subsequent therapeutic work to make sense of how the recollected experience has affected the patient. Therapists who believe that recovered memories are fabrications would probably not be using hypnosis. If they did and a recovered memory emerged, they would probably work to convince the patient that the "memory" was really metaphoric or symbolic, or even irrelevant. This difference in approach will obviously affect the patient's eventual perception of what the "memory" was all about. Therapists' attitudes, which may lie at any point between these two extremes, will affect both the process and the outcome of therapy.

Therapists need to examine their own belief systems and values to see how they are influencing their patients. Many try to convince themselves that they merely follow the patient's lead, but that is not what happens. Patients sense their therapists' attitudes and are greatly influenced by them. Most clinicians, for example, have heard such comments from their patients as, "I could never have shared that with my previous therapist because. . ." ". . . I knew that he was so strict about boundaries that he would not have come over to be nurturing or supportive, and it would have been too hard to discuss without that," or, ". . . he would get so upset and I would then feel like I had to take care of him," or ". . . I knew he would never have believed me." Patients evaluate and get to know their therapists just as therapists come to know them, no matter how neutral the therapist tries to remain. Therapists communicate their attitudes on all sorts of issues, including sexual abuse, both overtly and covertly. One patient remarked in her first meeting with me, "I'm glad that you are supportive about trauma issues." She had noticed some of the books on my shelf and concluded that I had an interest in the area, and had even noted that the particular authors I was reading agreed with her views.

2. Therapist's Preexisting Beliefs About Other Issues

I have spoken to many therapists who have been unwilling to discuss ritual abuse material with patients because they wish to avoid discussions about the devil or other matters that might be construed as disrespectful to strongly held religious beliefs. This can cause problems for a patient who is trying to sort out why such material is surfacing. Patients will readily pick up on a therapist's interest in an area or fear of it, which can then affect the patient's willingness to pursue the material further.

3. Therapist Who Projects a Personal Trauma History onto the Patient

In the past few years, I have seen a number of cases in which a therapist tried to persuade a patient that she was experiencing symptoms that were the result of incest by a family member, despite the patient's firm denials that any incest had occurred. Recently, a woman came to me for therapy after having seen a therapist for two years who utilized such an approach. After building a relationship with the patient, the therapist began to insist that the patient was in denial about having been sexually abused by her father. The patient had no repressed memories of any sort, and was very clear about having grown up in an alcoholic and violent family. She recalled her father beating her and many instances of his drunkenness causing her problems, but her therapist believed that this was not enough to cause her relationship problems and other symptoms, and insisted that she could tell that this patient had been sexually abused. The therapist disclosed her own sexual abuse history and explained that she had blocked and denied the abuse for a long time, and therefore recognized the patient doing the same thing. The therapist used a variety of strategies to get this patient to accept her sexual abuse history as truth. She went so far as to call the patient's family and "confront" them as well as instruct them and the patient to have no further contact until they all came out of "denial." The therapist's own history seems to have blinded her to the fact that the patient's symptoms could be understood in light of the experiences that she recalled, without resorting to such extreme hypotheses. This is not an isolated incident, unfortunately; one hears more and more such stories from patients. When patients respond to such interpretations with strong denial, the therapist will often tell them that the denial is proof that they were abused. The therapist may say that the patient does not remember the abuse because it occurred when the patient was "preverbal," and that instead of the memory being stored in words or pictures, it was stored in symptoms.

The patient described above had a very hard time trusting herself because of all of the invalidation that she had experienced in her life. She therefore found it hard to resist the interpretations of a strong and confident authority figure. She continued to doubt her own version of events even after learning that this therapist was being sued by four other patients for similar behavior. The damage done in this and similar cases is obviously major. This patient's adult relationships with her family (which had not been that bad) were ruined. She spent years in doubt and confusion, not to mention the time and money she wasted on ineffective therapy. Both of her parents suffered terribly with the accusations and loss of contact with their child.

It is important to note that this therapist is not a monster. She is very dedicated to her work and often goes well above and beyond what is required by her job. She cares deeply about her patients and truly believed that the only way that they could get well was to stop denying their sexual abuse. One should not assume that all therapists with their own traumatic histories are going to err in this way. Many of the best therapists in the trauma field have had their own traumatic experiences and are able to use them to understand their patients, sometimes far better than therapists who have never had such experiences. Better training and education, as well as supervision and consultation with complex cases, could avoid some of these problems.

4. Other Therapist Countertransference Problems

Most therapists who deal with traumatized patients have experienced the intense feelings generated in such work, in both the patients and themselves. Many therapists have been bullied by a patient to say that the patient's memories of abuse are real, making it difficult for them to remain neutral about this issue. The therapist has no way to know whether the memories are true, but is nonetheless frequently placed in the position of "arbiter of truth" in the patient's desire to settle his or her ambivalence. The therapist's refusal to validate a memory can incur a lot of hostility from the patient, whereas providing such validation, albeit prematurely, can lead the patient to view the therapist in a very positive light, as being helpful and supportive. The patient is almost always struggling, at least to some degree, with the veracity of recovered memories, even if they are based on historical fact. Denial, self-blame, confusion, the denial of others, and many other factors can create uncertainty, as can the errors or distortions in the memories, if there are any. The therapist needs to help the patient live with the uncertainty until the facts are clarified by internal work, external corroboration, or both.

Many therapists have committed a therapeutic error in deciding prematurely that the memories were either true or false. This is a problem even if the therapist turns out to be correct, because the patient is then not able to do the important work of seeing where his or her feelings come from and what meanings they have. The therapist who claims to know the truth is often operating out of his or her own needs, preexisting beliefs, or countertransference reactions to the patient. The latter can include a response to the patient's helplessness, a need to rescue the patient, or, at times, even an angry response to the patient.

Another example of countertransference that may emerge in this work is when the therapist becomes angry at the patient whose memory turns out to be either wholly or partially inaccurate. This is a natural response in certain ways, as the therapist has often strongly empathized with the patient about the memory, and then may feel duped if it turns out to be "false." It is important for both the patient and the therapist to understand why it was necessary for the patient to create a false memory in the first place. If they see that the distortions served some other need or fear, or occurred because of problems in the therapy itself, there will be less reason for anger and a greater ability to restore a therapeutic alliance complete with a sense of compassion and empathy. Many patients are, unfortunately, abandoned or not taken seriously if their memories turn out not to be completely accurate.

Countertransference anger can be a problem on another level as well. For example, many professionals in the field of psychiatry have moved away from the treatment of ritual abuse because many who claim to be survivors of ritual abuse have been unable to corroborate their more extreme memories. The fact that so many people have told such compelling stories that have not proven factually accurate would seem to be a very important phenomenon for the field of psychiatry to understand, but instead many professionals have begun to abandon this population. Whether these individuals are all ultimately credible or not, it is important to understand and treat them, both because they are clearly suffering and because in treating them, we may learn more about how such a phenomenon could have happened, especially on such a large scale.

In pursuing such powerful work, it is easy to make errors or to be seduced by a variety of intense feelings that can emerge. For example, most therapists who work in this area would not be doing such difficult and painful work if they did not have a need to fight perceived oppression and to advocate for the underdog. A therapist can, however, feel that he or she is fighting injustice, without actually taking on much risk, by battling nonexistent perpetrators (such as satanic cults). This, of course, entails great risk to the patient, whose sanity and ability to function may be jeopardized. Providing therapy to someone who is truly suffering injustice or abuse can be extremely gratifying work, but it can sometimes pose real dangers for the therapist. Protecting an abused patient may incur the anger of the perpetrator, for example. Fighting imaginary enemies, although a lot less risky in fact, may have some of the same excitement and rewards. Therapists can probably best prevent such countertransference problems (and best protect their patients) by obtaining supervision or consultation, or by having a psychotherapist of their own when working in this area.

5. Disturbed Therapists

Occasionally, a therapist with severe psychopathology obtains a license to practice. This can lead to terrible consequences for that therapist's patients.

I became aware of one such case when a patient came to see me for a one-time consultation after being told by her therapist that she was a ritual abuse survivor who was possessed by the devil. The patient was a fairly disturbed woman who was unsure whether or not to believe that diagnosis. Disbelieving that any therapist would say this, I requested permission to speak with the therapist. I then called the therapist, who confirmed what the patient had told me. She added that the patient had been doing spiritual warfare against her, had caused a group of men to come to her office and rape her, and had caused herself and some of her other patients to have emotional breakdowns. She told me (and had also told the patient) that she had done her own version of an exorcism with this patient and had witnessed an evil spirit, which looked like a reptile, leave the patient's body and fly out the office window. I strongly recommended to this therapist that she should discontinue her practice until such time as she could obtain psychiatric help for herself. Somewhat to my surprise, she agreed, and was actually hospitalized shortly thereafter.

This is an example of a disturbed therapist whose disturbance had a significant impact on her patient. The patient had come to treatment with delusions, but none had to do with ritual abuse. Because of her experiences in this "therapy," she had come to believe that she was evil, had survived ritual abuse, and was likely a hopeless case. Despite my attempts to discourage these perceptions and to explain my concerns about her therapist, she continued to be very much affected by this experience. When I met her by chance a year later in a day hospital treatment program, she was still convinced that she was a ritual abuse survivor, and was working on "memories" of having been a "breeder" for a cult. One hopes that this is an isolated case, but it shows that a disturbed therapist was able to pass along to a patient a delusional belief system that continued to influence the patient for a long period of time.

Severely disturbed therapists are not as unusual as one might imagine. I saw quite a few when I worked as a consultant to a hospital-based trauma program. One therapist was both disturbed and sociopathic. He had become sexually involved with his patient after he had become her conservator and had taken over all of her financial affairs. He convinced her that she was in danger from a satanic cult primarily sponsored by her parents. The patient had tape recorded some of their conversations and played the tapes for me after she was out of therapy with this man. The therapist, who was blatantly paranoid, had involved this disturbed and vulnerable young woman in his paranoid world. Every time she questioned his actions, he would bring up "the cult" and suggest that she was being "programmed" by her mother to question him. He was extremely loving and supportive to her at first but gradually became more and more controlling and hostile. He tried to forbid her to see friends and family members, and eventually became convinced that virtually everyone but himself was involved in a satanic cult conspiracy. She began to believe that her parents had been part of a satanic cult, and even wondered if she herself had been the cult's high priestess when she was younger. Her parents had been extremely neglectful of her as a child, being gamblers and drug abusers who moved around the country to escape gambling debts. She had grown up with a tremendous sense of loneliness and longing for a parent who would take care of her. The allure of this therapist and his promises to reparent her were extremely compelling. On some level, she knew that the satanic cult was unreal, but her need for a loving connection was so great that she began to believe it. It took a long time for her to extricate herself from this relationship, but once she did, the satanic cult memories gradually disappeared. Today, she talks about them as a crazy part of her past experiences created by that relationship.

B. External Influences

1. Analytic View of Incest as fantasy

I worked with a young woman who had a history of incest. When she went into treatment as a young adult, her analyst told her that the incest was her childhood fantasy and had never really happened. She went home and made an extremely serious suicide attempt. Denying someone's reality can be as dangerous as colluding with a fantasy. A competent therapist should do neither. Errors of the first kind are probably more common than one might expect in an era when so much attention is focused on child abuse.

For many years following Freud's abandonment of the seduction hypothesis, countless patients were told that their descriptions of incest were not reality-based. Sgroi described how, early in her career, she had seen physically abused children in hospital emergency rooms who were diagnosed with medical conditions that could account for spontaneous bruises or broken bones rather than having their abuse acknowledged.[21] It has not been that long since child abuse was largely a hidden phenomenon.

2. Beliefs About Abuse

Recently, a child psychiatrist told me that he does not believe that incest is harmful to children; it is only society's reaction to it that make it harmful because the child gets the message that he or she has been involved in something wrong, and that is what creates future problems. Clearly, a therapist's

---

21. Sgroi, S. (1990). Personal communication.

beliefs about abuse will influence what he or she examines in therapy and how symptoms get explained to the patient. The child psychiatrist referred to above would approach abuse very differently from most practitioners today.

3. Group Influences–Theoretical Orientation

A therapist's professional associates can influence his or her approach to treatment. I have been consulted by many therapists who had been discouraged from dealing with trauma by colleagues who believed that this would only create problematic regressions for their patients. I have also seen the reverse, where a therapist working in a trauma program would be encouraged to pursue "memory work" by colleagues in cases where it was questionable to do so. Unfortunately, knowing something about the therapist can better enable one to predict whether the therapist will believe or follow up on a "memory" than knowing a lot about the patient or the "memory" material.

C. Theoretical Influences

The therapist's theoretical orientation will often influence the decision of how to approach "memory work." The approach taken by a psychoanalyst is likely to differ from that of a biologically-oriented psychiatrist, which would in turn differ from that of a feminist therapist. The same patient would be treated very differently by each.

1. Misperceptions about Hypnosis, Memory, and the Effects of Trauma

One of the most insidious factors that I have seen affect the process of working with trauma memories is the belief of many therapists that physical abuse, neglect, emotional abuse, extreme invalidation, or even family chaos are not enough to have caused the patient's symptoms. Many clinicians believe that certain symptoms can only be accounted for by a sexual abuse history. This belief leads these clinicians to a search for recovered memories of sexual abuse whenever such symptoms are seen. While sexual abuse can create certain types of problems, that is not the same as saying that if one sees those problems, sexual abuse must have occurred. Just as doctors should be aware that headaches can be caused by a variety of factors (stress, vascular problems, muscle tension, head trauma, a brain tumor, a dissociative disorder, etc.), and should not assume that one of these factors is always responsible for a patient's headache, therapists should not ignore sexual abuse as a possible cause of problems, but neither should they assume it to be the root cause of every difficulty. It is an all too common experience and one of many that should be assessed, but there are many other important factors that can cause psychiatric disorders and they should not be minimized or ignored.

A patient's "memories" can also be influenced by the therapist's belief about what constitutes and what demonstrates a memory. A patient often comes into treatment looking for answers about complex and poorly integrated material and about puzzling symptoms. Interpreting these symptoms as indicators of "memories" can have a very strong impact on the patient's understanding of what has transpired. Any well-articulated explanation that seems to elucidate why the symptoms came about and offer hope that they can be resolved is likely to have a strong appeal to a patient who is in significant distress.

A 30-year-old man came to me for treatment after having moved to my area from the Midwest, where he and his wife had been seeing a therapist for four years, initially because of marital problems. The man had been sexually abused by his high school principal when he was a teenager and he knew that this had caused him problems. Although the principal had been arrested for abusing a number of boys at the school, my patient had never gotten help with his reactions to the abuse. When he went into therapy, he asked to be seen individually and explained his history. The therapist immediately scheduled three sessions per week and began to use hypnosis to search for other memories of trauma. She explained to him that his problems could not have been caused by the abuse with the principal and must have come from more extreme traumas. She also told him that hypnosis could get to the bottom of this and that anything he could imagine or see while in trance was a memory. She explained that people sometimes had trouble believing this, as such memories could be quite bizarre, but that it was known to be true. This young man was somewhat gullible and very desperate to get better. His family had been fairly distant, so it was both novel and appealing when the therapist showed such an interest in him.

During one of the hypnotic sessions, the therapist told him to try to imagine whether his mother or father had ever seduced him. He was able to develop an image of his mother approaching him in the crib and fondling him. He was horrified at this, but the therapist told him that he must deal with its implications. His mother must never be allowed to be alone with his or any other children and must be confronted about the abuse. When he refused to confront his mother, the therapist called the mother and told her that she had abused this man as a child. When the mother denied it, the therapist became incensed and instructed this patient to stop all contact with her since she was clearly in a dangerous degree of denial. He reluctantly agreed and instructed his siblings to do the same. When they refused, he stopped contact with them as well.

What came next was even more destructive. The young man wanted to talk about why he felt so uncomfortable with women. He described a hiking trip he had taken to San Francisco, where he had run into a pretty woman on the trail and had been too uncomfortable to speak to her. Later, he had seen her skinny-dipping at a small pond and, instead of staying and joining her, he had hurried off down the trail. He wanted to know why he had such difficulties and so much embarrassment, especially about sexual issues. The therapist's response was that clearly he had blocked what had really transpired that day and that he needed to look at it under hypnosis in order to understand his anxieties. She instructed him to get into a trance and to "remember the events." This time, he was able to see himself walking down the trail, but when he came upon her in the pond, he went into the water and strangled her, leaving her dead body on the shore. When he came out of the trance, he was mortified. Was he a killer? His therapist told him that she was very frightened. He must never allow himself to be alone with a woman. He must be very careful never to speak to anyone about this incident because he could go to jail, and he must work even harder in treatment, coming to sessions more often. By the time he had to move to the East Coast for work reasons, he was convinced that he was a child abuser himself, that he was a multiple murderer who had killed while in a dissociative state and then lost memory for the events, that he had slept with his mother and other relatives, and that he had committed numerous other crimes. (His wife, who had also entered treatment with this therapist, had become convinced that she had grown up in a satanic cult of which her parents were the high priest and priestess.)

After hearing his story, I corrected his understanding about the veracity of memories recovered by means of hypnosis. It took months before he would allow me to check the accuracy of any of his now deeply-held beliefs. Finally, he allowed me to call the San Francisco Police Department to find out if there had been a murder at the park that he had described, but I could only do so from a pay phone and under an assumed name, such was his terror. When we learned that no such murder had occurred, he began the slow process of recovering from this "therapy." He had for years believed himself to be a dangerous monster. It was extremely traumatic to realize that he had accused his mother of horrible things, especially because she was no longer living and he could not make amends. He was also now at odds with his wife, who was seeing a new therapist on the East Coast to work on "satanic ritual abuse" and had become involved in a social network of other cult survivors. It is a major understatement to say that this man's life had been ruined by his previous therapy experiences.

This man's therapist was not a mean or sadistic person. Apart from her obsession with abuse issues, she seemed quite reasonable in most respects.

She really believed that she was helping her patient and that what she told him about hypnotic recollections was true. She had confided to him that she herself had survived violent child abuse and had found healing through believing the memories that had come back to her. This may have been true, and may have led her to believe that the same process would happen for everyone else. It may have been what made her so convincing to her patients. It is also important to note that this young man was not stupid but had been desperate to understand and to heal his life circumstances. He went into treatment assuming that he would learn the causes of his symptoms and he believed what was presented to him.

2. Techniques Utilized

The specific techniques used in treatment can strongly influence a patient's memory. Some therapists continue to advocate the use of extremely leading questions despite warnings to the contrary by many experts in hypnosis. Gould, for example, recently encouraged the use of leading questions about ritual abuse with child patients because she believes that it is a frequent occurrence and that the victims have been so terrorized that they will not disclose it without a lot of encouragement by the therapist.[22] I have heard tapes of therapy sessions in which the therapist asked a sequence of questions similar to the following: "Did your abuse take place in a cult?" "Did they wear black robes?" "Did they stand in a circle?" "Were there thirteen people in the circle?" and so on. This was done without any previous indication that the patient was involved with such a group. The questioning sometimes included bribes, as where the therapist stated: "If you cooperate with me now and tell me about Ms. X doing these things to you too, I will give you the candy I showed you earlier." Most clinicians would find such leading questioning outrageous, but it does occur. It is important to address Gould's concerns, however, and develop other, nonleading, approaches that will allow terrorized patients to feel supported.

III. Perpetrator Factors

A. Internal Defenses

A full discussion of all of the defenses that abusers utilize is beyond the scope of this chapter, but the way the perpetrator deals with the abuse will

---

22. Gould, C. (1992). Diagnosis and treatment of ritually abused children. In D.K. Sakheim & S.E. Devine (Eds.), *Out of darkness: Exploring satanism and ritual abuse.* Lexington, MA: Lexington Books. pp. 207-248.

certainly have an impact on the patient. Denial is a very important defense for abusers as well as for the abused, especially for something as taboo as sexual abuse. If the abuser still has contact with the patient, the abuser's denial can either make the patient less sure about any recovered memories or it can infuriate the patient and make her feel that any memories that are recovered must be true. Conversely, a perpetrator's acknowledgment of the abuse can help to clarify any recovered memories. This does not guarantee accuracy, however, as some alleged abusers have confessed to things that later turned out to be false.

B. External Influences

There is little support for perpetrators of abuse to acknowledge their actions or to seek help. Most support groups for people who claim to have been wrongfully accused of abuse, such as the FMSF, would ask a member who acknowledged committing the abuse to leave.[23] This is unfortunate, as it is likely that at least some of the people who are accused of abuse have done at least some of what is alleged. There is no support group for True Memory Syndrome (TMS) parents. Just as the patient who realizes that she has created a false memory would be ejected from most "survivor" support groups, the parent who realizes that he has abused his child would be similarly treated. In both instances, this is probably the point at which support is most needed. Statistics on the prevalence of child abuse suggest that a great many parents could use such support.

As long as support for both accusers and accused remains contingent on their presenting themselves in certain specific and extreme ways, many support group members will be unable to examine the complexity of their memories and actions. This will affect the therapy process. Groups such as the FMSF should encourage a more complex view of events and acknowledge that some of their members may have been falsely accused of some things but accurately accused of others. Similarly, groups such as Incest Survivors Anonymous should acknowledge that their members are likely to have some memories that are accurate and others that contain distortions. Such a change in the structure of support would change the external pressures on the patient in therapy. It would relieve the pressure to maintain an extreme position and would encourage an environment where the goal is to help everyone involved to heal, as well as to accept a more realistic process of self understanding.

---

23. Freyd, P. (1997). Personal communication at conference on recovered memories of child sexual abuse, New Haven, Connecticut, November 14, 1997.

IV. Family of Origin Factors

Family members who are accused of abuse can have a major impact on the therapy process, depending on the amount of influence they have over the patient. Whether innocent or guilty, most accused family members deny abuse. The vehemence of this denial is not necessarily related to their guilt or innocence, but it can certainly influence the patient in ways noted above (see "Internal Defenses," above).

Whereas some accused parents are totally innocent, others may be even more guilty than the patient's descriptions imply. For most, however, the situation is likely to be considerably more complex. This was demonstrated by a family I met at a conference on memory in which the FMSF had been invited to participate. The mother and father (FMSF members) had been accused by their adult daughter of having sexually, physically, and emotionally abused her as a child. The couple acknowledged having physically and emotionally abused their children for many years. They stated that they had lived for a while in a commune where their daughter had been sexually abused by some of the other adults, but they vehemently denied that the husband had sexually abused the daughter. The father told me that he had been alcoholic and had had blackouts during which he was unsure of his actions, but he said that he could not have sexually abused his daughter, and that if he had, he would have to kill himself. His wife seemed able to accept that he had beaten the children, that he had been a severe alcoholic, and that they had raised the children in very problematic settings, but she too agreed that if he had sexually abused their daughter, she would have to divorce him.

It was striking to me how sexual abuse had been put into its own separate category, being seen as a behavior perpetrated only by monsters, whereas real people could beat their children or be alcoholic. These parents were amazingly open about how dysfunctional their family had been but at the same time vehement about calling their daughter's descriptions of abuse "false memories." Even if she had mislabeled the perpetrator of the sexual abuse (and that seems questionable), why did the parents focus solely on the "false" aspect of her memories, and ignore the aspects that were "true"? This family's story had been presented to other FMSF members, who shared this couple's outrage and horror about their situation. No one encouraged the parents to look at what abuse had gone on and to work with their daughter to understand any disagreements in memories between them. No one pointed out to them that they had abused their daughter and may have caused many of the problems with which she now had to deal. The sole focus of the discussions that I heard was on the unfairness of the parents being falsely accused of sexual abuse.

V. Current Family/Support System Factors

The patient's friends and current family can have a major impact on the therapy process by supporting or discouraging its progress. This can involve either emotional or financial support. When a patient recovers memories of abuse, especially if the patient is unsure what to make of them, the beliefs of significant others can have a major influence on how these memories are perceived.

VI. Societal Factors

The ways that various social factors can affect interpersonal processes such as psychotherapy have been discussed from both anthropological and sociological perspectives.[24] Several have pointed out how current approaches to diagnosis and psychotherapy direct which individuals and which factors will be considered appropriate for treatment. By assigning victims of child abuse psychiatric labels, for example, the field pathologizes the person who was injured and directs attention to his or her treatment as the way to solve the problem. This becomes even worse when, as noted earlier, these labels don't even recognize the traumatic etiology and when the stigmatizing labels are, strangely, assigned only to the victim.

There is no diagnostic label for the perpetrator of abuse, nor for the sexism and other social values that are responsible for the abuse of women and children in our culture. We accept this when it comes to child abuse but would be unlikely to accept it if it were about other phenomena. Faced with the problem of the "ethnic cleansing" rape camps in Bosnia, we would probably not create diagnostic labels for the individuals who were physically or emotionally injured in those camps and set up treatment programs for them without simultaneously labeling the camp guards as disturbed or as involved in problematic behaviors, as well as trying to stop them. More importantly, we would try to address the problematic racist and nationalist values which make such camps possible. By failing to do this with the issue of child abuse, we enable it to continue, and collude with social denial about the problem.[25]

---

24. See Miller, J.B. (1976). *Toward a new psychology of women.* Boston: Beacon Press; Jordan, J.V., Kaplan, A.G., Miller, J.B., Stiver, I.P., & Surrey, J.L. (1991). *Women's growth in connection: Writings from the Stone Center.* New York: Guilford Press; Boyd, A. (1991). *Blasphemous rumors: Is satanic ritual abuse fact or fantasy?* London: Fount; Mulhern, S. (November, 1990). *Training courses and seminars on satanic ritual abuse: A critical review.* Paper presented at the 7th International Conference on the Treatment of Multiple Personality and Dissociative Disorders, Rush Presbyterian-St. Luke's Medical Center, Chicago, IL; Noll, R. (1989). Satanism, UFO abductions, historians and clinicians: Those who do not remember the past. *Dissociation, 2,* 251-253; Richardson, J.T., Best, J., & Bromley, D.G. (1991). *The satanism scare.* New York: Aldine De Gruyter.

25. Sakheim, D.K., & Devine, S.E. (1995). Trauma related syndromes. In C.A. Ross & A. Pam (Eds.), *Pseudoscience in biological psychiatry: Blaming the victim's body.* New York: John Wiley and Sons. pp. 255-272.

If the focus of discussions were not only on the veracity of memory or the types of pathology shown by victims, we might also be discussing what social factors contribute to the epidemic of child abuse in our culture. Much of our resources are spent on diagnosing and treating victims or on disputing their claims, and little is actually spent on trying to understand and change the factors in our culture which teach boys and men about ownership of women and children, as well as other factors that lead to sexual and other violence.

A. Insurance Companies

Insurance coverage has a major impact on diagnosis and therefore on treatment. In the 1980s, as managed care began to limit coverage for most psychiatric problems, psychotherapy was becoming more and more limited in duration while treatment with medications and brief therapy was increasing. At that time, however, a diagnosis of multiple personality disorder could still result in coverage for long-term psychotherapy and even for lengthy hospital admissions. The research and clinical literature suggested that medications were only experimental and that psychotherapy was the treatment of choice for this condition. Insurance companies therefore had a hard time denying coverage. As managed care began to limit more and more treatment, MPD was one of the few diagnoses that could get such coverage. Not surprisingly, this led to a major upsurge in the diagnosis of this condition, whereas it had previously been seen as quite rare. Eventually, insurance companies began to find ways to deny coverage for this condition as well. (Interestingly, this was not based on any research or any new clinical information, but merely by on the gradual issuance of new "treatment guidelines" which suggested that long-term work or a focus on past trauma could be regressive and could decrease a patient's functioning, so only short-term or symptom-oriented approaches would be covered.) As these new rules went into effect, the diagnosis of MPD became less popular and it is now being diagnosed much less frequently. Clearly, this has nothing to do with science, research, or clinical wisdom, but rather with access to monetary resources.

A similar phenomenon is happening today. As this chapter is being written, a new parity law has just mandated that depression (along with a few other psychiatric diagnoses) be classified as a biological illness and therefore be covered by insurers in the same way as other medical problems. These kinds of political and monetary pressures make for poor science and, consequently, a poor image for the field. Many patients will be hurt in the process. It is fairly predictable that this will mean an upsurge in the diagnosis of depression because that will result in much better insurance coverage for treatment. Both patients and therapists will push for utilizing the depression diagnosis. As noted above, many patients with trauma histories meet criteria for a variety of disorders, including depression.

This new law will likely cause clinicians to overdiagnose depression in this population (and others) in order to get access to the improved coverage. This will create many problems for the field. For example, although initially trauma patients will get more insurance coverage, over the long term, it will move us further away from a much-needed, trauma-based diagnostic category, which would aid research and understanding of the effects of trauma and abuse. Many patients will be given antidepressant medications unnecessarily and will be given a diagnosis that can cause later problems in many areas (such as the ability to obtain life insurance). Studies of depression will be skewed and invalid because they will include subjects who are not really, or solely, depressed. Once again, the field will be following politics and money rather than science and the best interest of the patient. It seems fairly predictable that in five to ten years, we will again be looking at how the field harmed patients by misdiagnosing them, overprescribing medications and/or giving the wrong types of treatment.

While I was writing this chapter, I had a dispute with an insurance company's managed care department over the diagnosis of one of my patients. The patient had a dual diagnosis of depression and PTSD, but the company wanted the diagnosis to be PTSD alone because the depression diagnosis would mandate better coverage. I had to go through a number of levels of appeal to retain the depression diagnosis. What is fascinating is that I had the same argument five years earlier except that the sides were reversed. At that time, the same insurance company wanted to eliminate the trauma diagnosis because at that time a trauma diagnosis meant access to therapy while a depression diagnosis meant referral for medication with only a few therapy sessions allowed for cognitive behavioral teaching. In summary, it is probably safe to predict that there will be an upsurge of depression in the American populace, followed by some clever maneuvering by insurance companies to find ways around providing coverage for this condition, followed in turn by a miraculous recovery by the American people.

B. Lawyers and Courts

Lawsuits have increasingly influenced this field. Many therapists will no longer see trauma survivors because they fear being falsely accused of sexual abuse by the patient and they fear being sued by angry parents who claim to be falsely accused of abusing the patient because of false memories suggested by the therapist. Therapists also fear being dragged into court to testify for other reasons and having their practices disrupted. Many therapists try to stay away from trauma cases because they are afraid of being viewed as "one of those wacky trauma therapists." I get calls every week from patients who describe themselves as trauma survivors who cannot find therapists to treat them. There is no question that the legal system affects recovered memories—recently, by making therapy unavailable for many trauma survivors.

C. Society as an Influence on Memory

The subject of societal influences on recovered memory is beyond the scope of this chapter, but such influences clearly play a major role in shaping the expectations of all of the participants in the therapy process. Feminist writers have discussed the ways that society discounts the traumatic experiences of women and children because of power imbalances in the culture.[26] This certainly affects the ways that relationships such as that of psychotherapist and patient are structured and pursued. Other sociological research has addressed the question of how social contagion or rumor panics can occur and then influence patient reports and clinician opinion.[27]

The media clearly affect how problems are defined by the public and therefore who will seek help, under what circumstances and with what expectations. A recent mailing from the Oxford Health Plan directs physicians to instruct their depressed patients that "depressive disorder is a medical illness" and to "refer to a neurochemical dysregulation in the brain" when discussing the problem with them. A recent Oprah Winfrey program focused on how an individual can deal with psychiatric symptoms such as depression by focusing on her "inner child" and connecting the symptom to early trauma. Present symptoms were said to result from the triggering of old issues for the "inner child." Clearly, a public that learns about mental health from Oprah is going to be looking for the "inner child" and doing "recovered memory" work whereas a public that learns that symptoms merely reflect a chemical imbalance will seek other treatments. The model that gets adopted and portrayed by the media has a major impact on the kinds of treatment demanded by the public and offered by clinicians.

---

26. See Miller, J.B. (1976). *Toward a new psychology of women.* Boston: Beacon Press; Jordan, J.V., Kaplan, A.G., Miller, J.B., Stiver, I.P., & Surrey, J.L. (1991). *Women's growth in connection: Writings from the Stone Center.* New York: Guilford Press.

27. See Boyd, A. (1991). *Blasphemous rumors: Is satanic ritual abuse fact or fantasy?* London: Fount; Mulhern, S. (November, 1990). *Training courses and seminars on satanic ritual abuse: A critical review.* Paper presented at the 7th International Conference on the Treatment of Multiple Personality and Dissociative Disorders, Rush Presbyterian-St. Luke's Medical Center, Chicago, IL; Noll, R. (1989). Satanism, UFO abductions, historians and clinicians: Those who do not remember the past. *Dissociation, 2,* 251-253; Richardson, J.T., Best, J., & Bromley, D.G. (1991). *The satanism scare.* New York: Aldine De Gruyter.

SUMMARY

Clinicians must allow their patients to develop an understanding of their history and an awareness of its complexity, and they must do so unencumbered by outside forces but at the same time conscious of their influence. Instead of viewing memories as either true or false, they should accept that memory is a complex phenomenon that may involve both accurate and distorted elements. External corroboration of recovered memories can be helpful, especially if there is a specific need to verify what has been recovered (for example, for use in a court proceeding). Everyone involved in this debate should stop oversimplifying the memory recovery process and try to see the complex phenomena that are at work. Patients will be better served by clinicians who understand the potential impact of their own beliefs, orientation, values, techniques, and life experiences. Patients will benefit if they are seen, not as people with true or false memories, but rather as people who are struggling to understand and piece together lives that involved the interaction of complex internal defenses and external influences. Clinicians should appreciate how the process is affected by, and in turn affects, the family, the perpetrator, the current support system and any external players such as courts or insurance companies. Lastly, they should respect the limits of their ability to perceive their own place in the changing landscape of societal perspectives on this issue.

Editor's note: Mark Pendergrast wrote the following in response to several points made by Dr. Sakheim:

It is encouraging that David Sakheim and many others who have expressed a belief in massive repression, such as John Briere and Christine Courtois, now caution against the use of hypnosis to extract "memories." Sakheim's chapter is filled with horror stories of well-intended but misguided recovered memory therapy.

It is unfortunate, however, that Sakheim does not disavow the massive repression cases in which he was personally involved. He still apparently believes that MPD "alters" told him memories, and he continues to believe in "screen memories" and other odd interpretations of his own case studies. For instance, he describes a client who recovered a "memory" of satanic ritual abuse that came straight out of a picture she had seen. This is not surprising, since many such satanic abuse "memories" came directly from movies, books, or pictures. Rather than becoming skeptical of this patient's memories, however, Sakheim believed her when she "suddenly remembered" that her brother had raped her in the attic where she found the picture, and that she had used "her dissociative strategy of going into the nearest picture on the wall." Sakheim has no trouble believing that she had completely forgotten being raped by her brother until that moment.

Sakheim asserts that there was "external corroboration" for this case, but he is typical of recovered memory therapists in that he has not produced any evidence other than his second-hand word. It is entirely possible, as he asserts, that this client came from a violent home and that her brother was later convicted of rape, but this does not constitute corroboration that her brother raped her in the attic and that she forgot it. While I grant that he must respect client confidentiality, it would be possible for him to provide better documentation. If he has a truly corroborated case of massive repression, it is important that he at least ask his client whether she would be willing to grant an anonymous interview (and show the evidence) to a gentle skeptic such as me. Similarly, Sakheim claims to have a case in which a client recovered a corroborated memory from the age of 18 months, which is highly unlikely, since the period of infantile amnesia covers the first three years of life.[1]

It is distressing that Sakheim repeats an oft-heard assertion: "As long as trauma work was confined to therapists' offices, it mattered little whether such errors [false memories] occurred. Once the field of trauma therapy left the privacy of the therapy office and entered the courtroom and the media, however, the veracity of trauma memories became much more important." That is nonsense. The truth always matters, and it particularly matters when a client comes to believe, incorrectly, that her parents raped her all during her childhood. It is damaging for the client's mental health, and it is inevitably hurtful to family relationships.

Sakheim should heed his own words. "The memory recovery process is a very rewarding one for both the patient and the therapist. It brings two people together, makes them both feel very special, close and courageous, and it feels like very important and powerful work." That is why it is so seductive, and so very dangerous. "A therapist can...feel that he or she is fighting injustice, without acually taking much risk, by battling nonexistent

---

1. See Pendergrast, Mark (1995, 1996). *Victims of memory: Sex abuse accusations and shattered lives.* (2d ed.). Hinesburg, VT: Upper Access. pp. 113-115; Usher, J.A., and Neisser, U. (1993). Childhood amnesia and the beginnings of memory for four early life events. *Journal of Experimental Psychology: General, 122*(2), pp. 155-165; Howe, M.L., and Courage, M.L. (1993). On resolving the enigma of infantile amnesia. *Psychological Bulletin, 113*(2), pp. 305-326.

perpetrators (such as satanic cults)," Sakheim continues.[2]

Editor's note: Dr. Sakheim responded to Mark Pendergrast's remarks, above, as follows:

I did, in fact cite various forms of corroboration in the case I presented, including the brother's conviction for child abuse and the patient's school and hospital records, among other things. It is not my role as a therapist to ask a client to agree to an interview with a third party for the express purpose of establishing (for the interest of that third party) whether or not the client's recovered memory is valid. I would consider that to be an exploitation of the client.

Mark Pendergrast argues that there is no evidence for "massive repression" and that anyone presenting a case that appears to involve massive repression should have to present extreme amounts of proof along with it. (This appears to include the necessity for a one-man truth squad assessment by Mr. Pendergrast.) This battle was fought years ago in the field of psychiatry; it is Mr. Pendergrast's view that is outside of the mainstream today. There have been many clinical case presentations, clients who have agreed to be interviewed, research studies, theoretical papers written, and presentations of such cases from many different areas. There is now an International Society for the Study of Dissociation with chapters around the world. There is a journal specifically dedicated to research about the dissociative disorders (titled *Dissociation: Progress in the Dissociative Disorders*). The current edition of the APA's *Diagnostic and Statistical Manual* (DSM-IV) now contains a category for the dissociative disorders, which was included after extensive debate, research, and clinical documentation. It is therefore unfair to expect that every case discussion should necessitate Mark Pendergrast having to interview the patient. Just as there are people who doubt the existence of clinical

---

2. David Sakheim has come a long way since coediting the 1992 volume, *Out of darkness: Exploring satanism and ritual abuse,* in which he wrote: "In therapy it is not necessary to verify every detail. In therapy it may be enough to accept that a patient's post traumatic stress reactions indicate a history that must be explored—with the therapist present as an ally....Taken separately, the crimes that ritually abused patients report (child abuse, torture, infanticide, cannibalism, child pornography, drug abuse, cruelty to animals, and murder) are all known to occur. It is probably our own difficulty imagining the combination of horrors that makes us so skeptical." He wrote of the "sad reality of the extreme sadism and cruelty behind the problems that these patients experience." It is quite clear from reading all of Sakheim's writings in this 1992 volume—which I urge readers to verify for themselves—that he believed in the essential validity of many ritual abuse memories. "Each time such practices come to light," he wrote, "we try to avoid the pain of knowledge. Recent history is full of killing fields." In other words, because humans are capable of extreme cruelty, he urged readers to believe in ritual abuse memories, even though he gave lip service to cautions against believing EVERYTHING clients recalled. "It would be a major loss to our field if hysteria tempts us to go beyond our data," he wrote. Yet there WAS no data, no concrete evidence whatsoever to corroborate ritual abuse memories. (Sakheim, D. K., & Devine, S. E. (Eds). (1992). *Out of darkness: Exploring satanism and ritual abuse.* San Francisco: Jossey-Bass. pp. xiv-xv.)

depression or other psychiatric problems, there are those who doubt the reality of dissociative disorders. At this point in time, however, it is incumbent on the doubters to disprove something that is supported by so much history and evidence and so many clinical examples.

I have been writing about the complexity of memories for a long time. When I edited *Out of Darkness*, it was a plea for further investigation of these phenomena. At that time, there was little or no data to support either side of the polarized debate about these cases. I was trying to present what was then known and to encourage further study and debate. This is clear in the introduction, where I stated "All of these patients need to be understood and treated, but probably not all in the same fashion.

Unfortunately, our field has a tendency to become polarized, with some clinicians claiming that every patient's story is true and the rest of the field is heartless, and others claiming that every patient is delusional and the rest of the field is merely too gullible. Neither of these positions takes into account all of the data, and neither really furthers the understanding of this complex group of patients. We have tried to present the range of views in this volume in the hope that doing so may bring some integration to this area as well as some sensitivity to the complexities involved. Each 'side' in this debate has many valid and worthwhile points to make. Each could learn a lot from the other."

Mr. Pendergrast's use of selected quotations, taken out of context, from *Out of Darkness* misrepresents my views as favoring an acceptance of everything a client reports and believing that it does not matter if false memories occur. I presented a much more balanced and complex view of ritual abuse allegations in that essay, which can be seen if the passage from which the quotes are taken is read in its entirety. In that passage I was making a more complex point about problems with both hysteria and denial. That section is quoted below. I will leave it to the reader to judge whether Mr. Pendergrast was being unfairly selective in his quotes.

"Over the years the mental health profession has indulged both in hysterical overreaction to and denial of interpersonal violence. It will be very sad if the internal disagreements about how to approach the area of ritual abuse force therapists to take sides before the information is available to do so intelligently. If that occurs, each side will misdiagnose important clinical situations. 'Believing' a delusional patient can be as destructive as 'disbelieving' a traumatized one. It would be a major loss to our field if hysteria tempts us to go beyond our data. It would be equally tragic if our field ends up blaming the victims and dismissing their stories as fantasy rather than confronting the horrors of their experiences. This is not to imply that a therapist must believe every word of a survivor's descriptions, even if we know for a fact that she was abused. Research has shown that people in general are usually not very accurate witnesses even under ideal circumstances. Clearly, the observations of a young child who is deliberately being tortured, confused, drugged, and terrorized will be distorted. This is even more likely when the survivor is trying to reconstruct events that occurred twenty or more years in the past. However, in therapy, it is not necessary to verify every detail. In therapy, it may be enough to accept that a patient's post-traumatic stress reactions indicate a history that must be explored-with the therapist present as ally."

"However, the therapist must not be seduced by his or her own needs. The compelling material and the intensely projected affects must not be allowed to make the therapist into an advocate for either side of the patient's ambivalence. The therapist's role is to help the patient to better understand his or her own doubts and uncertainties. It is the patient's struggle to sort out what is real."

Chapter 4

REPRESSION, DISSOCIATION AND OUR HUMAN STREAM OF CONSCIOUSNESS: MEMORY AS A CONSTRUCTIVE, CREATIVE PROCESS

JEROME L. SINGER

SOME EARLY MEMORIES AND CLINICAL EXPERIENCE

As both a practicing clinician and a research scientist in psychology, I have long proposed that we should begin an inquiry with personal introspection and self-examination.[1] Analyzing our personal memories, fantasies, or experiences in daily life; recalling our own traumatic situations; or serving as participants in the same experiments we design for others cannot *resolve* scientific questions but they can point to issues we may need to explore more fully in formulating researchable hypotheses. In this volume, we are dealing with issues relating to the so-called reality of an adult's recovered memories of childhood experience and the possibility that some of these memories have been intentionally forgotten (repressed) or separated systematically from arrays of other memories (dissociated) only to be retrievable in adulthood under psychotherapy, hypnosis, or other special circumstances. While I cannot recall ever retrieving memories of abuse in the course of my own seven-year psychoanalysis, I do have childhood memories that to the best of my knowledge were sustained by me over about a seventy-year period.

Let me begin with an instance that sounds surprisingly like the "Lost in the Mall" experiments of which so much is made in the current debates over the validity of recovered memories.[2] When I was just a toddler, about two-and-a-half years of age, while traveling on a New York subway with my parents, I suddenly walked out of the train and onto the station platform. The doors shut and the train pulled out before my frantic parents could reach me. My

---

1. Singer, J.L. (1966). *Daydreaming.* New York: Random House.

2. Loftus, E., & Pickrell, J. (1995). The formation of false memories. *Psychiatric Annals, 25,* 720-725.

parents left the train at the next stop and my father rushed to the opposite platform to catch a train heading back to where I had walked off. Fortunately, when he got back to the platform where I had exited, he found me standing just at the same place, held firmly by the hand of a kindly gentleman who had appreciated the situation.

In my memory, I can picture myself walking off the train and waiting there with the man. But I have also had visual memories, for as long as I can remember, of my father's and mother's agitation after their train pulled out and of my father rushing to catch the train heading in the opposite direction—scenes that I could not possibly have witnessed. I also remember first hearing this story from my parents when I was about five years of age and at that time trying to imagine an incident of which I actually had no original recall. The story was repeated to me a few times over the next couple of years and during that period, I developed further visual images of the event. I grew up never believing I had actually remembered the original event *but only the narration of it by my parents*, to which I responded by trying to imagine what had happened.

Here, however, is a contrasting memory that I seem always to have remembered in privacy and which I never shared with anyone. I was about four years old, a veridical dating since I have many clear memories of the apartment in which we lived then. My mother was angry with me for a misdeed which I have completely forgotten. She locked me in a clothes closet, threatening me with the "Bogey Man." I remember crying and huddling down on the floor and then gradually calming down when nothing happened. Eventually she opened the door and let me out.

All my life, I remembered this event and thought about it occasionally along with other memories of the apartment and neighborhood where we lived at the time. The great majority of my memories were quite positive in affect and overall I almost always thought of my mother in those days as a loving, caring, and trustworthy person. Was this a veridical memory or a fantasy? When my mother was well into her nineties and living in a home for the aged, she often reminisced about the distant past. One day, she said, "You know, I remember the time when we lived on Franklin Avenue and I got mad at you and locked you in the closet, telling you the Bogey Man would come. When I opened the door, you weren't even crying. You were always such a good boy."

I mention these two early memories because they illustrate the complexities of our memory system and the difficulty in establishing the truth or falsity of such experiences. The subway incident, which bears similarities to the "Lost in the Mall" experiments of Loftus and Pickrell in that it was an adventure, suggested to a child by adults, is an instance where initially I had no recollection of the event.[3] Once told of it, I tried to picture it and fill in the visual details, including, of course, some I could never have witnessed. Yet I have never believed that I actually remembered that scene because I also recall being told about it by my parents. For all I know, it may never have happened, and my parents had some unfathomable motive for telling me this tale. Yet I can vividly picture the scene, borrowing the image of myself standing there, I can guess, from an old photograph of me at that age.

In the case of the "locked in the closet" memory, which I always remembered as a true event, albeit with nothing like photographic vividness, it appears to have been a "genuine" memory because my mother spontaneously reported its occurrence almost 68 years later. Even so, I can't be sure that she hadn't described it much earlier and I simply forgot her telling me the story.

Fortunately, I have no early memories of severe physical abuse or betrayal traumas.[4] This incident and another from the same period, when my mother packed up a little suitcase and locked me (weeping) out of the apartment, might qualify as early nonsexual betrayal traumas. They were never apparently repressed, however, and were so exceptional in an atmosphere I recall of parental love and trust that I was fortunately quite "securely attached" throughout childhood.

When I began clinical practice in the late 1940s, the received wisdom of the psychoanalytically-oriented and trained therapists of that period was that much of patients' reports of childhood incest that might arise in treatment would be manifestations of Oedipal fantasies (following Freud's post-1900 views). I remember a relative telling me that she had been regularly molested in middle childhood by another family member, whereupon I quickly asked her (to her indignation) whether this might not be imagined. As I began to see more clients in my practice, it was soon apparent that a significant number of the women spontaneously reported incidents of childhood or early adolescent sexual molestation. These accounts had not been repressed, but were reported in therapy because it was a first opportunity to bring up these shameful events to a nonthreatening adult. I soon realized, as did others of my colleagues at that time, that such incestuous incidents were indeed far more frequent and believable than we had expected and that we owed it to our patients to treat these events as genuine recollections. Data such as those reported by Herman, Herman and Schatzow, and Feldman-Summers and Pope are in keeping with the clinical observations a number of us were

---

3. Id.

4. Freyd, J. (1996). *Betrayal trauma theory: The logic of forgetting abuse.* Cambridge, MA: Harvard University Press.

making in the 1950s.[5, 6, 7] Such memories emerged unsolicited. They had not been forgotten and the events reported had occurred in middle childhood or adolescence when they could be stored as memory schemas by verbal labels as well as by images.

I stress these early clinical observations because it is important that we keep in mind, for both therapeutic and preventive mental health purposes, the seriousness for growing children of such early traumatic betrayals. We need better evidence of the frequency of such cases and the genuine likelihood of their occurrence when they have been reported as recalled only after decades of repression.

COGNITIVE PROCESSES, REPRESSION, AND DISSOCIATION

In 1988, I organized a conference on Repression and Dissociation at Yale University under the auspices of the MacArthur Foundation's Program on Conscious and Unconscious Mental Processes. The presentations by a panel of distinguished scholars and researchers in psychiatry and psychology were later published.[8] The conference focused on two major issues:

(a) Was there scientific evidence to support the concepts of repression and dissociation as forms of selective, motivated forgetting? Could such processes be incorporated into the current state of scientific knowledge about human cognitive functioning and memory?

(b) Was there evidence that such selective, motivated forgetting or information-avoiding processes could become crystallized into trait-like forms? Were there identifiable groups of normal or psychopathological individuals who could be characterized as "repressors," people who consistently sought to avoid attending to or remembering potentially unpleasant or psychologically-threatening stimuli? If so, what were the personality and health implications of such an avoidant cognitive style?

With a group of participants ranging from the psychoanalytically-oriented (such as Marshall Edelson, Mardi Horowitz, Sidney Blatt, and Helen Block Lewis) to the more cognitively-oriented (such as Kenneth Bowers, Gordon Bower, John Kihlstrom, Penelope Davis, and Matthew Erdelyi, among others), one might have anticipated a far-ranging and diffuse volume. I believe the result, reflecting the scientific, empirical research commitment shared by

---

5. Herman, J.L. (1981). *Father-daughter incest.* Cambridge, MA: Harvard University Press.

6. Herman, J.L. & Schatzow, E. (1987). Recovery and verification of memories of childhood sexual trauma. *Psychoanalytic Psychology, 4,* 1-14.

7. Feldman-Summers, S. & Pope, K.S. (1994). The experience of "forgetting" childhood abuse: A national survey of psychologists. *Journal of Consulting & Clinical Psychology, 62,* 636-639.

8. Singer, J.L. (Ed.) (1990). *Repression and dissociation.* Chicago: University of Chicago Press.

all the participants, was more in the direction of agreement than of chaos. The consensus was that there was a need for fundamental operationally-defined and experimentally accessible characterizations of differences between *procedural* and *declarative* knowledge, *episodic* and *semantic* memory, *explicit* and *implicit* memory, *short-term* and *working* memory, and the special role of *self-relevant* or *autobiographical* memory. All of the conference participants seemed to agree on the important differences in retrieval possibilities between recognition and recall memory, the usefulness of schemas and scripts as organizing mental structures and the role of cognition as an active process in which reminiscence, anticipation, and recurring imaginative activity all played a key role.[9]

Curiously, although most of the participants were also active clinicians, the subject of repressed memory concerning sexual trauma was practically unmentioned, even by Helen Lewis, whose own daughter, Judith Lewis Herman, was just then actively exploring that phenomenon in her groundbreaking work on father-daughter incest. The issues of the therapeutic uses of catharsis of repressed memory—so central to Freud's and Breuer's work on incest memories in the 1890s and, much more recently, to the clinical work of trauma therapists of sexual abuse survivors—were largely unmentioned, as if such approaches were scientifically passé. In view of the tremendous controversy over repressed memory of sexual trauma that has erupted in the past fifteen years, I wonder, were all of us at that conference somehow subject to a massive dissociation? Or was it possible that with all the accumulated clinical experience in that room, the phenomenon of *repressed* memory of sexual abuse had not surfaced sufficiently in our various practices?

There seemed to be some consensus about the difference between repression, a presumably *vertical* process, in which unpleasant material was "shoved down" into a less retrievable "unconscious" region, and "dissociation," a presumably *horizontal* process, in which sets of event memories and their contextual cues could be sustained "side by side" at a near conscious level, retrievable separately as called for by circumstances. The human capacity for *absorption*, a normal predictor of the likelihood of response to hypnotic induction, explains how, at a movie or during a play we can almost completely lose ourselves in the unfolding story, oblivious of the surrounding audience and theater, but can quickly shift attention to the "real" setting as the story ends. I have come to believe that dissociation is the more common process.

What follows is my summary of the implications I perceive to have emerged from that conference and from the recent literature on memory and ongoing cognitive processes.

---

9. Singer, J.L., & Sincoff, J.B. (1990). Beyond repression and the defenses. In J.L. Singer (Ed.), *Repression and dissociation* (pp. 471-496). Chicago: University of Chicago Press.

A COGNITIVE-AFFECTIVE PERSPECTIVE ON SELECTIVE MEMORY AND PERSONALITY COPING STRATEGIES

A General View of Memory and Emotion

A human being can be regarded as an information-seeking, information-processing organism. We need to assign meanings to the ambiguities we confront in each new physical or social setting.[10] Our emotional system is closely linked to the rate, ambiguity and complexity of the new information we must process from moment to moment.

Our established schemas or scripts, along with our wishes and fantasies, lead us to anticipate what we may confront in the next room or in the next social encounter.[11] We rarely get it exactly right, but we seem to be wired up so that moderate degrees of incongruity arouse interest and curiosity, motivating further exploration until we can match the new data with some stored array of prior schemas. Then we laugh, smile, or experience relief. More extreme degrees of incongruity or disconfirmation of expectancies evoke fear. The persistence over time of such unexpected information that cannot readily be assimilated evokes anger, distress, or sadness.[12] As Kihlstrom and Hoyt [13] suggest (and in keeping with much research on the self-concept), a special role is played by the relevance of information or beliefs about the self of memories defined as autobiographical.

We can propose that there are three major sources of stimulation that serve as settings for our encounters with new information. The first is the physical or social environment outside our skins, although this "real world" takes on a personal meaning based on our experiences and the complexity of our differentiated schemas, scripts, and prototypes for defining it. A second source of stimulation is the ongoing activity of our memory system – our stream of consciousness, which provides us with fleeting associations, elaborate and sometimes frightening fantasies, and odd but generally intriguing

---

10. Kreitler, H., & Kreitler, S. (1976). *Cognitive orientation and behavior.* New York: Springer.

11. Miller, G., Galanter, E., & Pribram, K. (1960). *Plans and the structure of behavior.* New York: Holt; Singer, J.L. (1984). *The human personality: An introductory text.* San Diego, CA: Harcourt, Brace, Jovanovich.

12. Mandler, G. (1984). *Mind and body.* New York: Norton; Singer, J.L. (1974). *Imagery and daydream methods in psychotherapy and behavior modification.* New York: Academic; Singer, J.L. (1984). *The human personality: An introductory text.* San Diego, CA: Harcourt, Brace, Jovanovich; Tomkins, S. (1962-63). *Affect, imagery, and consciousness* (Vol. 1). 2 vols. New York: Springer.

13. Kihlstrom, J., & Hoyt, I. (1990). Repression, dissociation and hypnosis. In J.L. Singer (Ed.), *Repression and dissociation* (pp. 181-208). Chicago: University of Chicago Press.

night dreams.[14] This is the domain that Edelson[15] proposes is the special area for psychoanalytic exploration. Finally, the ongoing machinery of our bodies presents us with a continuing series of signals, some fairly readily interpretable, as in alimentary, digestive, or excretory functions or reactive pains, but many a mere twitching or, in the case of autonomic or central nervous system functions (such as brain waves), largely outside an awareness level that permits effective communication to others. Evidence of conditioning of bodily activities or of voluntary control through biofeedback (often still without verbal labeling or descriptive awareness) suggests that such signals can be discriminated but not interpreted into a lexical or imagery system that permits the formation of schemas.[16]

Part of the human dilemma is that we must maneuver our way through life from moment to moment choosing which stimuli we wish to attend to at both the first and the second types of awareness.[17] Generally, we give highest priority to our own physical and social milieu (what Neisser has termed the "ecological self") because survival necessitates, for example, that we look before crossing city streets.[18, 19] We must, of course, slip back into the private self of memory or fantasy in order to interpret new experiences, but this is often an overlearned, automatic process. We can, however, give more attention to our memories, wishes, and fantasies when our external demands are reduced by redundant settings and overlearned situations such as routine chores, solitary environments, and waiting rooms.[20] Centrally generated

14. Bonanno, G. & Singer, J.L. (1990). Repressive personality style: Theoretical and methodological implications for health and pathology (pp. 435-470). In J.L. Singer (Ed.), *Repression and dissociation*. Chicago: University of Chicago Press; Singer, J.L. & Bonanno, G.A. (1990). Personality and private experience; Individual variations in consciousness and in attention to subjective phenomena. In L. Pervin (Ed.), *Handbook of personality* (pp. 419-444). New York: Guilford Press.

15. Edelson, M. (1990). Defense in psychoanalytic theory: Computations or fantasy? In J.L. Singer (Ed.), *Repression and dissociation* (pp. 33-60). Chicago: University of Chicago Press.

16. Schwartz, G. (1990). Psychobiology of repression and health: A systems approach. In J.L. Singer (Ed.), *Repression and dissociation* (pp. 405-434). Chicago: University of Chicago Press; Bonanno, G. & Singer, J.L. (1990). Repressive personality style: Theoretical and methodological implications for health and pathology (pp. 435-470). In J.L. Singer (Ed.), *Repression and dissociation*. Chicago: University of Chicago Press.

17. Baars, B. (1997). *In the theater of consciousness. The workspace of the mind.* New York & Oxford: Oxford University Press; Bower, G. (1990). Awareness, the unconscious and repression: An experimental psychologist's perspective. In J.L. Singer (Ed.), *Repression and dissociation* (pp. 209-232). Chicago: University of Chicago Press.

18. Neisser, U. (1988). The self: An ecological analysis. Keynote address, presented to the twenty-fourth International Congress of Psychology, Sydney.

19. See also Rapaport, D. (1960). On the psychoanalytic theory of motivation. In M.R. Jones (Ed.), *Nebraska symposium on motivation* (pp. 173-247). Lincoln, Nebraska: University of Nebraska Press.

20. Antrobus, J.S. (1993). Thinking away and ahead. In H. Morowitz & J.L. Singer (Eds.), *The Mind, the brain and complex adaptive systems* (pp. 155-174). New York: Addison-Wesley; Antrobus, J.S. (1998). Towards a neurocognitive processing model of imaginal thought. In J.A. Singer, & P. Salovey (Eds.) *At play in the fields of consciousness* (pp. 3-28). Mahaw, NJ: Erlbaum.

stimuli can divert our attention from the physical environment, as when we pass a flower shop while riding on a bus and suddenly remember that it is Mother's Day. This can happen even without external cues, as when the face of one's most recent romantic flame stares up at one from a pile of data analyses. Body signals generally receive lowest priority, except when a persistent urge to urinate leaves one wiggling and twisting while trying to conduct a serious conversation or when a pang of muscle pain suddenly interrupts a pleasant reverie about a future victory in tennis.

Styles of Selective Attention and Memory Retrieval

Growing up involves learning a variety of strategies for choosing where to focus attention, for determining under what circumstances we can give higher priority to private thoughts and wishes, for gaining control over bodily functions, and so on. We also begin to develop metastrategies (presumably through early socialization by family and culture as well as through management of constitutional temperamental proclivities) for determining the relative emphasis to place on internal and external signals, in what is believed to be the origin of an introversion-extroversion dimension of personality.[21] We need an automatic metastrategy for limiting the complexity and levels of inputs from all sources so that what Baars has called the global workspace or theatre of consciousness does not become too cluttered.[22]

Selective filtering thus becomes a critical human task and almost certainly the basis for what later emerge as avoidant strategies. Gradually, we learn not to divert too much attention to stimuli that we have learned are nonconsequential features of the environment in order that we may better focus on matters of special importance. We also learn avoidant strategies for reducing clutter in the workspace of consciousness even when the issue is not threatening, as when we turn away from the television set during the commercials. The procedures for voluntarily avoiding attention (and hence later encoding or storage) include the ways we learn to skim a newspaper, making judgments from headlines or sections of the paper so that we spend no time reading and later remembering material in which we have little interest. Luborsky's clever demonstration of certain individuals' (characterized as "repressors") avoidance of sexually provocative material in a picture they are looking at is a special case of such a skimming strategy.[23] Bower, Bowers,

---

21. Singer, D.G. & Singer, J.L. (1990). *The house of make-believe: Children's play and the developing imagination.* Cambridge, MA: Harvard University Press.

22. Baars, B. (1997). *In the theater of consciousness. The workspace of the mind.* New York & Oxford: Oxford University Press.

23. Luborsky, L., Crits-Christoph, P., & Alexander, K. (1990). Repressive style and relationship patterns-three samples inspected. In J.L. Singer (Ed.) *Repression and dissociation* (pp. 276-298). Chicago: University of Chicago Press.

Erdelyi, and Kihlstrom and Hoyt outline a variety of ways in which the forgetting feature of repression is constructed out of a series of cognitive processes from attention through encoding, rehearsal, and various retrieval strategies.[24, 25, 26, 27] Bower and Kihlstrom and Hoyt have also suggested how such avoidant strategies can become automatic.[28, 29]

One can also suppress unwanted thoughts by shifting one's attention in order to avoid spontaneous mental rehearsal. The pain or distress one might experience if one thinks for a while about a lost opportunity or lover can be quickly, if temporarily, avoided by busying oneself with making a drink, lighting a cigarette, turning on the television, or trying to engage one's neighbor at a cocktail party in light chatter. Such failures of rehearsal may, to some extent, reduce the probability of later spontaneous retrieval of the thought.[30]

Conscious suppression of thought may indeed be quite adaptive, as Erdelyi, Schwartz, and Vaillant suggest, in the interest of more effective timing or consideration of one's current unfinished issues.[31, 32, 33] We all confront the reality that, if we think too much about desired pleasures or about the dangers to human existence posed by nuclear armaments, terrorism, pollution, population density, and chemical hazards in food and at the workplace, then we can barely make it through the day, let alone get present work done. To suppress such thoughts about potential dangers, however, does not mean to minimize their importance. That would be the most primitive, and usu-

24. Bower, G. (1990). Awareness, the unconscious and repression: An experimental psychologist's perspective. In J.L. Singer (Ed.), *Repression and dissociation* (pp. 209-232). Chicago: University of Chicago Press.

25. Bowers, K.S. (1990). Unconscious influences and hypnosis. In J.L. Singer (Ed.), *Repression and dissociation* (pp. 143-181). Chicago: University of Chicago Press.

26. Erdelyi, M. (1990). Repression, reconstruction and defense: History and integration of the psychoanalytic and experimental frameworks. In J.L. Singer (Ed.) *Repression and dissociation* (pp. 1-33). Chicago: University of Chicago Press.

27. Kihlstrom, J. & Hoyt, I. (1990). Repression, dissociation and hypnosis. In J.L. Singer (Ed.), *Repression and dissociation* (pp. 181-208). Chicago: University of Chicago Press.

28. Bower, G. (1990). Awareness, the unconscious and repression: An experimental psychologist's perspective. In J.L. Singer (Ed.), *Repression and dissociation* (pp. 209-232). Chicago: University of Chicago Press.

29. Kihlstrom, J., & Hoyt, I. (1990). Repression, dissociation and hypnosis. In J.L. Singer (Ed.), *Repression and dissociation* (pp. 181-208). Chicago: University of Chicago Press.

30. Singer, J.L., & Sincoff, J.B. (1990). Beyond repression and the defenses. In J.L. Singer (Ed.), *Repression and dissociation* (pp. 471-496). Chicago: University of Chicago Press.

31. Erdelyi, M. (1990). Repression, reconstruction and defense: History and integration of the psychoanalytic and experimental frameworks. In J.L. Singer (Ed.) *Repression and dissociation* (pp. 1-33). Chicago: University of Chicago Press.

32. Schwartz, G. (1990). Psychobiology of repression and health: A systems approach. In J.L. Singer (Ed.), *Repression and dissociation* (pp. 405-434). Chicago: University of Chicago Press.

33. Vaillant, G. (1990). Repression in college men followed for half a century. In J.L. Singer (Ed.), *Repression and dissociation* (pp. 259-274). Chicago: University of Chicago Press.

ally more pathological, defense of denial.[34] Instead, one decides when one can fruitfully think of these issues and what practical actions one can take, whether by joining organizations, contributing money, changing dietary habits, or otherwise engaging in activities that insure that others are actively thinking and working on such issues and that one's government is not denying or repressing the dangers.

The same principle applies to more private yearnings, pains, and sorrows. We can temporarily refrain from dwelling on them in the interest of completing certain urgent tasks or obligations, but we must allow ourselves some opportunities to confront our recurrent wishes in order to discover whether at least some are attainable, to ponder over failures in order to do better, to mourn for people who have died, and to recognize through physical pain the possibility that we may require some form of medical attention.

With respect to bodily functions, we go through a phase of first noticing them a great deal in infancy, gradually differentiating those most important for survival or for avoiding the embarrassment of soiling. We achieve automatic control of our bodily functions; then we turn our attention away from them for many years of our lives until the aches and pains of old age become more insistent. Again, there may be interesting individual differences in awareness of some kinds of bodily functions or organ systems—in athletes, for example, with respect to their muscular and skeletal systems, and in individuals with more deviant narcissistic body fixations.[35] It remains to be determined whether the denial or repression discussed in the health psychology areas reflects a form of selective inattention to cardiovascular system signals or even to certain messages from the immune system.[36]

Although a search to trap classical repression as it happens may be a dubious approach, there is an heuristic opportunity for studying individuals who differ systematically in their reliance on avoidant processes. We need to know more about how such processes develop—in what kinds of families, under what social constraints, and in what domains of activity or around what kinds of problems. Blatt suggests that exaggerated avoidant strategies are more closely associated with early experiences emphasizing social concerns, fear of loss of love, abandonment or rejection, and experiences of shame.[37] Strategies that involve what he calls counteraction (e.g., isolation,

---

34. Blatt, S. (1995). Emotion, cognition and representation. In D. Cicchetti & S. Toth (Eds.), *Rochester symposium on developmental psychopathology,* Volume 6, pp. 1-33. Rochester, NY: University of Rochester Press.

35. Kunzendorf, R.G., Spanos, N., & Wallace, B. (Eds.) (1996). *Hypnosis and imagination.* Amityville, NY: Baywood.

36. Bonanno, G., & Singer, J.L. (1990). Repressive personality style: Theoretical and methodological implications for health and pathology (pp. 435-470). In J.L. Singer (Ed.), *Repression and dissociation.* Chicago: University of Chicago Press.

37. Blatt, S. (1995). Emotion, cognition and representation. In D. Cicchetti & S. Toth (Eds.), *Rochester symposium on developmental psychopathology,* Volume 6, pp. 1-33. Rochester, NY: University of Rochester Press.

reaction formation, and obsessive-compulsive rituals) are more likely to emerge from problems of excessive self-criticism, low self-esteem, guilt, and fear of failure.

Even so-called "counteractive" strategies may essentially be avoidant. Sullivan used the term "obsessional substitution" to suggest that ritualistic behavior, preoccupation with petty details, and rumination about trivial thought may serve to avoid confrontation with an idea, environmental cue, or needed action that either would be incapable of fulfillment or would involve social risk or inner conflict.[38]   Indeed, it might be arguable that many of the so-called "defense mechanisms" may be forms of systematic self-distraction to preclude attention to, or to prevent learning and rehearsal of, conflictual ideas and communications, thereby deceiving oneself and possibly other people about one's desires and intentions.[39]   As these become overlearned, they may indeed function outside awareness, but they may be identifiable fairly readily (sometimes with the help of a therapist-observer) in the same way that we can reconstruct the sequences in an overlearned motor act once we find it necessary to explain the process to someone else.[40]   As recent works on dissociation suggest, the human capacity for compartmentalizing complex sets of differentiated social, emotional, and motor behaviors is greater than we generally realize.[41]

The special role of avoidant strategies in the health or psychophysiological area beckons for greater exploration. Why should denial of illness or systematic avoidance of thought about one's worries or interpersonal skills be so often associated with physical problems? Schwartz uses the notion of "system deregulation" to suggest an approach to linking avoidant thought and behavior to body organ malfunction.[42]   Recently, there has been increasing attention paid to the role of the immune system. A study by Pennebaker, Kiecolt-Glaser, and Glaser demonstrated that simply asking undergraduates to write about the major traumas in their lives for four consecutive days led to significantly lower subsequent visits to health services and was also associated with changes in immune system functioning (compared to control subjects).[43]   The observation that the number of visits to the doctor's office was

---

38. Sullivan, H.S. (1956). *Clinical studies in psychiatry.* New York: Norton.

39. Singer, J.L. (1984). *The human personality: An introductory text.* San Diego, CA: Harcourt, Brace, Jovanovich.

40. Singer, J.L., & Salovey, P.S. (1991). Organized knowledge structures and personality: Person schemas, self-schemas, prototypes and scripts. In M.J. Horowitz (Ed.), *Person schemas and recurrent maladaptive interpersonal patterns* (pp. 33-79). Chicago: University of Chicago Press.

41. Spiegel, D. (Ed.) (1994). *Dissociation: Culture, mind and body.* Washington, D.C.: American Psychiatric Association.

42. Schwartz, G. (1990). Psychobiology of repression and health: A systems approach. In J.L. Singer (Ed.), *Repression and dissociation* (pp. 405-434). Chicago: University of Chicago Press.

43. Pennebaker, J.W., Kiecolt-Glaser, J.K., & Glaser, R. (1988). Disclosure of traumas and immune function: Health implications for psychotherapy. *Journal of Consulting and Clinical Psychology, 56,* 239-45.

significantly reduced after "confession" has now been replicated several times. This opposite effect of the avoidant strategy used by the repressor personality clearly merits further research. Indeed, Schwartz reported that repressive individuals showed more frequent visits to the college health service, despite the denial of problems reported on questionnaires.[44] Just what links there may be between the immune system and the central nervous system may be a question deserving of study not only for immunobiology but also for careful psychophysiological work. There may be ways in which some individuals have overlearned a cluster of avoidant strategies designed to maintain a constricted sense of well-being; these strategies may, however, yield a failure to identify subtle bodily signals of malaise or to engage in appropriate self-care behaviors.[45]

The reality of the so-called "repressor personality" style has been suggested by a considerable number of studies. Most recently, Schlimmack and Hartmann demonstrated that persons so classified (generally using the measures introduced by Weinberger et al. or in Weinberger's more recent scoring procedure) register *fewer* events as unpleasant and, hence, recall few unpleasant memories.[46, 47, 48] Work by Berger, Kircher and Groyle also points up the voluntary inhibitory style of repressors, which even affects physiological responsivity.[49] A recent series of studies by Bonanno and Siddique of bereavement reactions and persistence of distress suggest strongly that control of negative emotion leads to a less prolonged period of grieving and distress and that forms of the repressor strategy may prove adaptive following occasions of serious loss.[50] In addition, their work questions whether extensive sharing and "working through" of traumatic experiences,

---

44. Schwartz, G. (1990). Psychobiology of repression and health: A systems approach. In J.L. Singer (Ed.), *Repression and dissociation* (pp. 405-434). Chicago: University of Chicago Press.

45. Bonanno, G., & Singer, J.L. (1990). Repressive personality style: Theoretical and methodological implications for health and pathology (pp. 435-470). In J.L. Singer (Ed.), *Repression and dissociation*. Chicago: University of Chicago Press.

46. Schlimmack, U., & Hartmann, K. (1997). Individual differences in the memory representation of emotional episodes: Exploring the cognitive processes in repression. *Journal of Personality & Social Psychology, 73*, 1064-1079.

47. Weinberger, D.A., Schwartz, G., & Davidson, R. (1979). Low anxious, high anxious and repressive coping styles: Psychometric patterns and behavioral and physiological responses to stress. *Journal of Abnormal Psychology, 88*, 369-380.

48. Weinberger, D.A. (1990). The construct validity of the repressive coping style. In J.L. Singer (Ed.), *Repression and dissociation* (pp. 337-386). Chicago: University of Chicago Press.

49. Berger, S., Kircher, J., & Groyle, R. (1997). The effects of social context and defensiveness on the physiological responses of repressive copers. *Journal of Personality and Social Psychology, 73*, 1118-1128.

50. Bonanno, G.A., & Siddique, H.I. (1999). Emotional dissociation, self-deception, and psychotherapy. In J.A. Singer & P. Salovey (Eds.), *At play in the fields of consciousness* (pp. 249-270). Mahwah, NJ: Erlbaum.

as is encouraged in some therapies, is necessarily helpful.

It is probably best that we consider using other terminology than "repression" to describe persons who show systematic styles of avoiding thought or self-awareness of potentially troublesome life issues or who actively avoid situations that might remind them of such issues. We need to move toward newer constructs, newer models, and better integration of cognitive laboratory research with the observations by clinicians of their patients' self-defeating and pathological behaviors. We can acknowledge that all thought involves selectivity and filtering processes, that we may in given situations consciously assign differential priorities to processing material from the environment, from our memories and wishes, or from our bodies. We gradually develop strategies that permit us to perform many of these tasks so smoothly that they occur without conscious awareness. Selective inattention, avoidance of labeling, ruminative thoughts about trivialities all may interfere with the subsequent retrievability of troublesome experiences. Individual differences in types of selective, cognitive-affective strategies under certain circumstances and in particular domains of human concern may become the basis for differences in self-presentation, psychopathology, and physical health.

STUDYING THE STREAM OF CONSCIOUSNESS

Some forty-seven years ago, I set myself the task of "navigating" the stream of consciousness; that is, identifying methods to study this human phenomenon that would meet scientific standards of operational definition, hypothesis testing, and replicability. Starting with projective techniques, I moved on to self-report questionnaires that met more rigorous psychometric standards and then to a variety of laboratory procedures. John Antrobus and I developed laboratory procedures through which we could interrupt people as they worked on various auditory or visual signal detection tasks to determine to what extent and under what conditions they were experiencing thoughts and images unrelated to the very rapid processing of these signals. Such intrusive, task-irrelevant thoughts, manifestations of ongoing centrally-generated consciousness, have been the subject of dozens of experiments and have been labeled as "Task Unrelated Images and Thoughts" or TUITs.[51] The consistency of the TUIT phenomenon across a range of exper-

---

.51. Antrobus, J.S. (1998). Towards a neurocognitive processing model of imaginal thought. In J.L. Singer & P. Salovey (Eds.) *At play in the fields of consciousness* (pp. 3-28). Mahwah, NJ: Erlbaum; Giambra, L. (1995). A laboratory method for investigating influences on switching attention to task-unrelated imagery and thought. *Consciousness and Cognition, 4,* 1-21; Singer, J.L. (1998). Daydreaming, the stream of consciousness and self-representations. In R. Bornstein & J. Masling (Eds.), *Empirical perspectives on the psychoanalytic unconscious* (pp. 141- 186). Washington, D.C.: American Psychological Association.

imental variations in the signal detection situation confirms the insights about ongoing consciousness of William James, but it also provides us with opportunities to pin down how such experiences change predictably as a function of task complexity, simple social variation, such as sex differences between experimenter and study participant, sudden influxes of new information, level of emotional activation, the aging process, personality styles, etc.

Moving beyond the confines of the signal detection or vigilance laboratory paradigm, researchers exemplified by Pope, Csikszentmihalyi and Larson, Klinger, and Klos and Singer have increasingly employed thought-sampling methods in more natural environments.[52, 53, 54, 55, 56] Participants may carry pagers that randomly "beep" seven or eight times a day and to which they respond by marking on special data sheets their thoughts, emotions, and the contingent circumstances.

A major outcome of this line of investigation that is relevant to the issue of recovered memories is the frequency with which people report self-related thoughts that often take the form of imagining oneself in different social, play, or work situations and engaging in what Freud called "trial actions."[57] While philosophers or neurophysiologists seeking links between brain function and consciousness tend to emphasize externally-generated experiences such as pains, visual or auditory sensations and their qualia, the data from TUIT and thought-sampling studies suggest that much of consciousness is characterized by images constructed from long-term memory involving the self in past or potential future settings (memories, fantasies, anticipations, or daydreams).[58] The current data from laboratory studies of night dreaming

---

52. Pope, K.S. (1978). How gender, solitude and posture influence the stream of consciousness. In K.S. Pope & J.L. Singer (Eds.), *The stream of consciousness* (pp. 259-299). New York: Plenum.

53. Csikszentmihalyi, M. & Larson, R. (1987). The experience- sampling method: Toward a systematic phenomenology. *Journal of Nervous and Mental Disease, 175*, 526-536.

54. Klinger, E. (1978). Modes of normal conscious flow. In K.S. Pope & J.L. Singer (Eds.), *The stream of consciousness. Scientific investigations into the flow of human experience* (pp. 226-258). New York: Plenum; Klinger, E. (1990). *Daydreaming.* San Francisco: Jeremy P. Tarcher; Klinger, E. (1999). Thought flow: Properties and mechanisms underlying shifts in content. In J.L. Singer & P. Salovey (Eds.), *At play in the fields of consciousness* (pp. 29-50). Mahwah, NJ: Erlbaum.

55. Klos, D.S. & Singer, J.L. (1983). Determinants of the adolescent's ongoing thought following simulated parental confrontations. *Journal of Personality and Social Psychology, 41*, 975-987.

56. Singer, J.L., & Kolligian, J. (1987). Personality: Developments in the study of private experience. *Annual Review of Psychology, 38*, 533-574; Singer, J.L., & Bonanno, G.A. (1990). Personality and private experience; Individual variations in consciousness and in attention to subjective phenomena. In L. Pervin (Ed.), *Handbook of personality* (pp. 419-444). New York: Guilford Press.

57. Freud, S. (1911/1962). Formulations regarding the two principles in mental functioning. In J.L. Strachey (Ed.), *The Standard edition of the complete psychological works of Sigmund Freud.* (Vol. 12, pp. 218-226). London: Hogarth Press.

58. Searles, J. (1995). *The mystery of consciousness.* New York: New York Review of Books.

also point to continuities between TUIT-like waking thought and REM-sleep mentation, both emerging under comparable conditions of moderate arousal and reduced external stimulation.[59]

There has been an upsurge of research in cognitive and social psychology recognizing how many important features of *procedural* knowledge or information-processing strategies operate out of awareness.[60] What the TUIT and thought-sampling data suggest is that a great deal of our *declarative* knowledge is extensively rehearsed and reshaped during ongoing consciousness between (or even as some of our TUIT data suggests) in parallel with the processing of external stimuli.[61] The stream of consciousness as a reflection of the continuous activity of our brain provides us with an alternative stimulus field to which we respond much as we do to "objectively verifiable" external stimuli such as noises or colors. The associations that are traceable to external cues and those derived from more environmentally remote long-term memories lead us to react with surprise, fear, or delight and also to engage in active replays or new forms of trial action. This continuing activity, much like music or athletic practice, may lead to overlearning of organized mental structures that later on may seem to "pop out." TUITs indeed are the building blocks for INTUITION! I am suggesting, then, that conscious experiences are plentiful and that they yield the overlearned preparations for further thought, speech, and action that are the features of working memory.

Set against this background of continuous processing of memories, recasting them into possible futures or reshaping them in relation to Klinger's important concept of "current concerns," we may see most of the retrieval of past events as a constructive process.[62] With respect to the issue of recovered memories, I would take the position that for the most part, they are neither true nor false memories (unless someone is consciously lying). What we retrieve when we are actively seeking out past events, or even when such episodes occur spontaneously, are approximations. Some of these are independently verifiable, as, for example, when one revisits one's childhood home after many years and finds that it is built of tapetried brick, as one had recalled. Usually, however, such revisits also reveal differences between the reality and one's recollection. The arrangement of rooms, for example, may

---

59. Antrobus, J.S. (1993). Thinking away and ahead. In H. Morowitz & J.L. Singer (Eds.), *The mind, the brain and complex adaptive systems* (pp. 155-174). New York: Addison-Wesley; Antrobus, J.S. (1998). Towards a neurocognitive processing model of imaginal thought. In J.L. Singer & P. Salovey (Eds.) *At play in the fields of consciousness* (pp. 3-28). Mahwah, NJ: Erlbaum.

60. Kihlstrom, J. (1987). The cognitive unconscious. *Science, 237,* 1445-1452; Kihlstrom, J. (1993). The psychological unconscious and the self. In Ciba Foundation Symposium, 174, *Experimental and theoretical studies of consciousness* (pp. 147- 167). New York: Wiley.

61. Kihlstrom, J. (1987). The cognitive unconscious. *Science, 237,* 1445-1452.

62. Klinger, E. (1990). *Daydreaming.* San Francisco: Jeremy P. Tarcher.

be quite different, perhaps reflecting a childlike overemphasis on one's own bedroom or playroom relative to the other, "adult," rooms.

Certain episodes from one's past may recur frequently in one's ongoing thought. These frequent conscious replays may serve to "fix" the reality or sequence of the episode even if we can no longer pin down many specific details. Somewhere between the ages of four or five (1928-1929), my father and some uncles took me along to see a baseball game at what must have been the Yankee Stadium (we then lived nearby in the South Bronx of New York City). I recall nothing of the game, which I didn't understand, but I do recall an episode where the audience's shouting became tumultuous. When I asked what was happening, my family pointed to a tiny chubby man standing with a bat at what seemed to me, in those days before my "size constancy" had been firmly established, a very great distance. "It's the Babe, the Babe!" they shouted. I watched as the distant figure of Babe Ruth took three swings at the ball and then left the scene. That image has recurred dozens of times, not because it seemed important to me as a four-year-old, but because over seventy years, I have read hundreds of articles about Babe Ruth, have seen him swinging in hundreds of still photographs or newsreels, and have also recounted proudly to others that I once saw him play. All I can be sure of from asking my father and uncles in their old age is that they did take me to the game, but they could recall no details other than that Babe Ruth did play.

I want particularly to emphasize the role of contextual cues in stimulating memory retrievals. Vivid and, I believe, scientifically accurate examples appear in the literature or film depictions of the stream of consciousness. In James Joyce's *Ulysses,* the young student, Stephen Daedalus, gazing seaward at the crisscrossing waves, is reminded first of harp strings, then of an Irish song, then of his dying mother's request that he play the music for her and, finally, of his guilt that he refused her deathbed plea for him to return to the Catholic faith he had renounced. It is simple to demonstrate, as I have many times with students, that establishing a long-past context by such suggestions as, "Think about your first day at school," or "Try to picture your childhood bedroom and toys," will evoke a flood of memories that one believes he has not thought about for years.

The power of contextual cues for eliciting retrieval can also help us explain how defensive repression or dissociation may operate. Except for horrible, life-threatening events such as wartime experiences, which are characterized by recurring unwanted memories or flashbacks rather than forgetting, our natural human tendency is not to "dwell on" unpleasant events.[63]

---

63. Shobe, K., & Kihlstrom, J. (1997). Is traumatic memory special? *Current Directions in Psychological Science, 6,* 70-74.

We manage this, not necessarily by massive forgetting, as in Freud's classic repression, but often just by conscious attempts of not thinking about material—the sort of voluntary suppression that Ebbinghaus first demonstrated in his classic studies of memory.[64] One can sustain such memory loss by avoiding settings or environments that abound in cues sufficiently resembling the unwanted materials. As discussed above, repressor personalities learn quickly to turn attention away from potentially threatening scenes so they are not transferred from short-term memory to long-term memory or encoded for later retrieval.[65] As I also suggested above, however, we all practice dissociation simply to get on with our daily chores. We turn off TV news stories about environmental dangers and focus on sitcoms instead so as not to allow the threatening context to arouse our thoughts of our own mortality, the illnesses of our parents or children or even the embarrassment of our failure to become social activists.

The adaptive role of intentional dissociation (albeit not thorough forgetting) is evident from recent studies of bereavement and of other kinds of stress-coping responses.[66, 67] Such research argues against the widespread clinical belief, especially among practitioners of the "recovered memory" approaches, that recurrent rethinking and "working through," or "catharsis," is critical for mental health. Many survivors of the Holocaust have described how for years they avoided as much as possible contexts that could remind them of the traumas they had undergone. Such dissociations served them well in many cases for adjustment to new lives in other countries. Recently, veterans of World War II were in their old age attracted to watching the terrible opening scenes of the film "Saving Private Ryan" only to find no catharsis but great distress and an unwanted resurgence of frightening memories in waking and sleeping thought.

64. Erdelyi, M. (1996). *The recovery of unconscious memories: hypermnesia and reminiscence.* Chicago: University of Chicago Press.

65. Singer, J.L. (Ed.) (1990). *Repression and dissociation.* Chicago: University of Chicago Press.

66. Bonanno, G. (1995). Accessibility, reconstruction and the treatment of functional memory problems. In A.D. Baddeley, B.A. Wilson, & F.N. Watts (Eds.), *Handbook of memory disorders* (pp. 615-637). New York: Wiley & Sons;   Bonanno, G., & Keltner, O. (1997). Facial expressions of emotion and the course of conjugal bereavement. *Journal of Abnormal Psychology* 106, 126-137.

67. Berger, S., Kircher, J., & Groyle, R. (1997). The effects of social context and defensiveness on the physiological responses of repressive copers. *Journal of Personality and Social Psychology, 73,* 1118-1128; Fabes, R., & Eisenberg, N. (1997). Regulatory control and adults' stress-related responses to daily life events. *Journal of Personality & Social Psychology, 73,* 1107-1117; Fraley, R.C., & Shaver, P. (1997). Adult attachment and the suppression of unwanted thoughts. *Journal of Personality & Social Psychology, 73,* 1080-1091.

A recent fine work by Erdelyi has examined in detail how memories can be consciously avoided but also retrieved in experimental fashion.[68]   But Erdelyi also points out that frequent active efforts at retrieval, while leading to what he called "hypermnesia" or superior accuracy, also yield "false positives," that is, fanciful and sometimes creative, if inaccurate, reconstructions. A recent issue of *Current Directions in Psychological Science,* edited by Lynn and Payne, provides numerous instances from laboratory studies and some clinical evidence, including brain research, of the often confabulatory nature of memory.[69]

CONCLUSION: SOME CLINICAL COMMENTS

In summary, the position I believe is best supported by current research is that memories are not stored as quasi-audiotapes or videotapes in some area of the brain or mind only to be retrievable in pristine fashion under very special circumstances such as through hypnosis, psychoanalysis or guided imagery. Establishing a contextual cue framework (such as having a patient or research subject imagine early environments) can evoke a flood of memories, many of which have not appeared in conscious awareness for many years but were clearly not repressed. Asking normal participants in a study to retrieve memories linked to emotions like happiness, sadness, or anger or to events such as one's first awareness of racial prejudice can also lead to a series of rather specific, "self-defining" memories.[70] Even such specific memories may be veridical only in a general sense; they usually lack highly precise, demonstrable details or even the sense of conviction one finds in clinical reports.

During my almost fifty years of clinical practice (psychoanalysis and, later, cognitive-behavioral therapy), I very rarely encountered examples of repressed memories. More specifically, although I had a significant minority of my patients report instances of sexual molestation by family members or other adults, such instances were recounted to me early in therapy and had not been forgotten. All of the molestations had occurred in puberty or early adolescence. I never encountered a patient who reported retrieving a memory of molestation in the preschool years.

Because of my research on consciousness and ongoing thought, I began, in the 1970s and 1980s, to explore how imagery or conscious waking day-

---

68. Erdelyi, M. (1996). *The recovery of unconscious memories: Hypermnesia and reminiscence.* Chicago: University of Chicago Press.

69. Lynn, S.J., & Payne, D.G. (Eds.) (1997). Memory as the theatre of the past. Special Issue. *Current Directions in Psychological Science, 6*(3), 55-83.

70. Singer, J.A., & Salovey, P. (1993). *The remembered self: Emotion and memory in personality.* New York: Free Press.

dreaming was or could be used in psychotherapy. In all my scholarly surveys and those of many others concerning guided imagery, there were practically no accounts of retrieval of repressed memories of child abuse.[71] Leaders in Europe of the waking daydream approach did not emphasize the use of such methods to retrieve childhood repressed memories and they rarely gave accounts of uncovering preschool age sexual molestation.[72] The goal of most of these methods was to use our imaginative resources to help refocus the patient's attention on current life dilemmas.

In the case of hypnosis, both laboratory and research study points to the limited value of the technique in evoking accurate memories.[73] Even in the face of the many clinical reports of recovered memory of abuse one wonders why such reports have clustered in the 1980s and early 1990s.[74] A very careful analysis of the evidence by a clinician, C. Brooks Brenneis, led him to have serious concerns that many of these reports were indeed a consequence of a particular sociological and political culture of therapists' often unwitting suggestion and of patients' desperation to create a new and more meaningful life narrative.[75]

It is possible to question, on both ethical and methodological grounds, some of the early "lost in the mall" experiments that demonstrate how false beliefs can be inculcated.[76] More recent studies by Loftus and colleagues and by the late Nicholas Spanos conform to the general thrust of my own work on the constructive nature of ongoing consciousness in indicating the possibilities for creating vivid and deeply believed but nonveridical memories.[77, 78] It would be folly to deny that childhood sexual abuse occurs and

71. Singer, J.L. (1974). *Imagery and daydream methods in psychotherapy and behavior modification.* New York: Academic; Singer, J.L. & Pope, K.S. (Eds.) (1978). *The power of human imagination.* New York: Plenum.

72. Leuner, H. (1978). Basic principles and therapeutic efficacy of guided affective imagery. In J.L. Singer & K.S. Pope (Eds.), The power of human imagination (pp. 125-166). New York: Plenum.

73. Lynn, S.J., Lock, T.G., Myers, B., & Payne, D.G. (1997). Recalling the unrecallable: Should hypnosis be used to recover memories in psychotherapy? *Current Directions in Psychological Science, 6,* 79-83.

74. Alpert, J., Brown, L., & Courtois, C. (1996a). Symptomatic clients and memories of childhood abuse. What the trauma and child sexual abuse literature tells us. In L. Alpert, L. Brown, S. Ceci, C. Courtois, E. Loftus, & P. Ornstein, (Eds.), *Working group on investigation of memories of child abuse* (pp. 15-105). Washington, DC: American Psychological Association; Alpert, J., Brown, L., & Courtois, C. (1996b). Reponse to "Adult recollections of childhood abuse: Cognitive and developmental perspectives." In L. Alpert, L. Brown, S. Ceci, C. Courtois, E. Loftus, & P. Ornstein, (Eds.), *Working group on investigation of memories of child abuse* (pp. 198-220). Washington, DC: American Psychological Association.

75. Brenneis, C.B. (1997). Final Report of APA Working Group on Investigation of Memories of Childhood Abuse: A critical commentary. *Psychoanalytic Psychology, 14,* 531-547.

76. Pope, K.S., & Brown, L. (1996). *Recovered memories of abuse.* Washington, D.C.: American Psychological Association.

77. Loftus, E. (1997). Memory for a past that never was. *Current Directions in Psychological Science 6,* 60-64.

78. Spanos, N. (1996). *Multiple identities and false memories.* Washington, D.C.: American Psychological Association.

should be dealt with professionally. Such abuse, I believe, is likely to be remembered, even if temporarily dissociated for adaptive living reasons. Such persisting dissociations do involve periods of occasional recall of the memories followed by some rehearsal or mental elaboration. Scenes in movies or books or requests from therapists for a series of childhood-related images create a context for disrupting the dissociations and for retrieval of some forms of the memory. That is a far cry from the retrieval of repressed memories of abuse in very early childhood, which I believe rarely can be proven and which is subject to imaginative elaboration and confabulation for "current" motives by an adult striving to make sense of ongoing distress. My lifetime of research has convinced me that the powers of the human imagination can most often serve constructive, adaptive purposes. Alas, those very abilities of reshaping and reconstructing memories of past events or of current fantasies may also occasionally yield tragic instances of misunderstanding or demonstrably inaccurate accusations against family members.

Chapter 5

DISCOVERED MEMORIES AND THE "DELAYED DISCOVERY" DOCTRINE: A COGNITIVE CASE-BASED ANALYSIS

Jonathan Schooler

In this chapter I will use the term "discovered memories" to refer to what others have described as "recovered memories."[1] There are several reasons why I prefer the former term. The term "recovered memories" presumes that an individual is *recovering* something, i.e., that the event that is being recalled actually happened. In addition, it implies that the event was lost to memory and then somehow brought back. As will be shown, all of these aspects of the phenomenon may be in question, even for individuals who sincerely *believe* they have discovered a lost memory. In contrast, the term "discovered memories" focuses the discussion on *the memory discovery experience*, which is the discovery of the memory of an alleged traumatic event with the accompanying belief that the existence of this memory was not previously known. Additional advantages of the terms "discovered memory" and "memory discovery experience" is that they do not imply any specific mechanism of forgetting, such as repression, or that the memory itself is authentic. Often, discoveries are not what they at first appear to be.[2]

---

1. Cf. Schooler, J.W., Ambadar, Z., & Bendiksen, M.A. (1997). A cognitive corroborative case study approach for investigating discovered memories of sexual abuse. In J. D. Read & D. S. Lindsay (Eds.) *Recollections of trauma: Scientific research and clinical practices* (pp. 379-388). New York, N.Y.: Plenum; Schooler, J.W. (1997). Reflections on a memory discovery. *Child Maltreatment, 2*, 126-133.

2. Lindsay (this volume) prefers the term "recovered memory experiences" (RME's). This term is useful when talking about the phenomenology of a memory recovery; indeed, I have used it extensively myself in this context (e.g., Schooler, J.W. (1994). Seeking the core: The issues and evidence surrounding recovered accounts of sexual trauma. *Consciousness and Cognition, 3*, 452-469; Schooler, J.W., Bendiksen, M., Ambadar, Z. (1997). Taking the middle line: Can we accommodate both fabricated and recovered memories of sexual abuse? In M. Conway (Ed.) *False and recovered memories*, (pp. 251-292). Oxford, England: Oxford University Press.). As an alternative for the term "recovered memory," however, "recovered memory experience," in addition to being a bit unwieldy, still retains the questionable implication that an individual is recovering a memory that previously existed, was lost, and then was found. I hope that as the discussions on this topic mature the field will by consensus adopt new terms that are more precise and less burdened with potentially inappropriate assumptions. Although here I am casting my vote for the terms "discovered memories" (for such recollections) and "memory discoveries" (for the initial experience of discovery), "RME's" is certainly an improvement over the loaded term "recovered memories."

At present, there is a deep gulf between our scientific understanding of how people come to believe that they have discovered long-forgotten incidents of sexual abuse and the legal issues that must be resolved when claims of discovered memories of abuse are used as a foundation for litigation. Over half the states have passed special statutes of limitations for cases in which the plaintiffs purport to have recently discovered previously forgotten memories of sexual abuse. Although these statutes vary in their details, they all apply the "delayed discovery doctrine," which holds that the statute of limitations does not begin to run until the victim discovers the memory of abuse (or, in some cases, the causal connection between the abuse and her emotional injuries). As a consequence of such laws, individuals are able to file lawsuits long after the standard statutes of limitations would have expired. Plaintiffs do, however, have the burden of proving the recovery of a previously repressed memory of having been sexually abused as a child.[3]

On the surface, the issue of deciding whether a person has discovered a previously repressed memory of abuse might seem to be a simple matter of resolving whether the abuse occurred and, if it did occur, whether or not it was previously forgotten. Resolution of these issues is complicated, however, by several important considerations:

1. *The authenticity of the abuse.* Assessing whether or not the abuse itself occurred is difficult because there is now considerable research to suggest that it may be possible to vividly "remember" traumatic experiences that never actually happened. Furthermore, both time and the nature of the act work against the acquisition of incontrovertible corroborating evidence.

2. *The authenticity of the forgetting.* Assessing whether or not the abuse was forgotten is complicated by the fact that, as will be shown, individuals can misremember their prior states of forgetting.

3. *The authenticity of the discovery.* Central to the notion of a "delayed discovery" is the premise that at some particular time one "discovered" his or her abuse history. However, there are various reasons why this "discovery" may be suspect. Given the importance of the delayed discovery clause in many statutes of limitations, it is possible that individuals might deliberately mischaracterize the memory as a discovery in order to be able to seek legal recourse.[4] Even if an individual is sincere in reporting a memory discovery experience, it is still possible that the discovery itself is distorted. It may, as previously noted, be a "discovery" of an event that never occurred, or, as will be discussed, the individual may misconstrue what it is that was discovered. One may, for example, confuse a discovery of the interpretation of the experience with a discovery of the experience itself.

---

3. Taub, S. (1996). The legal treatment of recovered memories of child sexual abuse. *Journal of Legal Medicine, 17*, 183-214.

4. Taub, S. (1996). The legal treatment of recovered memories of child sexual abuse. *Journal of Legal Medicine, 17*, 183-214.

4. *The existence of special memory mechanisms.* Even if an event is deemed to have occurred and to have been forgotten, it is unclear whether it necessarily was "repressed." Implicit (and at times explicit) in the special status given to discovered memories of abuse is the notion that some type of special memory mechanism(s) (e.g., repression) caused the memory to be forgotten and that these mechanisms differ from those at work in the case of other types of events, for which the "delayed discovery doctrine" would not apply. Sound scientific evidence for such "special" repression mechanisms has so far eluded scientific documentation, however.

I will briefly review these four critical issues that must be considered in assessing the appropriateness of invoking the "delayed discovery doctrine" when memories of sexual abuse are alleged to have been discovered. I will begin with a general discussion of the research that suggests that discovered memories can be the product of suggestion, but the bulk of my analysis will focus on actual cases that I and my collaborators have investigated.[5] These cases demonstrate that individuals can have authentic memory discoveries that correspond to actual incidents of abuse. At the same time, they illustrate the complexities that surround the above issues and, as a consequence, suggest the need for great caution in invoking the delayed discovery doctrine in litigation on discovered memories.

THE AUTHENTICITY OF THE ABUSE

All too often, discussions of the authenticity of discovered memories of abuse will focus exclusively on either the reasons why we should be suspicious of such memories or on the reasons why should be accepting of them. There are, however, good reasons to believe that both sides of the issue have merit.

Evidence that Individuals Can Discover Memories for Abuse that Did Not Actually Occur

There are a plethora of reasons to be concerned that individuals can have sincere memory discovery experiences of abuse that may not have actually

---

5. Schooler, J.W., Bendiksen, M., & Ambadar, Z. (1997). Taking the middle line: Can we accommodate both fabricated and recovered memories of sexual abuse? In M. Conway (Ed.) *False and recovered memories* (pp. 251-292). Oxford, England: Oxford University Press; Schooler, J.W., Ambadar, Z., & Bendiksen, M.A. (1997). A cognitive corroborative case study approach for investigating discovered memories of sexual abuse. In J. D. Read & D. S. Lindsay (Eds.) *Recollections of trauma: Scientific research and clinical practices* (pp. 379-388). New York, : Plenum.

occurred. As there are a number of excellent reviews of these issues, I will simply allude to several of the key points brought out in the research.[6] First, one of the central findings of the past century of memory research is that memory is subject to distortion and change. From early research on the impact of schemas and retroactive memory interference to more recent research on misinformation and source monitoring, the converging finding is that memory is highly susceptible to change.[7, 8, 9, 10]

Of particular relevance is research on the impact of misleading suggestions on memory for events. Numerous studies have demonstrated that experimenters' misleading postevent suggestions can substantially alter individuals' recollections of prior events. Such studies have found that false memories of suggested details can be recalled with a vividness and confidence that is comparable to that of memories of actual details, and can be equally likely to be maintained in the face of contradictory information.[11, 12, 13]

One concern with the original misinformation paradigm is that it resulted in the generation of false details of events rather than of entire events that were false. There is now good evidence, however, that entire false events can be generated as a consequence of suggestions, including such events as being lost in a shopping mall, spilling punch on the bride's mother at a wed-

---

6. See, e.g., Loftus, E., & Ketcham, K. (1994). *The myth of repressed memory: False memories and allegations of sexual abuse.* New York: St. Martin's Press; Pendergrast, M. (1996). *Victims of memory: Sex abuse accusations and shattered lives.* Hinesburg, VT: Upper Access; Lindsay, D.S., & Read, J.D. (1994). Psychotherapy and memories of child sexual abuse: A cognitive perspective. *Applied Cognitive Psychology, 8,* 281-338.

7. See, e.g., Allport, G. W., & Postman, L. J. (1947). *The psychology of rumor.* New York: Henry Holt & Co.; Bartlett, F. C. (1932). *Remembering.* Cambridge: Cambridge University Press.

8. McGeoch, J. H. (1942). *The psychology of human learning.* New York: Longmans, Green; Barnes, J.M., & Underwood, B.J. (1959). "Fate" of first-list associations in transfer theory. *Journal of Experimental Psychology, 58,* 97-105.

9. Ceci, S.J., Loftus, E.F., Leichtman, M.D., & M., Bruck. (1994). The possible role of source misattributions in the creation of false beliefs among preschoolers. *International Journal of Clinical and Experimental Hypnosis, 42,* 304-320; Loftus, E. F., Donders, K., Hoffmann, H. G., & Schooler, J.W. (1989). Creating new memories that are quickly accessed and confidently held. *Memory and Cognition, 77,* 607-616.

10. Johnson, M. K., & Raye, C. L. (1981). Reality monitoring. *Psychological Review, 85,* 67-85; Johnson, M. K., Hashtroudi, S., & Lindsay, D.S. (1993). Source monitoring. *Psychological Bulletin, 114,* 3-28.

11. Schooler, J. W., Clark, C. A., & Loftus, E. F. (1988). Knowing when memory is real. In M. Grueneberg, P. Morris, & R. N. Sykes (Eds.), *Practical aspects of memory* (pp. 83-88): New York: Wiley; Schooler, J. W., Gerhard, D., & Loftus, E. F. (1986). Qualities of the unreal. *Journal of Experimental Psychology: Learning, Memory, and Cognition, 12,* 71-181.

12. Loftus, E. F., Donders, K., Hoffmann, H. G., & Schooler, J.W. (1989). Creating new memories that are quickly accessed and confidently held. *Memory and Cognition, 77,* 607-616.

13. Loftus, E. F., Korf, N., & Schooler, J. W. (1989). Misguided memories: Sincere distortions of reality. In J. Yuille (Ed.), *Credibility assessment: A theoretical and research perspective* (pp. 155-174). Boston: Kluwer.

ding, and going to the hospital after getting a finger caught in a mousetrap.[14, 15, 16] There is even evidence that people can come to recall false events that supposedly occurred over extended periods of time. For example, using a clever paradigm in which participants were given false feedback about their performance on various tests, Kelley and Lindsay were able to cause a sizable minority of their participants to "remember" having once been left handed but having changed their hand orientation as a result of parental coercion (see Lindsay, this volume).

In addition to the research on laboratory-induced false memories, there is also "real-world" evidence that individuals can come to "remember" events that are extremely unlikely to have actually happened, including alien abductions, fantastic satanic ritual abuse,and even being stuck in the fallopian tube while still a zygote.[17, 18, 19] As Heurer has noted, "there are a lot of things we don't know about memory but one thing we do know is that you need a nervous system to have a memory."[20] This is an attribute that is indisputably lacking in zygotes.

Several studies have documented the alarming frequency with which mental health professionals use recovered memory therapy on individuals who initially purport to have no recollection of having been sexually abused. Polusny and Follette, for example, found that a substantial minority of clinicians reported using a variety of memory recovery techniques with adult clients "*who have no specific memory of childhood sexual abuse but who [they] strongly suspected were sexually abused.*"[21] According to statements made by the respondents, 33 percent of them recommended books on sexual abuse, 27 percent used guided imagery, 20 percent used hypnosis, and 29 percent reported referring their patients to sexual abuse survivor groups. Such findings suggest that it is not just a few "bad apples" who use these kind of suggestive techniques. Rather, it appears that many clinicians are engaging in

---

14. Loftus, E.F. & Pickerel, J. (1995). The formation of false memories. *Psychiatric Annals, 25,* 720-724.

15. Hyman, I.E. (1995). False memories of childhood experiences. *Applied Cognitive Psychology, 9*(3), 181-197.

16. Ceci, S.J., Loftus, E.F., Leichtman, M.D., & M., Bruck. (1994). The possible role of source misattributions in the creation of false beliefs among preschoolers. *International Journal of Clinical and Experimental Hypnosis, 42,* 304-320.

17. Persinger, M. A. (1992). Neuropsychological profiles of adults who report "sudden remembering" of early childhood memories: Implications for claims of sex abuse. *Perceptual and Motor Skills, 75,* 259-266.

18. Ofshe, R., & Watters, E. (1994). *Making monsters: False memories, psychotherapy, and sexual hysteria.* New York: Scribners.

19. Loftus, E., & Ketcham, K. (1994). *The myth of repressed memory: False memories and allegations of sexual abuse.* New York: St. Martin's Press.

20. Heurer, F., personal communication, May 1995.

21. Polusny, M.A., & Follette, V.M. (1996). Remembering childhood sexual abuse: A national survey of psychologists' clinical practices, beliefs, and personal experiences. *Professional Psychology: Research and Practice, 27,* 41-52.

precisely the type of activities that cognitive psychologists would predict could produce false memories. (For evidence that these techniques are dangerously suggestive, see Lindsay, this volume.)

There are additional reasons to believe that individuals may, especially when in treatment with trauma-oriented therapists, come to recall abusive events that never actually occurred. Many "retractors" have come to the conclusion that their abuse memories were false.[22] Such conclusions do not demonstrate conclusively that the abuse was fictitious, but we certainly cannot accept these individuals' beliefs about their memories when they perceive them to be true and then reject their beliefs when they later conclude the memories were actually false.

It is well-known that individuals are tremendously persuadable when in the presence of authoritative individuals. Indeed, events of the twentieth century have shown that we previously underestimated just how persuadable people can be. No one would have expected that individuals in Nazi Germany could have been persuaded to do the things that they did. Few expected, in Milgram's classic studies, that the majority of experimental subjects could be persuaded to give their fellow subjects what they believed to be potentially lethal electrical shocks, and yet they did.[23] Similarly, it came as a great surprise that the majority of people could, following the suggestions of their peers, come to perceive distinctly different line lengths as the same.[24] Thus, we should be very careful not to make the same mistake again and assume that people cannot be persuaded that they possess memories of sexual abuse that did not in fact occur.

In short, although this brief review does not do justice to the full spectrum of evidence for the existence of false memories of abuse, it highlights some of the many reasons for concern. If an individual who has recovered a memory of abuse (1) originally had no reported knowledge of the abuse, (2) underwent extensive "recovered memory" therapy involving highly suggestive practices by an authoritative therapist who deeply believed that abuse did occur, and (3) currently has no corroborative evidence for that abuse, then there are very good reasons to view the memory with marked skepticism.

---

22. See, for example, Pasley, L. E. (1993). Misplaced trust. In E. Goldstein & K. Farmer (Eds.), *True stories of false memories* (pp. 347-365). Boca Raton, FL: Sirs Publishing.

23. Milgram, S. (1963). Behavioral study of obedience. *Journal of Abnormal and Social Psychology, 67,* 371-378. Horn, M. (1993, Nov. 29). Memories lost and found. *U.S. News and World Report,* 53-63.

24. Asch, S.E. (1956). Studies of independence and conformity: A minority of one against a unanimous majority. *Psychological Monographs, 70* (9, Whole No 416).

Evidence that Individuals Can Discover Memories of Actual Abuse

Although in many cases involving discovered memories of abuse there are good reasons to be skeptical that the alleged abuse occurred, there are other cases in which there are good reasons to believe the abuse was factual. In a number of publicly documented cases, there is compelling corroborative evidence of the alleged abuse. Ross Cheit, for example, whose case was originally reported in *U.S. News and World Report*, awoke one night to images of his former choir camp administrator, Bill Farmer, hovering over him.[25] The following day he recovered memories of being sexually abused by Farmer. The multiple sources of corroboration in this case included other individuals who had independently recorded instances of Farmer's sexual improprieties, both before and after Cheit's recovered memory experience, and most importantly, a tape-recorded confession by Farmer.[26] A second publicly-discussed recovered memory claim that has received corroboration in the public forum was featured in the 1993 court case of Commonwealth of Massachusetts v. Porter. In this case, Frank Fitzpatrick reported that he had been lying in bed with unexplainable anguish when he recalled being sexually molested many years earlier by Father James Porter. Corroboration of this case came from multiple sources. Church officials conceded that they had observed or heard of Porter's sexual improprieties. In addition, after Fitzpatrick made his charges public, nearly 100 people reported having been sexually abused by Porter.[27]

Although there have been a number of publicized cases of discovered memories with varying degrees of corroboration, there have been relatively few efforts by researchers to systematically document and corroborate actual allegations of recovered memories. Most investigations of discovered memories that have discussed corroboration have relied on the corroborative evidence that patients have *claimed* to find.[28] Clearly, patients may be

---

25. Horn, M. (1993, Nov. 29). Memories lost and found. *U.S. News and World Report*, 53-63.

26. Regretfully, a prior discussion of this case (Schooler, J.W., Bendiksen, M., Ambadar, Z. (1997). Taking the middle line: Can we accommodate both fabricated and recovered memories of sexual abuse? In M. Conway (Ed.) *False and recovered memories*, (pp. 251-292). Oxford, England: Oxford University Press) neglected to mention the existence of the tape-recorded confession and mischaracterized the evidence in this case as exclusively involving "multiple sources of indirect corroboration." (Schooler, et al., p. 261.)

27. Recently a web site has been established that currently cites 45 public cases that have some form of corroboration. Interested readers can find it at: www.brown.edu/Departments/Taubman_Center/Recovmem/Archive.html.

28. See, e.g., Andrews, A. (1997) Forms of memory recovery among adults in therapy: Preliminary results from an in-depth survey. In *Recollections of Trauma: Scientific research and clinical practices*. J.D. Read and D.S. Lindsay, Eds.). Plenum Press, NY; Herman, J. L., & Schatzow, E. (1987). Recovery and verification of memories of childhood sexual trauma. *Psychoanalytic Psychology*, 4, 1-14.

strongly biased to present their discoveries as being authentic. In the absence of more direct evidence, their claims of corroboration must therefore be viewed with some caution.

Recently, my collaborators and I have sought to investigate and seek independent corroboration of cases in which individuals alleged to have discovered previously forgotten memories of abuse.[29] These cases were identified through modest networking and are not in any sense a representative sample. In each case, the investigators sought independent corroboration of the abuse, usually by contacting other individuals who the victim indicated had prior knowledge of either the abuse itself or the abusive tendencies of the alleged perpetrator. In the following discussion, I will briefly review each of the cases and the corroborative evidence of abuse that was obtained.

Case 1: JR reported discovering a memory of being fondled by a priest at age eleven and subsequently discovering memories of additional incidents of abuse that took place over the next several years. He discovered the initial memory while lying in bed one night after seeing a movie involving sexual abuse. The corroboration: Another individual reported that he had been abused by the same priest. Although this individual only made his accusation *after* JR had discovered his memory, he indicated that he had maintained an intact memory of being abused by this priest. Thus, to the degree that the abuse memories of individuals who have maintained intact memories of abuse are not in question, this individual's allegations support the likelihood that this priest abused JR as well.[30]

Case 2: MB reported discovering a recollection of being raped while hitchhiking at age seventeen. The discovery experience occurred when MB was thirty-four years old after she heard a friend refer to a young woman as "certainly not a virgin." The corroboration: An individual who was present the day of the rape confirmed MB'S original recounting of the experience.

Case 3: TW reported discovering a memory at the age of twenty-four of being fondled by a family friend at age nine. The recollection was triggered after a friend suggested that they hear a talk on sexual abuse. The corroboration: TW's former husband reported that she had talked about the abuse several times prior to this memory discovery experience.

Case 4: DN reported discovering a memory of being raped in a hospital at the age of nineteen and then taking the case to court. She discovered the

29. Schooler, J.W., Bendiksen, M., & Ambadar, Z. (1997). Taking the middle line: Can we accommodate both fabricated and recovered memories of sexual abuse? In M. Conway (Ed.) *False and recovered memories,* (pp. 251-292). Oxford, England: Oxford University Press; Schooler, J.W., Ambadar, Z., & Bendiksen, M.A. (1997). A cognitive corroborative case study approach for investigating discovered memories of sexual abuse. In J. D. Read & D. S. Lindsay (Eds.) *Recollections of trauma: Scientific research and clinical practices.* (pp. 379-388) New York : Plenum; Schooler, J.W. (1998). Discovered memories of abuse: A cognitive corroborative case study approach. Invited manuscript in preparation for *Journal of Aggression, Maltreatment, and Trauma.*

30. Loftus, E. F. (1993). The reality of repressed memories. *American Psychologist, 48,* 518-537.

memory at age thirty-five, several hours after her group therapist remarked that survivors of childhood abuse, which DN had maintained an intact memory of being, often are victimized as adults. The corroboration: DN's former lawyer confirmed that the case had gone to court and that the perpetrator was found guilty.

Case 5: JN reported discovering a memory of being molested at age five. The discovery experience occurred when she was eighteen, soon after she became sexually active. The corroboration: JN's mother confirmed that this event actually did happen.

Case 6: CV reported discovering a memory of being molested and exposed to masturbation by her stepfather at age ten. This memory discovery experience occurred while CV was cleaning the bathroom at the age of twenty-seven. The corroboration: her sister stated that she had also been abused by the stepfather and had maintained intact memories of the abuse, although she had never discussed it with CV.

Summary. In each of these cases, there are compelling reasons to believe that the individual's memory discovery experiences corresponded to actual abuse events because the investigators were able independently to obtain corroborative evidence of the abuse. It is important to emphasize that this corroboration does not absolutely guarantee that the events took place. Indeed, how strongly one views the corroborative evidence is likely to depend in part on one's a priori views regarding the likelihood that such discovered memory experiences could in fact correspond to actual events. If the likelihood of such events is viewed as comparable to, say, alien abductions, then none of the corroborative evidence described here is likely to be persuasive. On the other hand, if one views discovered memory experiences as at least plausible, then the corroboration presented here is apt to be compelling. It is therefore important to explore the scientific factors that could potentially explain memory discovery experiences in order to better assess how plausible or implausible they really are (see subsequent section).

The present attempts at corroboration illustrate the complexities of relying on such discovered memory experiences for purposes of litigation. Collectively, the corroborative evidence suggests the strong likelihood that discovered memories really can correspond to actual events. From a legal standpoint, claims of discovered memories should therefore not be dismissed out of hand. In no single case, however, was the evidence absolutely incontrovertible. Thus these findings also illustrate the difficulty of relying on a specific discovered memory as the foundation for litigation.

THE AUTHENTICITY OF FORGETTING

In the previous discussion I focused on the corroborative evidence for the original abuse. An additional critical component of the delayed discovery doctrine is the claim that knowledge of the abuse (or its negative effects) was absent for some period of time. Assessing prior degrees of forgetting is, unfortunately, extremely difficult. Individuals' assessments of forgetting are based on their estimations of what they knew at an earlier period of time. They must therefore guess what they would have known had they been queried about the abuse at an earlier time. This point is clearly illustrated by JR (Case 1) who, in characterizing his forgetting prior to the discovery experience, observed:

> If you had done a survey of people walking into the movie theater when I saw the movie...asking people about child sexual abuse, "have you ever been, or do you know anybody who has ever been?" I would have absolutely, flatly, unhesitatingly said "no."

It is clear from this characterization that JR unambiguously believes that prior to the discovery he had absolutely forgotten the experience. As his testimony illustrates, however, this belief is based on his estimation of what he thinks *would have happened* had he been queried about his abuse prior to his remembering it. In fact, he was not actually asked about the abuse prior to remembering it and so we cannot ascertain the full degree to which he had previously forgotten the abuse.[31]

Case 4 similarly illustrates the difficulty in assessing prior degrees of forgetting. As with JR, ND unambiguously believed that she had forgotten her rape and ensuing court case prior to her memory discovery experience. She observed:

> It's like, how could I forget this? As horrible as it was having to go to court....and having to tell what happened and everything, how could I forget that? I had no idea when I did forget it but I really feel that it had been totally forgotten until that night.

In support of her claim of forgetting, DN noted that on intake for therapy for childhood abuse she had described various incidents of childhood abuse but had failed to report her adult rape. This lack of reporting, although potentially attributable to her having forgotten it, could also have occurred because she was not thinking of her adult rape in the context of childhood abuse.

---

31. Of course, even if he had recalled the memory following a direct query this would not prove that the memory had not been forgotten up until that point, as the query itself could have triggered the memory. Such observations further illustrate the fundamental difficulty of assessing forgetting and, indeed, in even conceptualizing what forgetting really means in these situations.

Although it is extremely difficult to document true forgetting in these types of cases, it is possible to demonstrate overestimations of forgetting. In cases 2 and 3, for example, there was clear evidence of misconstrual of prior forgetting. In each of these cases the victim's ex-husband reported discussing the event with the victim during a time in which the victim later believed that she had completely forgotten it. In both of these cases the individuals were truly shocked to discover that they had been aware of, and had talked about, the abuse at that time. TW (Case 3) described her reaction upon learning that she had previously told her husband about the abuse as follows:

> I felt like falling over. Absolutely shocked and floored that it happened. And I still am...I can't remember telling him, I can't think of anything about the memory before [the recovery], and it's very disturbing, actually.

The fact that individuals can believe that they had entirely forgotten abuse at a time at which they are known to have been aware of it illustrates the difficulty in relying on individuals' assessments of their own prior memory states. Scientifically, this finding suggests that there may be some very interesting hindsight bias effects that may distort individuals' assessments of their prior degree of forgetting. (I will return to this issue later.) From a legal perspective, this demonstrates that we cannot assume that a memory was necessarily completely forgotten even if an individual sincerely believes that it was.

THE AUTHENTICITY OF THE DISCOVERY EXPERIENCE

Given the centrality of the "discovery doctrine" in allowing discovered memories to be considered in court, it is easy to see why an individual might be motivated to characterize an always intact memory as recently discovered in order to be able to pursue legal action. In the present cases, however, there is relatively little reason to suspect that such deliberate misconstrual of the discovery experience is occurring. In five of the cases, the individuals did not pursue legal actions subsequent to the memory discovery. JR (Case 1) did pursue legal action after having his discovery experience, but at the time that he made his accusations (1988), the discovery doctrine had not been applied to discovered memories; the case therefore did not go to court because of the statute of limitations. JR's discovery thus occurred prior to the time at which there was a legal advantage for characterizing a memory as "discovered" and prior to the time in which it was publicly appreciated that such memory discoveries occurred.

Another compelling aspect of the memory discovery experiences reported here is the striking similarity of the phenomenology of discovery reported in all of these cases. Three distinctive qualities characterized the discovery experiences that we investigated: sudden surprise, immediate unpacking of the memory, and an emotional onrush. With respect to the sudden surprise quality of the discovery, JR described the discovery as occurring "fairly suddenly," WB described a "sudden and clear picture," TW noted that "the whole thing was evident and immediate to me," and DN observed that "all at once I remembered."

An unpacking of the experience also typified many of the accounts. TW observed "It was like...a package of some sort...something there that's completely unwound instantly, and not only the experience but the sequel of the experience". DN recounted "All at once I remembered...not only that I had been a victim, but that I had to go to court." CV described this unpacking as occurring visually, noting "Suddenly a whole reel of pictures started running through my mind."

The emotional impact of the experience was also noted in the majority of cases. JR described his experience as being "stunned." WB noted "complete chaos in my emotions." DN characterized her reaction as "just this extreme emotion of fear and disbelief."

Although the striking parallels among the phenomenological accounts of these memory discovery experiences cannot serve incontrovertibly to validate these experiences, they do (especially given the lack of evidence for deliberate deceit) lend credence to the notion that these individuals reported authentic discovery experiences; i.e., they truly believed they were discovering previously forgotten incidents of abuse. The fact that individuals can have authentic memory discovery experiences in which they truly believe they are remembering long-forgotten incidents of abuse does not necessarily demonstrate that the abuse was as forgotten as they thought it was, however. When the evidence regarding prior forgetting is considered, these cases suggest that it may well be possible to have full-blown discovery experiences for memories that may not have been entirely forgotten, a finding that may have important legal implications.

THE EXISTENCE OF SPECIAL MEMORY MECHANISMS

The fourth critical consideration in considering the appropriateness of applying the delayed discovery doctrine to discovered memory experiences involves assessing whether unique memory processes (e.g., repression) are involved. If the alleged forgetting and remembering associated with discovered memory experiences involves the same basic memory mechanisms involved in other types of forgetting situations, then it is unclear why special status should be given to the recollection of abuse. When one considers whether special memory mechanisms need to be invoked in accounting for the cases described above, a number of observations emerge. First, as will be seen, there are a number of relatively standard memory mechanisms that may readily apply to these cases. Second, these cases suggest the possible existence of other memory mechanisms, not heretofore scientifically examined, that may well apply both in these cases and in a variety of more "standard" forgetting situations. Finally, although unique trauma-related processes (e.g., repression, dissociation) cannot be inferred on the basis of the present evidence (and indeed such processes may well not be required at all), the present evidence does not allow us to dismiss the possibility of their existence.

Well-Established General Memory Mechanisms

There are quite a few well-documented memory mechanisms that seem readily applicable to the cases described here. In prior writings I have outlined how a number of well-established memory mechanisms may contribute to discovered memory experiences.[32] I will limit my discussion here to three standard memory mechanisms that seem likely to be especially important.

1. Directed Forgetting

It has been well demonstrated in the cognitive literature that individuals can forget information when they actively attempt to do so.[33] In short, much of the forgetting in these cases could be a consequence of individuals' active attempts to forget the experience. MB explicitly recalls that "I tried not to think about it." In other cases, individuals report no recollection of actively trying to forget the experience. In Case 4, for example, DN observed "I really don't remember putting it out of my mind, I really don't know when I forgot it, I really didn't try to forget it, it was just like it never happened. Then all at once it came back." If one can forget about being raped and going to court, however, one clearly should be able to forget about having tried to put such memories out of mind. Thus the lack of recollection of directed forgetting provides little evidence that such processes did not occur.

---

32. See, e.g., Schooler, J.W. (1994). Seeking the core: The issues and evidence surrounding recovered accounts of sexual trauma. *Consciousness and Cognition, 3*, 452-469; Schooler, J.W., Bendiksen, M., & Ambadar, Z. (1997). Taking the middle line: Can we accommodate both fabricated and recovered memories of sexual abuse? In M. Conway (Ed.) *False and recovered memories*, (pp. 251-292). Oxford, England: Oxford University Press.

33. See, e.g., Bjork, R.A. (1989). Retrieval inhibition as an adaptive mechanism in human memory. In H.L. Roediger & F.I.M. Craik (Eds.). *Varieties of memory and consciousness: Essays in honor of Endel Tulving.* (pp.309-330). Hillsdale, NJ: Lawrence Erlbaum.

2. Reinterpretation

Another potentially very important mechanism is reinterpretation.[34] Changes in the interpretation of an event can activate previously inaccessible information. An individual who comes to interpret an event in a different way could, as a consequence of the new interpretation, remember more information about the event and also have a more emotional account of it. This is clearly applicable in Case 2, in which MB said, "In a way I've managed to repress the meaning of what happened all these years. I may not have completely forgotten the experience but I pushed it away, minimized it; it wasn't a real rape." When MB had her discovery experience it was framed specifically in terms of the interpretation of the experience. She exclaimed, "Oh, my God, I was raped!" Although individuals in the other cases were not specifically aware of the possible role of reinterpretation of their experience in driving the discovery, it seems quite plausible that such processes may have been involved. Accordingly, in some of these cases individuals may have had a discovery of the meaning of the event and may have then misconstrued the discovery of the meaning of the event as a discovery of the memory itself.

3. Encoding Specificity

Another very important mechanism is encoding specificity.[35] The basic principle at work here is that the probability of retrieving a memory is maximized when retrieval conditions correspond to the encoding conditions. Strikingly, in all six cases there was a notable correspondence between the original abuse situation and the situation in which the memory was ultimately cued: Case 1, seeing a movie about abuse; Case 2, mentioning the virginity of the young woman (this woman was a virgin when she was raped); Case 3, the prospect of seeing a talk on abuse; Case 4, the mention of adult sexual abuse; Case 5, becoming sexually active; and Case 6, cleaning a bathroom (CV's abuse originally occurred in the bathroom). In all of these cases there is some significant overlap between the initial experience and the cuing conditions.

---

34. See, e.g., Anderson, R.C., & Pitchert, J.W. (1978). Recall of previously unrecallable information following a shift in perspective. *Journal of Verbal Learning and Verbal Behavior, 17,* 1-12.

35. See, e.g., Tulving, E., & Thompson, D. M. (1973). Encoding specificity and retrieval processes in episodic memory. *Psychological Review, 80,* 352-373.

Previously Uninvestigated but Potentially General Memory Mechanisms

1. The "Forgot It All Along" Effect

One potentially pertinent general memory mechanism that is suggested by these cases is what we have termed the "forgot it all along" effect. In several of these cases the individuals underestimated their prior knowledge about the event. At present little is known about the processes that might lead to the underestimation of prior knowledge, but much is known about why people often overestimate their prior knowledge, a phenomenon quite aptly termed the "knew it all along" effect.[36] The premise of the "knew it all along" effect is that a person who is told something will then believe that he knew it all along. This happens because individuals use their current knowledge state to infer their earlier knowledge state. In effect, one reasons, "I know it now, therefore I must have known it before." Although there has been little research to date on cases of underestimations of prior knowledge, it seems reasonable to suppose that if one can use one's current knowledge state to make overestimations of prior knowledge, one may also use it to make underestimations of prior knowledge. Accordingly, in the context of the emotional onrush associated with thinking about memories of abuse individuals may assume that they had no previous knowledge about their abuse. They may reason, "If I'm this shocked and surprised now, then I must have previously completely forgotten about the experience."

In short, individuals may misattribute the emotional onrush associated with thinking about the event to the emotional onrush of discovering the memory itself. In reality, there are a number of other reasons why an individual might experience an emotional onrush besides discovering a long forgotten memory. The person may be accessing the emotional content that had, for whatever reasons, not been accessed on prior retrievals. Consistent with this view, although both WB and TW had spoken about their memories prior to their memory discovery experiences, they reportedly did so in an emotionally flat manner. Individuals may also reinterpret the experience, redefining it as abuse and confusing the emotion stemming from this new and more upsetting characterization with the experience of discovering the memory itself. Yet another possibility is that prior attempts at putting the memory out of mind may have resulted in an emotional "rebound effect" when it was once again thought about. The revisiting of previously suppressed thoughts can induce a strong emotional punch.[37] The emotion

---

36. Fischoff, B. (1982). For those condemned to study the past: Heuristics and biases in hindsight. In D. Kahneman, P. Slovic, & A. Tversky (Eds.), *Judgment under uncertainty: Heuristics and biases* (pp. 335-351). New York: Cambridge University Press.

37. Wegner, D.M & Gold, D.B. (1995). Fanning old flames: Emotional and cognitive effects of suppressing thoughts of a past relationship. *Journal of Personality and Social Psychology, 5,* 782-792.

resulting from the rebound of suppression could thus also be confused with the discovery of the memory. In short, there are a variety of reasons other than the actual discovery of a long forgotten memory that could cause individuals to retrieve the memory with great emotion. These alternative sources of emotional punch might nevertheless mislead individuals into believing that they were just now remembering the experience for the first time.

2. Precipitous Forgetting of Nocturnal Experiences

The above mechanisms, or some combination thereof, could, at least in principle, readily account for many of the elements of the discovery experience phenomena illustrated in the reviewed cases. However, there is one element of some characterizations of discovered memories that these mechanisms clearly cannot accommodate: the claim that abuse was precipitously forgotten nearly immediately after it occurred. Characterizations of forgetting as precipitous are certainly not ubiquitous. In the majority of the cases reported here individuals believed they had remembered the experience for at least some period of time following the event. In the case of JR, however, who reported repeatedly going on overnight camping trips with his abuser, the element of precipitous forgetting was central to his account. JR observed:

> When I woke up in the morning I didn't have any knowledge of what had happened the night before, which is why I could continue to go on trips with him and enjoy it.

In one of the best documented cases of discovered memories involving corroborated abuse, Ross Cheit similarly characterized the forgetting as having been complete the morning after the abuse. As noted in the *Providence Journal Bulletin*, May 8, 1995:

> When morning came, life at Camp Wallace Alexander would slide back into its familiar grooves, the nocturnal ritual would fade into the shadows. In the daytime, Cheit says, he was my friend.

In a personal communication, Cheit further substantiated this claim, saying "I am confident as I can be that I did not think of the abuse in the daytime."[38]

How can it be that a person is abused in the middle of the night and wakes up the next morning having completely forgotten it? One possibility is that the person's belief in precipitous forgetting represents another instance of mischaracterizing prior forgetting. Such sincere mischaracterizations could result from a reinterpretation of the experience. At the time, these experi-

---

38. Cheit, R., personal communication, November 15, 1997.

ences may have been associated with greater ambivalence than they are today. In order to account for how they could continue interacting with the perpetrators, victims may infer that they must have forgotten the experience during the day.

Is it possible that precipitous forgetting could be real? In exploring the claims of precipitous forgetting of abuse, it may be helpful to ask two related questions: (1) Are there any known situations in which individuals do immediately forget traumatic experiences? (2) If so, do such situations have anything in common with sexual abuse situations? The standard answer to the first question is "no." We do not typically forget traumatic experiences unless there is actual physical trauma to the brain (e.g., a concussion). This observation overlooks one striking anomaly to this seemingly sound generalization, however. There is at least one situation in which individuals often, indeed usually, forget traumatic and disturbing events: when they occur during dreams. It is well-known that individuals typically forget the content of dreams and nightmares despite the fact that dreams are often disturbing and even traumatic.[39, 40] Could the processes that lead to the precipitous forgetting of dreams be related to claims of precipitous forgetting of sexual abuse?

There are a number of striking parallels between dream forgetting and allegations of forgetting of sexual abuse. First, in contrast to virtually all other types of traumatic experiences, sexual abuse, like dreams, often occurs at night while the individual is in bed. Thus, various physiological nocturnal processes that may contribute to dream forgetting may also contribute to the forgetting of nocturnal abuse.[41] Second, like dreams, sexual abuse experiences (especially when perpetrated by a known care giver) are bizarre, occur in isolation, and may be difficult to reconcile with preexisting schemata and other events. These parallels between dreams and nocturnal abuse may both contribute to the forgetting of such abuse and to the dismissal of such recollections as being merely "bad dreams."

Although the clinical literature does not provide an experimental basis for claims of precipitous forgetting of nocturnal abuse, sleep research provides some evidence that precipitous forgetting of more mundane events can and does occur. A number of laboratory studies have examined memory for

---

39. See, e.g., Hobson, J.A. (1988) *The dreaming brain.* New York: Basic Books; Kramer, M. (1979). Dream disturbances. *Psychiatric-Annals, 9,* 50-68.

40. Hobson, J.A. (1988) *The dreaming brain.* New York: Basic Books; Hobson, J.A. (1997). Consciousness as a state dependent phenomenon. In Cohen, J.D. & Schooler, J.W. *Scientific approaches to consciousness.* Mahwah, N.J.: Erlbaum.

41. Cf. Hobson, J.A. (1988) *The dreaming brain.* New York: Basic Books; Hobson, J.A. (1997). Consciousness as a state dependent phenomenon. In Cohen, J.D. & Schooler, J.W. *Scientific approaches to consciousness.* Mahwah, N.J.: Erlbaum.

material encoded immediately prior to sleep. Anthony et al. reported "anterograde and retrograde amnesia" for verbal materials presented immediately prior to sleep onset.[42] Other studies have examined memory for material introduced upon awakening from sleep. Bonnet examined immediate and morning recall in individuals who were awakened from either stage 2 (light sleep) or slow-wave sleep (deep sleep) and presented with word lists.[43] All participants showed relatively poor morning retrieval, especially those awakened from slow-wave sleep. These studies have documented precipitous forgetting of mundane materials encountered in close proximity to sleep onset and awakenings from sleep.

If precipitous forgetting of abuse is associated with its nocturnal occurrence, the critical question that arises is whether such experiences can be recovered. Although there is some, albeit limited, evidence for precipitous forgetting of nocturnal experiences, there is no direct empirical evidence that such memories can later be recovered. The lack of evidence may simply result from the fact that no one has yet directly investigated this issue. We are currently conducting a study to determine the extent of forgetting and recovery of nocturnal events. While the issue of recovery of precipitously forgotten nocturnal events is clearly still an open question, it should be noted that in both of the reviewed cases in which precipitous forgetting was alleged, the alleged abuse occurred at night and was purportedly forgotten by morning. Moreover, in both JR's case and Cheit's case, the memories were discovered while they were lying in bed at night. JR reported, "I couldn't sleep, I tossed and turned. After a couple hours of not sleeping, that's when I had my first memory." Cheit reported "having had something like a dream. He woke with a baffling sense that a man he had not seen or thought of in twenty-five years was powerfully present in the room."[44] These anecdotal reports raise the possibility that some type of state- dependence may contribute to both the forgetting of and subsequent remembering of nocturnal abuse.[45]

---

42. Anthony, J., Wyatt, J.K., Bootzin, R.R., Oswald, V., & Allen, J.J. (1994). Retrograde and anterograde amnesia at sleep onset: A conceptual replication. *Sleep Research, 23,* 502-511.

43. Bonnet, M.H. (1983). Memory for events occurring during arousal from sleep. *Psychophysiology, 20,* 81-87.

44. Horn, M. (1993, Nov. 29). Memories lost and found. *U.S. News and World Report,* 53-63.

45. In addition to being a potential cause of precipitous forgetting of actual abuse, nocturnal dream-related processes may also contribute to the fabrication of false memories. It has been suggested, for example, that alien abduction reports may result from the misinterpretation of nightmares (Karon, B. (1996). On being abducted by aliens. *Psychoanalytic-Psychology, 3,* 417.) and that bizarre accounts of sexual abuse may be the product of a confusion between nightmares and reality. (Dalenberg, C. J. (1996). Fantastic elements in child disclosures of abuse. Paper presented at the Conference on Responding to Child Maltreatment, San Diego.) Although this is another issue for future research, it seems quite plausible that individuals might be much more suggestible regarding events purported to have happened at night. Those who appreciate that nocturnal experiences are apt to be recalled less clearly than other experiences may be more apt to accept a suggested and perhaps initially "fuzzy" false memory as having actually occurred.

Further research is necessary to determine whether the nocturnal characteristics of some sexual abuse incidents may contribute to the alleged precipitous forgetting of such experiences. Although at present, we must consider this hypothesis rather speculative, it seems at least plausible that the
precipitous forgetting alleged in some discovered memory cases could be the
consequence of the unique forgetting processes associated with nocturnal
events and in particular the forgetting of dreams. Like dream forgetting,
such nocturnal abuse forgetting might result from difficulties in the full con-
solidation of memories due to brain states and/or a lack of schematic coher-
ence due to the fact that the nocturnal event is bizarre and unattached to
everyday experience. In addition, because nocturnal abuse may be "dream-
like," individuals may upon awakening dismiss their experiences as being
nothing more than a very bad dream.

3. Trauma-Specific Memory Mechanisms

Given the various mechanisms outlined above, it seems quite plausible
that it may ultimately be possible to account for all authentic discovered
memories without having to call on mechanisms unique to trauma. At the
same time, however, there are a number of hypothesized special mechanisms that might ultimately prove to be exclusively associated with traumatic experiences, although at present they have not been adequately demonstrated. Possible candidates include:

a. *Dissociative Processes*. It has been suggested that during trauma individuals may separate themselves from the experience. Such complete distancing of oneself from ongoing events could alter the manner in which such
experiences are encoded and later retrieved.[46]

b. *Physiological Processes*. There is evidence (primarily from animal studies) to suggest that highly arousing situations may increase the involvement
of the amygdala-based storage of memory and decrease hippocampal-based
storage, resulting in the production of fragmentary affective memories.[47, 48, 49]

c. *Psychodynamic Processes*. There could be automatic processes (e.g.,
repression) that limit access to recollections that are excessively disturbing or

---

46. See, e.g., Spiegel, D., & Cardena, E. (1991). Disintegrated experience: The dissociative disorders revisited. *Journal of Abnormal Psychology, 100*, 366-378.

47. LeDoux, J.E. (1992). Emotion as memory: Anatomical systems underlying indelible neural
traces. In S.A. Christianson (Ed.), *The handbook of emotion and memory: Research and theory* (pp. 269-
288). Hillsdale, NJ: Erlbaum.

48. See, e.g., Nadel, L., & Jacobs, W.J. (in press). Traumatic memory is special. *Current Directions
in Psychological Science.*

49. See also Metcalfe, J., & Jacobs, W.J. (1998). Emotional memory: The effects of stress on "cool"
and "hot" memory systems. *The Psychology of Learning and Motivation, 38*, 187-222.

threatening to the ego.[50] At present, there is simply insufficient evidence to assess the role of these mechanisms in mediating discovered memories.[51]

Summary of special mechanisms. The existence of unique processes that could be involved in the forgetting and subsequent discovery of memories of abuse remains an open question. The cases documented here can potentially be accounted for on the basis of nontrauma-based memory mechanisms, particularly if we add to the list hindsight biases that may distort individuals' assessments of their degree of prior forgetting and nocturnal forgetting processes. On the other hand, we cannot at present rule out the possibility that psychological and/or physiological processes that are unique to trauma may be involved in at least some discovered memory experiences. Although the presence of unique forgetting processes is clearly of great legal importance in assessing whether discovered traumatic memories should be given special consideration in litigation, the scientific jury is still out.[52]

CONCLUSIONS

Although many issues remain to be resolved regarding the scientific status of discovered memories and their applicability to the discovered memory doctrine, a few unambiguous conclusions seem warranted. First, there seems little question but that individuals are capable of generating and believing false memories. Moreover, the aggressive memory therapies in which some discovered memories are elicited involve precisely the type of suggestive and coercive conditions that are known to produce false memories. On the basis of such observations, it seems clear that we cannot assume that an abusive episode occurred simply because an individual sincerely recalls it. Second, although we must be skeptical of discovered memories in the absence of corroboration, attempts at independently corroborating some of these recollections indicate that they can (at least sometimes) correspond to actual events. Thus we can neither accept nor reject discovered memories out of hand. Third, even when individuals have the experience of discovering a seemingly long-forgotten memory for a corroboratable abuse, it is possible that the memory was not entirely forgotten prior to its discovery. Thus, an individ-

---

50. See, e.g., Vaillant, G. (1992). *Ego mechanisms of defense: A guide for clinicians and researchers.* Washington, D.C.: American Psychiatric Press.

51. See also Schooler, J.W. & Hyman, I.E. (1997). Investigating alternative accounts of veridical and non-veridical memories of trauma: Report of the cognitive working groups. In J. D. Read & D. S. Lindsay (Eds.) *Recollections of trauma: Scientific research and clinical practices* (pp. 531-540). New York: Plenum.52. For recent opposing views on this topic, see Shobe, K. K., & Kihlstrom, J. F. (1997). Is traumatic memory special? *Current Directions in Psychological Science, 6*, 70-75; and Nadel, L., & Jacobs, W.J. (in press). Traumatic memory is special. *Current Directions in Psychological Science.*

ual's convictions regarding his or her prior forgetting of an experience cannot alone demonstrate that the memory was actually inaccessible. Fourth, even if the memory was not entirely forgotten, the experience of discovery may be profound. The individual may, for example, be discovering previously unappreciated emotions or understanding of the experience and confusing this discovery with a discovery of the memory itself. Although precisely what aspect of the experience the individual has discovered is unclear, it may still be reasonably argued that some type of discovery regarding the *significance* of the event occurred. Thus, following discovery experiences of corroboratable abuse, a newfound concern with an abuse experience may be authentic, even if the prior degree of forgetting may have been unwittingly exaggerated.

Finally, the specific processes that lead to discovered memory experiences corresponding to actual events have yet to be fully determined. It may be that the forgetting and recollection of traumatic memories involve the very same processes that are associated with the forgetting of nontraumatic experiences. Indeed, the present discussion elucidated a number of mechanisms, both standard ones typically considered in memory discussion and newly proposed ones (e.g., the "forgot it all along" effect and nocturnal forgetting processes), that may apply to the discovery of both traumatic and nontraumatic memories. At the same time, however, it must be conceded that additional trauma-specific mechanisms may also be at play. Thus, at present, we cannot assert with confidence that discovered memories of abuse draw exclusively on the same mechanisms as other types of experiences, nor can we claim that unique mechanisms are involved.

In reviewing the scientific evidence surrounding discovered memories of abuse it is easy to become discouraged. Investigations of both the production of false memories and the discovery of true memories of abuse are hampered by important ethical concerns. We cannot ethically attempt to implant memories of severe trauma, nor can we induce actual trauma and then investigate its subsequent forgetting and recollection. Thus, we must rely on indirect approaches such as the implanting of nontraumatic or, at most, only mildly traumatic false memories in the laboratory and the investigation of uncontrolled case studies in the field. Though imperfect, such approaches provide our best current approximations of the phenomena at hand. Given these limitations, it might be tempting to simply ignore our present scientific knowledge in making legal determinations on this topic. In my opinion, however, the legal system will be far better served by relying on our current, albeit incomplete, scientific understanding of discovered memories rather than on mere intuition and folk theories of memory. At the same time, it is imperative that scientists who communicate our current understanding of the topic maintain humility by articulating clearly both what we do and don't know about discovered memory experiences.

Chapter 6

RECOVERED-MEMORY EXPERIENCES

D. STEPHEN LINDSAY[1]

During the last ten years, substantial numbers of North Americans have reported emotionally wrenching experiences of "remembering" histories of childhood sexual abuse (CSA) of which they were previously unaware. Cases differ one from another in important ways, but the defining feature of the phenomenon is the *subjective experience* of "recovering" memories of extremely distressing childhood events that contradict the persons' prior beliefs about their childhoods. I use the term "recovered-memory experiences" (RMEs) to refer to such cases.

How best can RMEs be explained, and how should psychologists, other professionals, and society at large respond to them? Until recently, answers to these questions have tended to cluster at two polar extremes. Critics of trauma-oriented therapies argued that RMEs are usually pseudomemories developed in response to suggestive forms of therapy and self-help. In contrast, trauma-oriented clinicians and other countercritics argued that RMEs are usually essentially accurate memories of previously repressed or dissociated CSA and that the claims of critics should be dismissed as antifeminist backlash. Recently, however, there has been growing support for a middle-ground position that acknowledges the existence of both essentially accurate and essentially illusory RMEs.

It is useful to think of RMEs as ranging along a continuum. At one extreme are cases in which RMEs of multiple instances of violent and often bizarre forms of incestuous abuse (sometimes including events in early infancy and/or extending into late adolescence) arise in the context of powerful suggestive influences and in the absence of compelling corroboration. I will refer to such cases as "implausible RMEs." At the opposite extreme are cases in which RMEs of one or a few isolated instances of relatively high-base-rate kinds of childhood sexual abuse arise more or less spontaneously and are subsequently corroborated. I will refer to cases of this sort as "plau-

---

1. Some paragraphs in this chapter were adapted from paragraphs in the following papers: Lindsay, D. S. (1998). De-polarizing views on recovered-memory experiences. In S. J. Lynn & K. McConkey (Eds.), *Truth in memory*. New York: Guilford Press; Lindsay, D. S. (1997, November). Recovered-memory experiences: Explaining true and false delayed memories of childhood sexual abuse. *Psychology Place* (www.psychplace.com).

sible RMEs." The central thesis of this chapter is that it is likely that qualitatively different mechanisms underlie RMEs at the two ends of this continuum. To anticipate, my claim is that RMEs at the "implausible" end of the continuum usually reflect illusory memories or false beliefs, whereas RMEs at the "plausible" end of the continuum more often involve essentially accurate recollections of long-forgotten CSA. Different sorts of ordinary cognitive mechanisms may account for both types of RMEs.

As an example of highly implausible RMEs, consider the case that initially sparked my interest in the controversy about recovered memories. In 1992, a man in his early seventies contacted me and related what at the time seemed an extraordinary story. His forty-ish daughter (X) had sought therapy after the break-up of a relationship. After 2 years of therapy, she accused her father of multiple violent abuses, for which he was facing criminal charges. Initially, I did not know what to make of his claims—he cried his innocence, but the guilty often do that. I later learned that the therapist had no formal training or qualification. The therapist's notes recorded that, after the very first session, she formed the opinion that X's problems were likely caused by "repressed" CSA. The therapist used a variety of techniques to encourage X to recover memories, and after about 100 sessions (many of which were several hours long) conducted over a one-year period, X did indeed begin to report new "memories" of CSA. Over the next 100 sessions she came to report more and more violent and bizarre instances of abuse (e.g., being manacled to the kitchen table at 2 years of age and raped by neighborhood men; watching her father strangle babies and bury them in the snow in the yard). No remotely credible evidence for these allegations emerged.[2]

The well-known case of Ross Cheit provides a contrasting example of highly plausible RMEs. In 1992, at age 36, Cheit recalled being repeatedly sexually molested by William Farmer, a counselor at a boys' summer camp. Cheit claims (and cites reasons for believing) that before he recovered these memories, he would have honestly denied that he had ever been molested.

---

2. For other examples of highly implausible RMEs, see: Bass, E., & Davis, L. (1988). *The courage to heal: A guide for women survivors of child sexual abuse.* New York: Harper & Row; Bottoms, B. L., Shaver, P. R., & Goodman, G. S. (1996). An analysis of ritualistic and religion-related child abuse allegations. *Law and Human Behavior, 20,* 1-34; Coons, P. M. (1994). Reports of satanic ritual abuse: Further implications about pseudomemories. *Perceptual and Motor Skills, 78,* 1376-1378; Loftus, E. F., & Ketcham, K. (1994). *The myth of repressed memory: False memories and allegations of sexual abuse.* New York: St. Martin's Press; Qin, J., Goodman, G. S., Bottoms, B. L., & Shaver, P. R. (1998). Repressed memories of ritualistic and religion-related child abuse. In S. J. Lynn & K. McConkey (Eds.), *Truth in memory.* New York: Guilford Press; Newman, L. S., & Baumeister, R. F. (1996). Toward an explanation of the UFO abduction phenomenon: Hypnotic elaboration, extraterrestrial sadomasochism, and spurious memories. *Psychological Inquiry, 7,* 99-126; Pendergrast, M. (1996). *Victims of memory: Incest accusations and shattered lives* (2nd ed.). Hinesburg, VT: Upper Access; Yapko, M. (1993, September/October). The seductions of memory. *Networker,* 31-37.

Shortly before his RMEs began, Cheit had learned that a young boy who is a close relative was about to go to a similar camp. The new memories arose while Cheit was on vacation (the first holiday of his adult years) during the same time of year that, nearly 30 years previously, he had attended the camp. Cheit confronted Farmer in a surreptitiously tape-recorded telephone conversation, and Farmer admitted molesting him and other boys. Subsequently, other men who had attended the camp as boys confirmed that Farmer had sexually molested them too.[3]

When critics of trauma-oriented therapies refer to RMEs, they typically have in mind cases like X's, in which RMEs of numerous instances of bizarre abuse arose in the context of highly suggestive therapy. In contrast, when countercritics refer to RMEs, they often (although not always) have in mind cases like Cheit's, in which memories of sadly common forms of CSA arose more or less spontaneously. This difference in the kinds of cases different individuals have in mind when they talk about recovered memories has added to the contentiousness of the debate and hampered efforts to understand the phenomenon (or, as I will argue, phenomena) of RMEs.

IMPLAUSIBLE RMEs

Suggestive Forms of "Memory-Recovery Work" in Psychotherapy

As part of a long-overdue response to the appalling reality of CSA, many North American therapists have become sensitized to the likelihood that some of their adult clients were sexually abused during childhood. There are both theoretical and empirical grounds for believing that CSA can contribute

---

3. For other examples of plausible RMEs, supported by varying degrees and kinds of corroborating evidence, see: Schooler, J. W., Ambadar, Z., & Bendiksen, M. (1997). A cognitive corroborative case study approach for investigating discovered memories of sexual abuse. In J. D. Read & D. S. Lindsay (Eds.), *Recollections of trauma: Scientific research and clinical practice* (pp. 379-387). New York: Plenum; Williams, L. M. (1995). Recovered memories of abuse in women with documented child sexual victimization histories. *Journal of Traumatic Stress, 8,* 649-673; and Cheit's internet-based "Recovered Memory Project," http://www.brown.edu/Departments/Taubman_Center/ Recovmem/.

It is worth noting that the best-documented cases typically involve one or a few instances of relatively common forms of abuse (although in Cheit's case the sexual molestation allegedly occurred numerous times). This is not to say that the abuse in such cases was harmless or in any way acceptable, but rather to note that it did not involve the sorts of repeated, bizarre, and vicious acts (e.g., satanic rituals) that often feature in "implausible" RMEs.

to the development of psychopathology in adulthood.[4] A variety of psychotherapeutic perspectives hold that it is reasonable to assume that individuals with such histories can be assisted by therapeutic "working through" of the abuse, and there is at least some evidence to support that view.[5] A natural extension of these quite reasonable ideas is that some adults with psychological problems may be suffering aftereffects of CSA that they do not consciously remember.

In the late 1980s and early 1990s, many authors propounded the thesis that a substantial percentage of adults with psychological problems suffer the aftereffects of hidden memories of CSA.[6]
This idea, first proposed by Freud in 1896, together with the belief that therapeutic "working through" of abuse histories is helpful, laid the groundwork for trauma-oriented therapies that explicitly or implicitly encourage clients to search for hidden memories of CSA.[7] In addition to being widely disseminated to practitioners, these ideas were promulgated in the self-help litera-

---

4. See, for example, Beitchman, J. H., Zucker, K. J., Hood, J. E., daCosta, G. A., & Cassavia, E. (1992). A review of the long-term effects of child sexual abuse. *Child Abuse & Neglect, 16*, 101-118; Kendall-Tackett, K. A., Williams, L. M., & Finkelhor, D. (1993). Impact of sexual abuse on children: A review and synthesis. *Psychological Bulletin, 113*, 164-180.

See the following for arguments that the long-term effects of CSA have sometimes been exaggerated: Bauserman, R., & Rind, B. (1997). Psychological correlates of male child and adolescent sexual experiences with adults: A review of the nonclinical literature. *Archives of Sexual Behavior, 26*, 105-141.

5. See, for example, Foa, E. B., Rothbaum, R. O., Riggs, D. S., & Murdock, T. B. (1991). Treatment of posttraumatic stress disorder in rape victims: A comparison between cognitive-behavioral procedures and counseling. *Journal of Consulting and Clinical Psychology, 59*, 715-723; Resick, P. A., & Schnicke, M. K. (1992). Cognitive processing theory for sexual assault victims. *Journal of Consulting and Clinical Psychology, 60*, 748-756.

6. See, for example, Bass, E., & Davis, L. (1988). *The courage to heal: A guide for women survivors of child sexual abuse.* New York: Harper & Row; Blume, E. S. (1990). *Secret survivors: Uncovering incest and its aftereffects in women.* New York: Ballantine; Claridge, K. (1992). Reconstructing memories of abuse: A theory based approach. *Psychotherapy, 29*, 243-252; Clark, K. R. (1993). Season of light/season of darkness: The effects of burying and remembering traumatic sexual abuse on the sense of self. *Clinical Social Work Journal, 21*, 25-43; Courtois, C. A. (1988). *Healing the incest wound: Adult survivors in therapy.* New York: Norton; Courtois, C. A. (1992). The memory retrieval process in incest survivor therapy. *Journal of Child Sexual Abuse, 1*, 15-32; Fredrickson, R. (1992). *Repressed memories: A journey to recovery from sexual abuse.* New York: Simon & Schuster; Herman, J. L., & Schatzow, E. (1987). Recovery and verification of memories of childhood sexual trauma. *Psychoanalytic Psychology, 4*, 1-14; Maltz, W. (1990, December). Adult survivors of incest: How to help them overcome the trauma. *Medical Aspects of Human Sexuality*, 42-47; Olio, K. A. (1989). Memory retrieval in the treatment of adult survivors of sexual abuse. *Transactional Analysis Journal, 19*, 93-100.

For arguments against the belief that a substantial percentage of psychotherapy clients are suffering the aftereffects of non-remembered CSA see Lindsay, D. S. (1997). Comments on Courtois. In J. D. Read & D. S. Lindsay (Eds.), *Recollections of trauma: Scientific research and clinical practice* (pp. 361-368). New York: Plenum.

7. Freud, S. (1962). The aetiology of hysteria. In J. Strachey (Ed. and Trans.), *The standard edition of the complete psychological works of Sigmund Freud* (Vol. 3, pp. 191-221). Toronto: Clark, Irwin and Co. (Original work published 1896.)

ture (e.g., Bass & Davis's, 1988, self-help book, *The Courage to Heal*, which includes a substantial emphasis on ideas about the psychological benefits of searching for hidden memories of CSA, sold hundreds of thousands of copies and was given a five-star rating in Santrock, Minnett, & Campbell's 1994 guide to self-help books).[8] Even more extravagant versions of these ideas were presented in the popular media (e.g., one book claimed that in 1992, *The Oprah Winfrey Show* had 10 million viewers per show, and that the combined audience of this and similar shows, which often featured accounts of horrific RMEs, was 54 million viewing hours per day).[9]

Trauma-oriented approaches to therapy may become dangerously suggestive when they combine several of the following practices: communicating to the client (directly or indirectly) that she or he has symptoms of nonremembered abuse, that many survivors do not remember abuse, that remembering is an important step toward or sign of psychological healing, and that doubt may reflect denial; using techniques that enhance imagery and lower memory-monitoring criteria, such as hypnosis, sodium amytal, or guided imagery, as means of helping clients search for hidden abuse memories; and recommending that clients with suspected non-remembered abuse read popular books on memory recovery and/or attend survivors' support groups. I refer to such practices and techniques as "memory-recovery work" (to distinguish them from "memory work," which includes talking about never-forgotten childhood events). Note that such approaches need not be overtly coercive, neither in their intent nor in the client's perception. Indeed, suggestive influences may be more powerful when they are not overt.[10]

How prevalent are therapies that include a focus on memory-recovery work? The answer to this question is not known with any precision. It is incontrovertible that some therapists have used techniques that combine all of the suggestive elements enumerated above, but it is difficult to specify

---

8. Santrock, J. W., Minnett, A. M., & Campbell, B. D. (1994). *The authoritative guide to self-help books.* New York: Guildord Press. There's an amusing story regarding how I learned of Santrock et al.'s (1994) "authoritative" guide to self-help books. A friend who was going through some rough times showed me a self-help book that he was reading, and asked me what I thought of the following statement therein: "According to my experience with clients, in over 90% of all cases we find that our parents were our lovers or mates in former lives. Freud was not all that mistaken." (The just- quoted passage is from Griscom, C. (1988). *The healing of emotion: Awakening the fearless self.* New York: Fireside. P.42.) Dismayed, I asked a clinical colleague for help locating a more rational self-help book, and she kindly loaned me Santrock et al. Their book looked very promising, because rather than just offering their own opinions on self-help books, the authors based their recommendations on surveys of 500 members of the American Psychological Association. I was less impressed when I found that *The Courage to Heal* was "strongly recommended" for any women client who has "the slightest inkling that she might have been sexually abused" (Santrock et al., p. 12).

9. Heaton, J. A., & Wilson, N. L. (1998). Memory, media, and the creation of confusion. In S. J. Lynn & K. McConkey (Eds.), *Truth in memory.* New York: Guilford Press.

10. Bowers, K. S. (1984). On being unconsciously influenced and informed. In K. S. Bowers & D. Meichenbaum (Eds.), *The unconscious reconsidered* (pp. 227-273). New York: Wiley.

exactly which approaches used in which ways constitute dangerous risk and exactly how many therapists have used such approaches with some or all of their clients. There are some relevant survey data that justify the conclusion that in the early to mid 1990s a nontrivial minority of the hundreds of thousands of North American therapists made at least some use of therapeutic approaches that many memory researchers view as dangerously suggestive.[11, 12] It can also be said with some confidence that even at the height of their popularity the vast majority of qualified psychotherapists did not focus on highly suggestive memory-recovery approaches. Various theoretical and methodological difficulties (including the happy fact that it is likely that use of suggestive approaches to trauma-oriented therapies has declined steeply in recent years) prohibit a more precise or confident estimate of the prevalence of risky approaches to memory-recovery work in therapy and self-help.

Mechanisms of Essentially False RMEs

Beginning with research by Elizabeth F. Loftus and her colleagues in the mid-1970s, hundreds of studies have explored the mechanisms by which suggestions can lead to false memories. This research reveals that false memories are most likely when (a) suggestive influences are strong and (b) the time period about which suggestions are given is poorly remembered. A single passing suggestion can lead to false memories of trivial details, but more powerful suggestive influences are required to create illusory memories of dramatic life experiences. Suggestions increase in strength if they are given by an authority figure, are perceived as plausible, are encountered repeatedly, or are presented in ways that evoke vivid images or encourage the recipient to accept thoughts, images, and feelings as accurate memories. It is also likely that some individuals are more susceptible to suggestive influence than others (perhaps because they are more responsive to authority, less analyti-

---

11. See, for example, Bottoms, B. L., Shaver, P. R., & Goodman, G. S. (1996). An analysis of ritualistic and religion-related child abuse allegations. *Law and Human Behavior, 20,* 1-34; Polusny, M A., & Follette, V. M. (1996). Remembering childhood sexual abuse: A national survey of psychologists' clinical practices, beliefs, and personal experiences. *Professional Psychology: Research and Practice, 27,* 41-52; Poole, D. A., Lindsay, D. S., Memon, A., & Bull, R. (1995). Psychotherapy and the recovery of memories of childhood sexual abuse: U.S. and British practitioners' beliefs, practices, and experiences. *Journal of Consulting and Clinical Psychology, 63,* 426-437; Yapko, M. (1993, September/October). The seductions of memory. *Networker,* 31-37.

12. The data from the study by Poole et al. (Poole, D. A., Lindsay, D. S., Memon, A., & Bull, R. (1995). Psychotherapy and the recovery of memories of childhood sexual abuse: U.S. and British practitioners' beliefs, practices, and experiences. *Journal of Consulting and Clinical Psychology, 63,* 426-437.) have sometimes been mischaracterized by proponents on both sides of the recovered-memories controversy. For a rejoinder to such misinterpretations, see Lindsay, D. S., & Poole, D. A. (in press). The Poole et al. (1995) surveys of therapists: Misrepresentations by both sides of the recovered memories controversy. *Journal of Psychiatry & Law.*

cally critical in their thinking style, or have more vivid imagery than other individuals).[13]

For ethical reasons, no experiment has tested the hypothesis that suggestions can lead to false memories of CSA. Some authors have argued that it is therefore inappropriate to generalize from the research on suggestibility to memory-recovery work in therapy.[14] Arguments against generalizability have taken three major forms.

Some have argued that because the participants in research on suggestibility are not all trauma survivors, the research findings cannot be generalized to trauma survivors. This argument entirely misses the point: Concern about suggestive memory-recovery work focuses primarily on its potential ill-effects for clients who are *not* trauma survivors but who may be led mistakenly to believe that they are trauma survivors. In any case, there is little reason to believe that trauma survivors are less suggestible than other people–indeed, some psychologists believe that the opposite is the case.[15]

Others have argued against generalizing from studies of memory suggestibility because the studies do not involve psychotherapy clients in situations that directly mirror therapy. I see little reason to assume that therapy clients are less suggestible than other people, and the suggestive power of some trauma-oriented therapy situations dwarfs that of any research study of which I am aware.

A third argument against generalization is that the false memories created in research studies are not false memories of childhood sexual abuse. As noted previously, existing evidence and theory on suggestibility indicate that, all else being equal, more powerful suggestive influences are required to create false memories of significant life events, so there is no debate about the inappropriateness of *quantitative* generalization of laboratory findings involving trivial details to the therapy situation. For example, the fact that 75 percent of subjects who received a misleading suggestion regarding a peripheral detail in a slide show later reported that they saw the suggested detail in the slides would never be taken to indicate that 75 percent of clients who receive a suggestion regarding CSA will subsequently report false memories

---

13. See Hyman, I. E., Jr., & Billings, F. J. (1998). Individual differences in the creation of false childhood memories. *Memory, 6,* 1-20.

14. See, for example, Berliner, L., & Williams, L. M. (1994). Memories of child sexual abuse: A response to Lindsay and Read. *Applied Cognitive Psychology, 8,* 379-388; Enns, C. Z., McNeilly, C., Corkery, J., & Gilbert, M. (1995). The debate about delayed memories of child sexual abuse: A feminist perspective. *The Counselling Psychologist, 23,* 181-279; Pezdek, K. (1994). The illusion of illusory memory. *Applied Cognitive Psychology, 8,* 339-350.

15. See Ditomasso, M. J., & Routh, D. K. (1993). Recall of abuse in childhood and three measures of dissociation. *Child Abuse and Neglect, 17,* 477-485; see also Rhue, J. W., & Lynn, S. J. (1995). Dissociation, fantasy, and imagination in childhood: A comparison of physically abused, sexually abused, and non-abused children. *Contemporary Hypnosis, 12,* 131-136.

of abuse. The question, then, is whether the *general principles* discovered in the lab can be generalized to the therapy situation.

The question of whether or not the same general principles that govern suggestibility for laboratory events also govern suggestibility for CSA will never be directly addressed by experimental research, because ethics bar researchers from testing the hypothesis that suggestions can lead people falsely to believe that they were sexually abused by their parents. But the argument against generalization is not very strong. At a theoretical level, it is a basic tenet of science to prefer more parsimonious theories, and to resort to the postulation of special mechanisms only when the data compel them. There is no compelling evidence in favor of the argument that illusory memories or false beliefs of CSA cannot arise via the same mechanisms involved in the creation of illusory memories of other kinds of experiences.[16]

Support for the claim that suggestive influences can lead to false memories of significant (and even traumatic) life events comes from real-world cases in which people experienced RMEs that are demonstrably false or extremely implausible. Examples include reported memories of bizarre and murderous satanic cult rituals; memories of abusive events during the first days of life, in the womb, or during past lives; memories of UFO abductions; and memories of events that would have left unambiguous physical evidence in the absence of such evidence. The point of citing such examples is not to imply that all RMEs should be attributed to the same mechanisms that give rise to illusory memories and false beliefs such as these; rather, the point is merely that such cases demonstrate that people can experience illusory memories of traumatic childhood events.[17]

This anecdotal evidence is supported by recent studies that provide relatively close analogies to false memories of childhood sexual abuse. Examples include Loftus and Pickrell's "lost in the mall" study, Pezdek, Finger, and Hedge's follow-up of the "lost in the mall" paradigm (which demonstrated the importance of the perceived plausibility of misleading suggestions), similar studies using less common suggested events by Hyman and his associ-

---

16. This question is similar to the debate about whether "flashbulb memories" (i.e., vivid recollections of the circumstances under which one first learned of a highly surprising and consequential event, such as Kennedy's assassination) reflect the operation of a qualitatively different memory mechanism than do memories of more mundane events (see for example, Winograd, W., & Neisser, U. (Eds.). (1992). *Affect and accuracy in recall: Studies of "flashbulb" memories* (Emory Symposium on Cognition). New York: Cambridge University Press.). For a more detailed discussion of this analogy, see Lindsay, D. S. (1997). Jane Doe in context: Sex abuse, lives, and video tape. *Child Maltreatment, 2,* 187-192.

17. Readers who believe in past-life regression, fetal memories, Satanic cults, and UFO abductions will not, of course, find this argument compelling. Unfortunately, such individuals are unlikely to find *any* argument compelling, because they have accepted a belief system that is conveniently non-falsifiable (e.g., the very invisibility of the vast network of intergenerational Satanists is said to demonstrate the cult's enormous power).

ates, experiments by the late Nick Spanos and his colleagues demonstrating false memories of past lives (and of CSA in past lives) and Garry, Manning, Loftus, and Sherman's finding that merely asking people to imagine having had particular childhood experiences (e.g., breaking a window and cutting themselves) inflates their estimates of the likelihood that they actually did have those experiences.[18, 19, 20, 21, 22]

Additional evidence comes from an as-yet-unpublished experiment by Kelley, Lindsay, and Amodio, in which right-handed undergraduates performed a series of tests that, they were told, might be able to detect right-handed adults who were born with a left-hand preference. Some participants were told that the test results indicated that they were probably born left-handed, whereas others were told that the results indicated they were right-handed from birth. All participants were then asked to spend an hour on their own time attempting to remember any childhood experiences that might have discouraged them from being left-handed. Participants given the left-handed diagnosis more often reported such memories and, equally important, were more likely later to indicate belief that they started life as left-handers. Thus a single suggestive session, followed by a single hour of memory-recovery work, had a dramatic effect on both reported memories and reported beliefs about childhood events.

Skeptics can always argue that the analogy from research studies demonstrating false memories to the clinical situation is imperfect, but the onus shifts to explaining why one should *not* generalize in the interest of parsimony. Moreover, when in doubt therapists have a moral responsibility to minimize the risk of harming their clients. By analogy, if a drug was shown to cause blindness in rats, ophthamologists would not continue prescribing the drug on the grounds that the studies differed too much from the clinical situation; rather, they would be very cautious in using the drug until it was shown to be safe. This advice seems particularly sound when there is little if any compelling evidence that the treatment in question (i.e., looking for abuse memories in clients who initially indicate that they were not abused) has any beneficial effects.

---

18. Loftus, E. F., & Pickrell, J. (1995). The formation of false memories. *Psychiatric Annals, 25*, 720-724.

19. Pezdek, K., Finger, K., & Hedge, D. (1997). Planting false childhood memories: The role of event plausibility. *Psychological Science, 8*, 437-441.

20. Hyman, I. E., Jr., Husband, T. H., & Billings, F. J. (1995). False memories of childhood experiences. *Applied Cognitive Psychology, 9*, 181-197; Hyman, I. E., Jr., & Pentland, J. (1996). The role of mental imagery in the creation of false childhood memories. *Journal of Memory and Language, 35*, 101-117.

21. See Spanos, N. P., Burgess, C. A., & Burgess, M. F. (1994). Past-life identities, UFO abductions, and satanic ritual abuse: The social construction of memories. *The International Journal of Clinical and Experimental Hypnosis, XLII*, 433-446.

22. Garry, M., Manning, C., Loftus, E., F., & Sherman, S. J. (1996). Imagination inflation. *Psychonomic Bulletin and Review, 3*, 208-214.

Summary: Implausible RMEs

A number of prominent trauma-oriented psychologists have recently published statements acknowledging that highly suggestive forms of memory-recovery work are ill-advised and may put clients at unacceptable risk of developing illusory memories or false beliefs. For example, Courtois provided a detailed and thoughtful set of guidelines for therapy with clients with possible CSA histories, in which she acknowledged the excesses of some past practices and the difficulty of differentiating between historically accurate and inaccurate recovered memories, and cautioned against unduly suggestive approaches to memory-recovery work.[23] Similarly, Briere wrote:

> There is little question that a minority of therapists have used questionable "memory recovery" techniques . . . Such errors can create victims both of clients who have come to believe nonexistent abuse histories and those who have been falsely accused based on such pseudomemories.[24]

In summary, evidence and theory on memory suggestibility help account for cases like X's, in which an authority figure (a therapist, often augmented by self-help literature and/or a support group) presents repeated suggestions regarding the plausibility of long-ago CSA and uses techniques that enhance imagery, lower memory-monitoring criteria, and increase compliance (e.g., hypnosis or guided imagery). Such prolonged and socially influenced searches for CSA memories combine all of the factors known to increase the likelihood of false memories or beliefs regarding dramatic life experiences.

PLAUSIBLE RMEs

How can psychology account for cases like that of Ross Cheit, in which RMEs appear to have arisen more or less spontaneously and to be essentially accurate? As outlined in this section, ordinary cognitive mechanisms may lead some individuals who experienced CSA to forget about it for years or even decades and then later recover essentially accurate memories of the abuse.

---

23. Courtois, C. A. (1997). Informed clinical practice and the standard of care: Proposed guidelines for the treatment of adults who report delayed memories of childhood trauma. In J. D. Read and D. S. Lindsay (Eds.), *Recollections of trauma: Scientific research and clinical practice* (pp. 337-361). New York: Plenum.

24. Briere, J. (1997). An integrated approach to treating adults abused as children, with specific reference to self-reported recovered memories. In J. D. Read & D. S. Lindsay (Eds.), *Recollections of trauma: Scientific research and clinical practice* (pp. 25-41). New York: Plenum. pp. 26-27.

Mechanisms of Forgetting CSA

In my view, there is no compelling evidence for a special "repression" mechanism that "deep freezes" memories of traumatic events, shielding them from consciousness unless they are recovered. But there is no need to presume such a mechanism to account for accurate RMEs. For one thing, forgetting of dramatic, and even traumatic, experiences may be more common than intuition would lead us to believe. In this case, intuition is indeed likely to lead us astray, because we are (by definition) unaware of events that we have forgotten and therefore rarely encounter evidence of not remembering them. Systematic research indicates that people sometimes do fail to report (and, in some cases, to fail to remember) significant life events such as serious motor vehicle accidents, hospitalizations, crime victimizations, and CSA.[25] Much of childhood is poorly remembered in adulthood (perhaps partly because people rarely work at remembering childhood). For example, Chambliss found that only 12 percent of a sample of 340 college students said that they could recall ever having sat on a parent's lap when they were under 5 years of age; doubtless virtually all had done so on innumerable occasions, but few could remember even a single such occasion.[26] Research suggests that traumatic childhood experiences (especially repeated ones) are more likely to be remembered than mundane childhood events, but in many cases, children may not experience CSA (especially the more common forms of CSA, which do not involve physical violence) as a life-threatening trauma but rather as an upsetting, unpleasant event.[27] Moreover, it is likely that even genuinely traumatic childhood events are sometimes forgotten in adulthood.

Ordinary cognitive mechanisms may sometimes hasten forgetting of negative events relative to otherwise comparably memorable neutral or pleasant events. For example, some victims of CSA may divert their attention to other things when the abuse occurs (or become panicked in ways that grossly disrupt attention), which would impair memory for the trauma. Furthermore, victims of CSA may be threatened against speaking of the abuse, and may avoid thinking about it, which would limit rehearsal and thereby increase the likelihood of forgetting the abuse over a period of time. Some abused children may develop habits of avoiding environmental and internal (thoughts and feelings) cues that remind them of the abuse; such habits could, via ordinary memory mechanisms, lower the likelihood that abuse is later recollect-

---

25. See sources cited in Loftus, E. F., Garry, M., & Feldman, J. (1994). Forgetting sexual trauma: What does it mean when 38% forget? *Journal of Consulting and Clinical Psychology, 62*, 1177-1181.

26. Chambliss, C. (1996). *Less is sometimes more in therapy: Avoiding the false memory syndrome.* ERIC Research Report.

27. For a review, see Koss, M. P., Tromp, S., & Tharan, M. (1995). Traumatic memories: Empirical foundations, forensic and clinical implications. *Clinical Psychology: Science and Practice, 2*, 111-132.

ed. Forgetting of severe CSA beyond early childhood is probably relatively rare, especially if the abuse occurred on multiple occasions, but very likely does sometimes occur.[28]

The mechanisms of forgetting described above are similar to mechanisms hypothesized by some trauma-oriented clinicians. For example, "dissociative amnesia" is said to occur because, in essence, the victim does not attend to the abuse in ways that would support recall-appropriate encoding.[29] There are, however, important differences between attributing forgetting of child abuse to ordinary mechanisms of memory and attributing such forgetting to a special traumagenic amnesia mechanism. As argued by Read and Lindsay, use of the term "amnesia" may inappropriately pathologize forgetting of abuse (consequently leading it to be construed as a condition in need of treatment), and some hypothesized mechanisms of traumagenic amnesia also include dubious claims to the effect that the same mechanism that impairs conscious recollection of abuse also maintains unusually vivid and veridical unconscious memories.[30] Thus use of the term "amnesia" may foster therapeutic approaches that encourage clients (if only indirectly and subtly) to search for hidden histories of CSA. In any case, the central point for present purposes is that regardless of the precise mechanisms involved, it is almost certainly true that some people who experienced CSA later fail to recollect those events, even when asked.

Evidence for the claim that some people who experienced CSA later do not remember it comes from a study by Williams, who interviewed 129 women who 17 years previously had been judged by hospital staff to have suffered an instance of sexual abuse.[31] In response to questions about childhood sexual experiences, 88 percent reported one or more instances of CSA, but 38 percent did not report the documented "target" event. As critics have pointed out, it is likely that some nonreporters were cases in which the abuse occurred in the first few years of life (and hence would not be expected to be recalled due to infantile amnesia; others may have involved relatively non-

---

28. It may be, as some traumatologists have argued, that in moments of extreme, abject terror (e.g., violent, life-threatening torture), the minds of some individuals "shut down" in ways that totally disrupt encoding and hence produce a genuinely amnestic state for the traumatic episode. This is not a hypothesis that can easily be supported or refuted by empirical investigation. In any case, (a) it seems unlikely that events whose encoding was so totally disrupted could subsequently be recovered and (b) there are many reasons to believe that such experiences are rare among North American psychotherapy clients.

29. See, for example, Courtois, C. A. (1997). Informed clinical practice and the standard of care: Proposed guidelines for the treatment of adults who report delayed memories of childhood trauma. In J. D. Read & D. S. Lindsay (Eds.), *Recollections of trauma: Scientific research and clinical practice* (pp. 337-361). New York: Plenum.

30. Read, J. D., & Lindsay, D. S. (1998). *"Amnesia" for summer camps and high school graduation: Memory work increases reports of prior amnesia.* Manuscript submitted for publication.

31. Williams, L. M. (1994). Recall of childhood trauma: A prospective study of women's memories of child sexual abuse. *Journal of Consulting and Clinical Psychology, 62,* 1167-1176.

memorable kinds of abuse, and yet others may have reflected decisions on the part of the women not to disclose the abuse during the interview rather than failures to remember it.[32, 33] Williams presented evidence indicating that these factors do not tell the whole story, however, and it may well be that in some cases even quite severe forms of postinfancy abuse were simply not remembered during the interview. This is particularly likely for those women in the sample (the substantial majority) who reported other instances of CSA. When people have had multiple experiences of a particular kind, ability to recall any given instance is sharply curtailed. For example, if your parents frequently spanked you when you were a child, you probably know that such spankings occurred and recollect a few particularly memorable episodes, but if I asked you to report on your history of such childhood experiences, you would likely fail to remember some episodes. If, in contrast, you received only one spanking during childhood, the uniqueness, distinctiveness, and salience of that event would make it relatively recallable (although you might nonetheless fail to recall it).

Widom reported a prospective study similar to theWilliams study, except that it included individuals with a documented history of physical abuse and neglect as well as individuals with a documented history of CSA.[34, 35] Widom too found evidence that a substantial minority of participants did not report (and appeared not to remember) the documented abuse. Moreover, many denied having any abuse history at all. For example, of 75 women with documented CSA, 32 percent claimed not to have any CSA history. As in the Williams study, Widom's participants were not asked directly about the recorded instance, so it is possible that some would have recalled it if given such direct and detailed probes, but it may be that some would have indicated no memory of the documented abuse even if asked directly.

Thus there is ample evidence that adults who experienced CSA sometimes do not remember the abuse later in adulthood, even when asked if they have such a history. In my view, the likelihood of such forgetting declines sharply as the frequency, severity, and recency of the abuse increase, leading me to be deeply skeptical of any case in which a person reports newly discovered memories of years of bizarre abuse.[36] Nonetheless, for present pur-

---

32. See Pendergrast, M. (1996). *Victims of memory: Incest accusations and shattered lives* (2nd ed.). Hinesburg, VT: Upper Access; Pope, H. G. Jr., & Hudson, J. I. (1995). Can memories of sexual abuse be repressed? *Psychological Medicine, 25*, 121-126.

33. Eacott, M. J., & Crawley, R. A. (1998). The offset of childhood amnesia: Memory for events that occurred before age 3. *Journal of Experimental Psychology: General, 127*, 22-33.

34. Widom, C. S. (1997). Accuracy of adult recollections of early childhood abuse. In J. D. Read and D. S. Lindsay (Eds.), *Recollections of trauma: Scientific research and clinical practice* (pp. 49-70). New York: Plenum.

35. Williams, L. M. (1994). Recall of childhood trauma: A prospective study of women's memories of child sexual abuse. *Journal of Consulting and Clinical Psychology, 62*, 1167-1176.

36. See review by Koss, M. P., Tromp, S., & Tharan, M. (1995). Traumatic memories: Empirical foundations, forensic and clinical implications. *Clinical Psychology: Science and Practice, 2*, 111-132.

poses, the point is that there are good reasons to believe that significant kinds of CSA can be forgotten in adulthood.

Mechanisms of Recovering Essentially Accurate Memories of CSA

Given that an adult had forgotten CSA, how could she or he later "recover" accurate memories? According to Tulving's encoding specificity principle, the likelihood of recalling an event is determined by the similarity of current cognitive processes to those performed when the event occurred. For example, if your current cognitive processes become similar to those you performed at breakfast this morning, you are likely to retrieve memories of breakfast. I can increase the similarity of your current cognitive processes to those you performed at breakfast merely by asking you to think about this morning's breakfast. Alternatively, I could show you a picture of your kitchen or waft the smell of frying bacon, either of which could lead you to engage cognitive processes similar to those you performed at breakfast and hence cue retrieval of breakfast memories. Research also shows that reinstatement of an unusual emotional or physiological state can facilitate recall of past experiences of that state (although such effects are neither large nor robust).[37]

The encoding specificity principle helps us to understand cases such as that of Cheit, in which current environmental and emotional conditions (e.g., being on vacation, at the same time of year as the molestation experiences; having recently learned that a close relative was going to a similar camp) may have set the stage for essentially accurate RMEs. It also fits at least reasonably well with a number of other cases in which people appear to have experienced essentially accurate RMEs.[38]

Several surveys have shown that adults who report a CSA history often report prior periods of less or no memory for the abuse.[39] Although such findings are consistent with the claim that people can forget and then later re-remember CSA, interpretation of these results is so problematic that they will not be further considered here.[40] More persuasive evidence comes from

---

37. Eich, E. (1995). Searching for mood dependent memory. *Psychological Science, 6,* 67-75.

38. See, for example, Schooler, J. W., Ambadar, Z., & Bendiksen, M. (1997). A cognitive corroborative case study approach for investigating discovered memories of sexual abuse. In J. D. Read & D. S. Lindsay (Eds.), *Recollections of trauma: Scientific research and clinical practice* (pp. 379-387). New York: Plenum.

39. See, for example, Elliott, D., & Briere, J. (1995). Post traumatic stress associated with delayed recall of sexual abuse: A general population study. *Journal of Traumatic Stress, 8,* 629-647.

40. See Melchert, T. P., & Parker, R. L. (1997). Different forms of childhood abuse and memory. *Child Abuse and Neglect, 21,* 125-135; Read, J. D., & Lindsay, D. S. (1998). *"Amnesia" for summer camps and high school graduation: Memory work increases reports of prior amnesia.* Manuscript submitted for publication.

a study by Williams, who found that, of 75 women in her prospective study who did report the target instance and who were asked follow-up questions regarding prior memory for that abuse, 10 (16%) reported a prior period during which they did not remember the event.[41] Williams found equivalent accuracy in the reports of those who did versus did not indicate such a prior period of not remembering. As Williams noted, however, it was not altogether clear what the women meant when reporting a prior period of not remembering, and it appears that some of them meant simply that they avoided thinking about the abuse.[42] This is quite different from cases in which people appear to be confident that they have no abuse history and then later have dramatic RMEs. It does appear that some women in Williams's study were reporting prior periods during which they had no awareness of having an abuse history, but the Williams finding should not be taken as evidence that RMEs, in general, are as accurate as continuously accessible memories. As Freyd pointed out, in the Williams study all of the cases involved a documented instance of abuse, so by definition reports of the target event could not be essentially false.[43] Also, there is no indication that the women in Williams's sample had engaged in prolonged and suggestive searches for hidden memories. Finally, as noted below, there are reasons to be skeptical of the accuracy of retrospective assessments of prior ability to remember. Nonetheless, for present purposes the important point is that at least some of the 10 women in Williams's sample reported prior periods of having no awareness of an abuse history, followed by recovery of essentially accurate recollections of the documented abuse. Even if these women's reports of a prior inability to remember were erroneous, these findings support the claim that people can have the subjective experience of recovering previously nonremembered CSA when those memories are accurate.

Dalenberg reported on 17 of her own clients who entered therapy with continuously accessible memories of CSA by their fathers and who subsequently remembered additional instances of abuse that increased the severity of their abuse histories.[44] Dalenberg interviewed the fathers and other witnesses and sought other kinds of evidence to assess the accuracy of both the continuously available and new abuse memories, and reported that 75 percent of the content of both kinds of reports was supported by such evidence.

---

41. Williams, L. M. (1995). Recovered memories of abuse in women with documented child sexual victimization histories. *Journal of Traumatic Stress, 8*, 649-673.

42. See also Melchert, T. P., & Parker, R. L. (1997). Different forms of childhood abuse and memory. *Child Abuse and Neglect, 21*, 125-135.

43. Freyd, P. (1998, March). Dear friends. *FMSF Newsletter, 7*(2), 1. (http://advicom.net/~fitz/fmsf/fmsf-news/0137.html)

44. Dalenberg, C. J. (1997). The prediction of accurate recollections of trauma. In J. D. Read and D. S. Lindsay (Eds.), *Recollections of trauma: Scientific research and clinical practice* (pp. 449-453). New York: Plenum.

Dalenberg's study is interesting and important, but it is not clear that it is appropriate to classify her patients' reports as RMEs, because all of the women initially reported that they had always remembered having an abuse history. As noted at the outset of this chapter, the defining featuring of RMEs is that the new memories dramatically contradict the person's prior beliefs about childhood. As mentioned above, basic research on autobiographical memory has long established that when people have had multiple experiences of a particular kind, it is often difficult for them to retrieve many of the individual instances. To return to the previous example, if you were frequently spanked as a child, you probably cannot recollect all of those experiences now, but if you worked at remembering additional instances, you probably could do so. Your new memories of spankings would not qualify as RMEs unless the newly remembered punishments qualitatively differed from those you have always "known" about (e.g., you always remembered a few episodes of "mild" spanking, but now remember being whipped with a belt). Although Dalenberg's clients' new memories did tend to be of more severe forms of abuse than their continuous memories, the degree and nature of this shift is not clear from her report. It is also worth noting that, presumably, Dalenberg did not use the sorts of suggestive memory-recovery approaches that have most alarmed critics. Dalenberg's data support the claim that new reports of CSA that emerge in therapy can be just as accurate as continuously accessible memories for clients who enter therapy with such memories, but they should not be misconstrued as evidence for a more general claim that "recovered memories" are just as accurate as continuously available memories.

Schooler et al. reported several case studies in which emotionally wrenching RMEs were subsequently substantiated by various kinds of evidence.[45] Most interestingly, Schooler et al. described two cases in which women reported very powerful experiences of remembering abuse of which they believed they had previously been utterly unaware, but that other individuals reported the woman had previously talked about. Schooler et al. speculated that the emotional impact of remembering abuse may sometimes give rise to a "forgot it all along" effect, in which the person mistakenly believes that the memories had not previously been accessible. Relatedly, Dalenberg found that her clients were extremely poor at remembering, after therapy,

---

45. Schooler, J. W., Ambadar, Z., & Bendiksen, M. (1997). A cognitive corroborative case study approach for investigating discovered memories of sexual abuse. In J. D. Read & D. S. Lindsay (Eds.), *Recollections of trauma: Scientific research and clinical practice* (pp. 379-387). New York: Plenum.

which reports of CSA they had remembered prior to versus during thera-py.[46, 47]

RMEs of Non-traumatic Childhood Experiences

RMEs are almost certainly not restricted to traumatic childhood experiences. That is, people may have compelling subjective experiences of remembering other kinds of significant childhood events that, they feel, they had not previously remembered and that powerfully contradict their prior beliefs about their childhoods. Except in cases in which people have been exposed to prolonged, multifaceted, socially powerful suggestive influences, such memories are likely to be essentially accurate (not perfect and complete, any more than other recollections are, and a small proportion essentially false, but most essentially accurate). Salaman discussed numerous anecdotal examples from literature and from her own autobiographical reminiscences of involuntary recall of long-forgotten childhood memories, saying, "Subjectively the feeling is miraculous, as miraculous as a moment of love, the first sight of a newborn healthy baby to a mother" (p. 50).[48] Of Proust's famously "recovered" childhood memories (inspired, a la the encoding specificity principle, by eating a Madeleine cookie dipped in tea as he had often done as a child), Salaman wrote:

> The echo of his tears, in his traumatic memory of demanding his mother's kiss, never ceased, but was not audible until life grew quiet, like those convent bells which are drowned in the noise of daytime, and sound out again in the silence of the evening.[49]

Salaman argued that such involuntary recollections tend to be of traumatic childhood events, but as is clear from the above example, she used the term "traumatic" in a quite broad sense that might be translated as "emotionally evocative." Indeed, many of the examples Salaman described were of strongly positive rather than negative events (e.g., "They [involuntary recollections of a particular period of her life] brought me great joy"). Thus, poignant and vivid as they may be, involuntary recollections of childhood experiences do not always qualify as RMEs as I have defined them (because the experiences are not necessarily emotionally wrenching and their content does not neces-

46. Dalenberg, C. J. (1997). The prediction of accurate recollections of trauma. In J. D. Read & D. S. Lindsay (Eds.), *Recollections of trauma: Scientific research and clinical practice* (pp. 449-453). New York: Plenum.

47. For basic research on the mechanism by which people differentiate between memories with different origins, see Johnson, M. K., Hashtroudi, S., & Lindsay, D. S. (1993). Source monitoring. *Psychological Bulletin, 114,* 3-28.

48. Salaman, E. (1976). A collection of moments. In U. Neisser (Ed.), *Memory observed* (pp. 49-63). San Francisco: W. H. Freeman.

49. *Id.* at p. 51.

sarily contradict prior beliefs about childhood). The point, however, is that autobiographical writers and introspectionist psychologists such as Salaman have often observed that adults are sometimes (especially in their later years) visited by sudden and intense involuntary recollections of emotionally charged childhood experiences. I see no reason to assume that long-forgotten experiences of CSA could not sometimes similarly be dramatically recollected.

In more systematic research, Read found that a substantial minority of adults in a community sample reported experiences of "recovering" memories that surprisingly contradicted their previous beliefs about their childhoods.[50] For example, one respondent reported having completely forgotten ever having studied piano as a child, with subsequent recovery of the memory that she had taken piano lessons for 5 years! Some reported recovered memories concerned traumatic events (including CSA), but many did not.

Lindsay, Schooler, Hyman, and Read recently collected data in a new paradigm that speaks to the issues of forgetting and re-remembering significant life events.[51] Participants in this study were recruited via newspaper advertisements seeking individuals who had kept a personal diary at some time years in the past and had not reviewed that diary in recent years. During an initial screening interview, we identified a target year for each individual. Participants were subsequently asked to read eight entries from the target year of their diary and to report, for each entry read, on three kinds of subjective experiences that might arise: "Ordinary-memory experiences," in which reading the entry reminds the person of an event that they feel they have always known and remembered (even though they might not have thought of it recently); "No-memory experiences," in which there is a surprising failure to have any memory whatsoever of a seemingly memorable event described in the diary; and "recovered-memory experiences," in which there is a surprising feeling of recovering a previously forgotten memory. We have only begun to analyze these data, but a preliminary scan of the responses reveals that most of the 19 participants reported one or more "No-memory experiences" and one or more RMEs.

In another new study, Lindsay and coworkers asked undergraduates about 28 common childhood experiences, some relatively positive (e.g., "As a child, did you ever play with a piñata?") and some relatively negative (e.g.,

---

50. Read, J. D. (1997). Memory issues in the diagnosis of unreported trauma. In J. D. Read & D. S. Lindsay (Eds.), *Recollections of trauma: Scientific evidence and clinical practice* (pp. 79-100). New York: Plenum.

51. Lindsay, D. S., Read, J. D., Schooler, J. W., & Hyman, I. E. Jr. (1998, Nov.). *Remembering, forgetting, and re-remembering significant childhood experiences.* Paper presented at the meeting of the Psychonomic Society, Dallas, TX.

"As a child, did you ever get bitten by a dog?").[52] For each event, respondents were asked whether or not they thought they had experienced the event during childhood and, if so, to characterize their memories of the event. Respondents were also asked to rate the emotional quality of the event, and to indicate whether or not they thought they would be able to remember more about the experience if they worked at it. Here again, we have only just begun to analyze these data, but it is worth noting that all respondents indicated that they thought they had experienced childhood events for which they had no specific memories.

Summary: Plausible RMEs

Much of childhood is poorly remembered in adulthood (and perhaps especially in mid-life). A variety of ordinary cognitive mechanisms may speed forgetting of negative childhood experiences. When oriented and cued appropriately, adults who have long forgotten instances of CSA may recover essentially accurate recollections of the abuse. The encoding specificity principle suggests that psychotherapies that are not unduly suggestive may sometimes create conditions that foster such RMEs (e.g., simply by orienting adults to reminisce about their childhoods, by sanctioning thinking about and feeling rare affective states that may cue memories of childhood traumas, etc.). It seems tremendously unlikely that these ordinary cognitive mechanisms can account for cases in which people who initially believed they had "normal" childhoods later "recover" memories of years of bizarre and violent abuse–for such cases, I believe that the mechanisms of illusory memories described in the preceding section provide a better explanation–but ordinary cognitive mechanisms can well account for a wide range of cases, like that of Ross Cheit, in which people report newly recovered memories of instances of less extreme (but criminal and deeply upsetting) forms of abuse.

Just as trauma-oriented psychologists such as Briere and Courtois have made increasingly clear expressions of concerns regarding highly suggestive forms of memory-recovery work, critics of memory-recovery work have made increasingly explicit acknowledgments of the existence of essentially

---

52. Lindsay, D. S., Read, J. D., Schooler, J. W., & Hyman, I. E. Jr. (1998, Nov.). *Remembering, forgetting, and re-remembering significant childhood experiences.* Paper presented at the meeting of the Psychonomic Society, Dallas, TX.

accurate RMEs.[53, 54, 55]   Freyd, founder of the False Memory Syndrome Foundation, wrote, "Some memories are true, some a mixture of fact and fiction and some are false—whether the memories are continuous or remembered after a period of being forgotten."[56]

PREVALENCE OF TRUE AND FALSE RMEs

There is little doubt about the existence of cases such as X's, in which highly suggestive influences appear inadvertently to lead people to develop illusory memories of CSA. Likewise, there is little doubt about the existence of cases such as Cheit's, in which individuals appear to experience essentially accurate RMEs. Experts disagree, however, about the relative prevalence: Trauma-oriented clinical psychologists often argue that false RMEs are rare, whereas critics of memory-recovery work often argue that accurate RMEs are rare.

We do not have solid data on the prevalence of accurate and illusory RMEs (emotionally wrenching experiences of recovering memories of extremely distressing childhood events that contradict prior beliefs), but I believe that *both* phenomena are rare in the general population. On the one hand, it is likely that most adults who experienced CSA beyond the first few years of life remember it, and that only some of those who forget ever encounter appropriate cues; thus it is likely that essentially accurate RMEs are rare. On the other hand, people are unlikely to develop illusory memories of CSA unless they are exposed to very powerful suggestive influences, and so it is likely that essentially false RMEs are also rare.

Even a tiny percentage of North Americans translates into a large number of individuals. For example, if a condition occurs in only .01% of the gener-

53. Briere, J. (1997). An integrated approach to treating adults abused as children, with specific reference to self-reported recovered memories. In J. D. Read & D. S. Lindsay (Eds.), *Recollections of trauma: Scientific research and clinical practice* (pp. 25-41). New York: Plenum.

54. Courtois, C. A. (1997). Informed clinical practice and the standard of care: Proposed guidelines for the treatment of adults who report delayed memories of childhood trauma. In J. D. Read & D. S. Lindsay (Eds.), *Recollections of trauma: Scientific research and clinical practice* (pp. 337-361). New York: Plenum.

55. See, for example, Loftus, E. F. (1993). The reality of repressed memories. *American Psychologist, 48*, 518-537. p. 524, p. 533; Loftus, E. F. (1997). Dispatch from the (un)civil memory wars. In J. D. Read & D. S. Lindsay (Eds), *Recollections of trauma: Scientific evidence and clinical practice* (pp. 171-194). New York: Plenum; Pendergrast, M. (1996). *Victims of memory: Incest accusations and shattered lives* (2nd ed.). Hinesburg, VT: Upper Access. pp. 89-94, p. 536; Underwager, R., & Wakefield, H. (1998). Recovered memories in the courtroom. In S. J. Lynn & K. M. McConkey (Eds.), *Truth in memory* (pp. 394-434). New York: Guilford Press. p. 403.

56. Freyd, P. (1997, May). Dear friends. *FMSF Newsletter, 6*(6), 1. (http://advicom.net/~fitz/fmsf/fmsf-news/0053.html)

al population (1 in 10,000), then approximately 28,000 people in the U.S. and Canada have that condition. Try making 28,000 dots on a sheet of paper. If you make one dot per second, it will take you 7.7 hours and the sheet will be a smooth, dark grey. If you think of each dot as representing a person who has gone through an emotionally devastating experience, and think of each such person being connected to a family whose members often also go through an extraordinarily painful experience, you can appreciate the point: Even if RMEs (true and false) are rare, many people are affected by them.

It is likely that the prevalence of false RMEs is declining. From the mid-1980s to mid-1990s there was a fad that led a small but nontrivial minority of the hundreds of thousands of therapists in North American to use suggestive memory-recovery techniques. I suspect that most therapists in the United States and Canada have now become more cautious in the use of such techniques (although suggestive therapies may be becoming popular in parts of Europe). Absent suggestive influences, essentially accurate RMEs would be much more common than essentially illusory ones.

TENTATIVE CRITERIA FOR WEIGHING ALLEGATIONS BASED ON RMEs

As argued above, it seems extremely likely that some RMEs are essentially accurate and that some are essentially illusory. In my view, RMEs range along a continuum of plausibility. Even in cases in which individuals initially disclaimed an abuse history, some RMEs are relatively plausible (i.e., the kind of abuse reported is relatively common and not extremely memorable and is said to have happened a small number of times and after the first few years of life; highly suggestive memory-recovery work was not involved in recovering the memories; and there is at least some evidence in support of the report). Others are relatively implausible (i.e., the reported abuse is bizarre and extreme and is said to have happened on numerous occasions over a period of many years; the reports emerged via extensive suggestive memory-recovery work; and there is little or no evidence supporting the report).

We may be able crudely to estimate the accuracy of RMEs by weighing a constellation of kinds of evidence including (a) how the RME came about (the less evidence of suggestive memory-recovery work the greater the confidence), (b) the nature and clarity of the RMEs (with more credence given to detailed, integrated recollections than to vague feelings), (c) the likelihood of the alleged events being forgotten (e.g., when and how often the abuse is said to have occurred; probability that the person would have encountered reminders, overall memorability of the alleged events, etc.), (d) the plausibility of having memories to recover (e.g., less credence given to reports of events said to have occurred before 2 years of age), and (e) the base rate of the alleged type of abuse. Future research may also enable the development of valid and reliable individual difference measures that might be useful, along with other information, in evaluating RMEs. At this point, it is not known exactly how these factors should be weighted, nor how well this approach would work. It is likely that even an optimal solution would sometimes erroneously reject essentially accurate RMEs as false and erroneously accept essentially illusory RMEs as accurate. Nonetheless, I believe that this approach has major advantages over perspectives that imply that virtually all RMEs are false or that virtually all RMEs are accurate.

SUMMARY AND CONCLUSIONS

Psychological science describes mechanisms that may account for both accurate and illusory RMEs. It is likely that both types of RMEs are relatively rare, and that the prevalence of false RMEs is declining as trauma-oriented therapists develop an appreciation for the vulnerability of memory to suggestive influences. This does not mean that RMEs are unimportant. Their effect is often devastating, and repercussions of the recovered-memories controversy will continue to resound for years as lawsuits against parents accused of abusing their children and against therapists accused of implanting false memories drag on.

In my view, searching for childhood sexual abuse in psychotherapy is akin to searching for tumors in medical therapy. Cancer tumors are real; many people suffer from them, and detecting and treating them is one of many aspects of good medical care. One would be justifiably alarmed, however, if a fad developed in medical care of using multiple sessions of powerful x-rays on a wide variety of patients on the grounds that a broad range of symptoms is caused by cancer and that tumors are difficult to detect without multiple x-ray sessions. One would be alarmed about such a fad because x-rays themselves can cause cancer. This would not lead one to view all positive x-ray results as iatrogenic cancers, because there would be little reason to question positive x-ray results by physicians who were not using high-risk approaches, and even those who were using high-risk x-ray techniques would sometimes detect real (preexisting) tumors. It would, however, inspire one to attempt to persuade those caught up in the fad that it is a bad idea.

Similarly, childhood sexual abuse is real; many adults suffer from it, and detecting and treating its aftereffects is one of many aspects of good psychotherapy. I am alarmed by therapies that involve multiple sessions of highly suggestive searches for suspected hidden memories of childhood sexual abuse, because I believe such approaches can inadvertently lead clients who were not abused to come falsely to believe that they were abused. This does not, however, lead me to dismiss all reports of memories of childhood sexual abuse that emerge in therapy as iatrogenic illusions–it just leads me to want to persuade those caught up in the memory-recovery fad that suggestive searches for trauma memories are risky and unwarranted.

The important thing–for psychology and for society more generally–is that psychologists develop a balanced and scientifically grounded approach to this topic that seeks to address accurate and illusory RMEs simultaneously.[57] Such an approach aims to maximize support for victims of CSA (including those who experience delayed recall of the abuse), minimize the risk of inadvertently fostering illusory RMEs, and improve support for people who have suffered from false RMEs.

---

57. See Lindsay, D. S., & Briere, J. (1997). The controversy regarding recovered memories of childhood sexual abuse: Pitfalls, bridges, and future directions. *Journal of Interpersonal Violence, 12,* 631-647; Read, J. D., & Lindsay, D. S. (1997). *Recollections of trauma: Scientific research and clinical practice.* New York: Plenum.

Chapter 7

RECOVERED MEMORIES IN THE COURTS

ANITA LIPTON

OVERVIEW OF REPRESSED MEMORY LITIGATION

In 1992, the False Memory Syndrome (FMS) Foundation began its Legal Survey project to track the response of courts and legislatures to the rising tide of litigation based on claims involving the alleged recovery, usually during psychotherapy, of long-repressed memories of incest and child abuse.[1] By 1998, the project had accumulated sufficient data to paint a graphic picture of the rise and fall of a troubling social problem that has torn families apart and set off a widening controversy in the mental health field. The history of this phenomenon bears the hallmarks of an early rush to judgment followed by a more measured response, as courts, legislatures, clinicians, memory researchers, and many professional organizations reacted to growing concerns about the reliability of memories recovered in therapy.

At the time the legal survey was initiated, the problem of recovered memories of sexual abuse was little understood. Initial contacts of the FMS Foundation by family members reporting false allegations of sexual abuse were doubling every three months. By March 1993, one in sixteen persons who had contacted the FMS Foundation had been in court because of such allegations. Increasingly, this drama was being played out in courtrooms. Data collected early in 1993 indicated that the number of new filings of "repressed memory" lawsuits was growing exponentially. A number of states had recently amended their statutes of limitations to allow adults to sue for childhood sexual abuse many years after the abuse allegedly occurred. Juries were being asked to consider uncorroborated testimony of recovered memories that had been allegedly repressed for years, and often decades. There was very little case law from appellate courts addressing how trial courts should handle the novel evidentiary questions posed by repressed memory claims. Defendants who felt wrongly accused had few resources with which to defend themselves in the face of this new kind of "evidence." Many juries apparently accepted the notion that a recovered repressed memory must be true.

---

1. For a discussion of the history and activities of the False Memory Syndrome Foundation, see Freyd, this volume.

The picture is very different today. At the time of this writing (January, 1999), few new repressed memory claims are being filed. A substantially larger percentage of repressed memory claims are now being dropped or dismissed rather than going to trial. Courts have increasingly found repressed memory testimony to be unreliable and therefore inadmissible. A growing number of jurisdictions are making it more difficult for plaintiffs to bring repressed memory claims, citing the suggestive circumstances under which "repressed memories" are often "recovered" and the lack of any reliable scientific basis for the notion that memories can be repressed and later recovered intact. In the last decade, clinicians, memory researchers, and professional organizations have issued guidelines recommending the avoidance of suggestive therapy techniques. In recent years, psychotherapy clients injured by repressed memory therapy have begun to file malpractice claims against their therapists and many have won substantial awards. State agencies have also become involved, bringing criminal fraud charges and delicensure proceedings against some therapists who have engaged in repressed memory therapy.

In repressed memory cases, often the only evidence that abuse occurred is the plaintiff's subjective belief that it did. Because of the length of time that has elapsed between the alleged abuse and the trial, memories may have faded and witnesses, records, and any evidence that might have been available may be lost. All aspects of the allegation–the claimed memory loss and recovery, the date of supposed "discovery" of the abuse, the causal link to a subsequent injury, and even the alleged abuse itself–rest on the complainant's subjective assertions. A growing number of courts have recognized that the problem of proof is compounded in these cases because many inferences are based on a speculative theory of memory and repression whose reliability has not yet been proven. Courts facing repressed memory claims attempt to balance the legal needs of victims of childhood sexual abuse with the duty to ensure that defendants receive a fair trial. Society's justifiable repugnance for the crime of incest should not preclude the requirement of reliable proof that the alleged act did indeed occur.

The dissonance between a repressed memory belief and the evidentiary requirements of the legal system is, at times, jarring. The following excerpt from the deposition taken from a woman who had accused several family members of childhood sexual abuse on the basis of a recovered repressed memory is illustrative.[2]

---

2. *Daughter v. Father*, U.S. Dist. Ct., Western Dist. Mich., No. 91-CI-132; included in FMSF Brief Bank #106. Names of parties omitted at family's request.

Attorney: On what facts do you rely that it occurred over and over again?
X: Because my memory occurs over and over again . . . it's just a feeling.

Attorney: You have no witnesses that would support that your feeling is accurate, do you?
X: No.

Attorney: You have no physical evidence, scars on your body or conditions on your body that a physician has certified as the result of child abuse or sexual abuse when you were a child, do you?
X: Nothing [they] have found yet.

Attorney: Okay. anything else that you can give to me and give to the court in support of your allegations that you were sexually abused by B. from 18 months to 11 years of age than you've given me already?
X: Just today's disassociation. That's all . . . just what's wrong with me today . . . [and] I'm still afraid of spiders.

Attorney: You are suing your father for damages and you are saying only that, "I assume[I was abused there] . . . You must understand that makes me most uncomfortable.
X: We don't share the same pattern of logic.

Attorney: All you are relying upon is your memory that these alleged events of sexual abuse, physical abuse-even to expand your complaint, abandonment, child neglect, poor supervision, these are based upon witnesses to them, there are no other forms of physical evidence, documents, letters, correspondence to help you support your belief system; is that correct?
X: That I know of, yes.

Attorney: That you know of. Are you searching for some of these?
X: No.

Figure 7-1. DEPOSITION EXCERPT.

This complainant dropped her lawsuit the day before the case was to be heard in court, but hundreds of other complainants have made similar arguments before juries in all 50 states.

THE FMSF LEGAL SURVEY PROJECT

The FMSF Legal Survey is a compilation of reports of litigation related to repressed memory claims.[3] The FMSF legal staff collects information from

---

3. We have used the term, "repressed memory" because it is used most often by claimants and by the courts in discussing an alleged memory loss. We recognize that the term may be misleading in that it assumes the existence of an actual event as the object of memory (see discussions by Lindsay, Schooler, and Singer, this volume). Even in court records referring to "repressed memory," there is a great deal of variation in how the term is defined and in the underlying mechanisms thought to be responsible for the memory loss.

several sources: court filings, telephone interviews and follow-up written surveys from affected individuals and attorneys, media reports, and published appellate opinions.   The staff then codes each case according to the claimant's stated reason for the delay in filing. A "repressed memory" coding represents a case in which the claimant alleged a temporary memory loss for long past event(s).[4] The FMSF legal staff attempts to identify demographic information about the parties, specifics of the claim, circumstances surrounding the "memory recovery," any evidence that supports the claim, the positions of the litigants, and the final outcome of the case. Once a case has been identified, the FMSF makes every effort to track it to its conclusion.

By July 1998, the FMSF Legal Survey contained well over 1,800 records of litigation related to repressed memory claims. This collection is unlikely to contain all relevant cases, as 119 of the repressed memory cases reported below first became known to the FMSF only when an appellate decision was issued, suggesting that the number of repressed memory lawsuits filed in this country that never reach an appellate court is probably much higher than the number of such lawsuits uncovered in the FMSF Legal Survey.

Records in the FMSF Legal Survey represent the range of legal issues surrounding repressed memory claims. They include 1174 cases (termed "delay-filed" cases throughout this report) brought in the United States in which adults claimed that sexual abuse took place many years earlier but that they were unaware either that the abuse took place or that the alleged abuse had caused their current psychological problems. In seven cases, individuals were charged with murders that allegedly took place many years ago, after persons came forward who claimed to have witnessed the murder but subsequently repressed all memory of it. Fifteen additional criminal cases were filed after an adult claimed to have recovered memories of long-past childhood sexual abuse and the adult's minor children made similar allegations against their grandparents after being questioned. The FMSF Legal Survey also contains records from 262 foreign delay-filed cases (148 of which are repressed memory claims) that were filed in eight other countries. Most of these are criminal cases.

If one excludes from the 1174 delay-filed cases those cases in which the complainant does not specifically allege a memory loss and those cases for which court records do not clarify the reason for the delay in filing, the Legal Survey contains 803 repressed memory claims that have led to litigation in the United States. This group includes 633 civil suits, 103 criminal actions,

---

4. A lawsuit is coded as a "repressed memory" claim if any of the following are true: (1) the claimant alleged a memory loss for the event, even if the court subsequently decided that the facts showed the claimant to have ongoing awareness of the events; (2) the claimant initially claimed memory loss but subsequently, under questioning, admitted ongoing knowledge of the events; or (3) the claimant alleged "repression" or "dissociation" rendered her of unsound mind.

and 67 restraining orders and the like. The data reported here are based on the subset of 736 civil and criminal cases, which will be referred to hereafter as "repressed memory" cases. A subsequent section of this chapter will consider malpractice actions brought against mental health care providers by former patients and by third parties who claim that therapeutic negligence led to the development of false memories, with resulting injury to a patient, a third party, or both.

CHARACTERISTICS OF "REPRESSED MEMORY" CLAIMS

Who Are the Claimants?

Ninety percent of the claimants are female, and most are between the ages of 25 and 45.[5] The typical claimant alleges that her father sexually abused her repeatedly beginning at an early age and continuing for much of her childhood, yet most claimants allege they had no memory of the abuse until three to five decades after it ended. Nineteen individuals filed a claim at the age of 50 or older and one did not file until age 68.

When Did the Alleged Abuse Take Place?

Of the 736 repressed memory claims, 305 specified the time span over which the sexual abuse allegedly took place. In that subgroup, over 98 percent (298/305) claimed the abuse had lasted at least 2 years, over 70 percent (216/305) claimed the abuse had lasted at least 6 years, and nearly 20 percent (58/305) claimed the abuse had lasted at least 14 years. Twenty-three claimants alleged ongoing abuse that continued after they reached adulthood. Each alleged that she had temporarily lost all memory of the abuse that occurred during her adult years.

One 44-year-old woman sued her father for sexually abusing her from the time she was one year old until she reached the age of 23, saying she had had no knowledge of the abuse over that entire period. A 42-year-old woman alleged she had repressed memories of abuse lasting from age 4 to age 39. A 35-year-old man sued his uncle for sexually abusing him from age 8 to age 30, claiming he had only discovered the molestation at the time he was standing trial for murder.[6]

Many complaints fail to indicate the dates and duration of the alleged abusive events, causing some repressed memory claims to be dismissed for lack

---

5. Because most claimants are female, I will use the female pronoun to refer to claimants unless the specific claimant cited is male.

6. *Dattoli v. Yanelli*, 911 F.Supp. 143 (D.N.J. 1995).

of specificity. Of the 340 complaints that indicated the plaintiff's age for at least some of the alleged events, over half (178/340, or 52%) of the claims alleged that severe sexual abuse took place during the first 5 years of life. Approximately 30 percent (101/340) of the accusers claimed that the recovered memories of abuse included memories from infancy to three years. These complainants relied on early childhood images as the basis of their lawsuits despite the recognized improbability of accurate memories of events from such an early age (see Lindsay, Singer this volume). Most of these claimants were in therapy at the time they recovered "memories" of abuse during their infancy. Fourteen percent (47/340) claimed they were unaware of severe, invasive abuse occurring during their teen years and young adulthood.[7]

Who Is Being Sued?

In nearly 70 percent (422/612) of all repressed memory cases (civil, criminal, and restraining orders) in which the relationship between the accuser and defendant is known, an adult child made an accusation against a parent or parents.[8] Of the 505 repressed memory cases in which the defendant was in the same family as the plaintiff, only 16 percent (83/505) involved accusations against a family member other than a parent. The remaining cases (i.e., those in which the defendant was not a family member) involved accusations against family friends, baby sitters, foster parents, big brothers and members of almost every profession that works with children, including psychologists and other therapists, teachers and school administrators, pediatricians and other physicians, and priests and religious workers. Several plaintiffs have accused as many as 45 people of having abused them (although not all accused were eventually sued), and two plaintiffs independently claimed that the entire membership of their respective local Masonic Lodge abused them as children, but that they had subsequently lost all memory of the events.

Some adult children have filed repressed memory lawsuits against parents who were in their eighties or who were terminally ill or in nursing homes. In several cases, abuse allegations were not made until a parent's will went to probate and the plaintiff sought a sizable portion of her siblings' inheritance.

---

7. Some courts have found it unreasonable to believe that a teenager would not be aware of sexual contact as it was happening. See, e.g., *Ernstes v. Warner*, 860 F. Supp. 1338, 1341 (S.D. Ind. 1994).

8. This percentage may be affected by the fact that parents may be somewhat more likely to contact the Foundation than other accused persons.

What Were the Circumstances Under Which These "Memories" of Childhood Abuse Were Developed?

Nearly 80 percent (579/736) of the complainants in both civil and criminal cases stated that their memories were recovered while they were in therapy.[9] For an additional 18% (146/736) of claims, the record does not specify whether or not the complainant was in therapy. Many complaints state that "it was not until plaintiff felt safe in therapy that the images could emerge." Fewer than 2 percent (11/736) of the complaints specifically state that the complainant was not in therapy at the time the images of long past sexual abuse developed. Many courts have discussed the possible role of certain suggestive therapy techniques in the emergence of recovered memories of abuse; some of their findings are discussed below.

Some claimants stated that the process of memory recovery began with a dream that the therapist interpreted to be an indication of hidden trauma.[10]

What Do We Know About the Therapy?

Hypnosis or sodium amytal was used in 17 percent (98/579) of the cases in which repressed memories developed during therapy. Hypnosis or sodium amytal was part of the therapy of just over 7 percent (8/103) of the alleged victims in criminal cases. If hypnosis-like techniques were counted, this figure would be even higher. In some cases, the complainant initially denied that hypnosis played a role in the memory recovery process, but subsequent information contradicted this claim. This is a point of some significance because testimony based on memories recovered under hypnosis is inadmissible in most jurisdictions.

Of those repressed memory claimants who were in therapy, approximately 18 percent (103/579) were diagnosed as having Multiple Personality Disorder (MPD).[11] Approximately 18 percent (19/103) of all claimants in criminal cases and 13 percent (84/633) of all plaintiffs in civil suits were diagnosed as having MPD. If the related diagnosis of dissociative identity disor-

---

9. Eighty percent (512/633) of the civil claimants recovered "memories" of abuse while in therapy and nearly two-thirds (67/103) of the criminal cases were based on "memories" allegedly recovered while the claimant was in therapy.

10. See, e.g., *Nuccio v. Nuccio*, 673 A.2d 1331 (Me. 1996); *State v. Walters*, 698 A.2d 1244 (N.H. 1997).

11. MPD is a highly controversial diagnosis that was made exceedingly rarely until recent years. The fact that the personalities' expression often become more severe and the number of alter "personalities" increases during therapy has led many critics to conclude that manifestations of MPD are largely products of hypnosis-like techniques and therapists' interactions with their patients. These issues are often raised in psychiatric malpractice cases related to the development of false memories.

der were included, these percentages would be higher. Hypnosis was used in the therapy of at least one-third (34/103) of the complainants who had been diagnosed with MPD.

Why Is the Source of Repressed Memories of Concern to Courts?

To date, most case law relating to hypnosis deals with its use in a forensic setting, ostensibly to enhance the memory of a witness to a crime. Hypnotically enhanced memory is inadmissible in most jurisdictions because researchers have found that hypnosis affects the character of memories and the subjects' perceptions of recollected experiences, rendering them unreliable. Hypnosis has been shown to lead to an overconfidence in and uncritical acceptance of hypnotically-generated images, a phenomenon referred to as "memory hardening." Subjects may also experience so-called "source amnesia," in which hypnotically elicited images become divorced from context so that the individual is unable to determine accurately the source of the image. These factors, some courts have concluded, may render cross-examination of posthypnotic testimony ineffective.

In jurisdictions that allow posthypnotic testimony, the party who offers it into evidence generally has the burden of demonstrating its reliability, which may be done by establishing that the hypnotic session was conducted following guidelines recommended by courts and/or professional associations to minimize the effects of suggestion.

In 1992, a 38-year-old Connecticut woman sued relatives who, she claimed, had sexually abused her some 30 years earlier. She also testified that she recalled years of "abuse and rituals" by many relatives and family friends. Although she initially testified that most of the memories "unfolded on their own" and surfaced in "bits and pieces," other court records showed that she had first reported the alleged abuse to her unlicensed therapist during a hypnotic session. Her therapist, it turned out, had only a high school diploma and no formal training in psychiatry or psychotherapy, though he did have years of experience as a stage hypnotist.

The case eventually made its way to the U.S. Second Circuit Court, which affirmed dismissal of the case.[12] The court observed that "the literature has not yet conclusively demonstrated that hypnosis is a consistently effective means to retrieve repressed memories of traumatic, past experiences accurately." The court added that the plaintiff's "far-fetched, uncorroborated" claims against other parties, including allegations that she was raped and sex-

---

12. Borawick v. Shay, 68 F.3d 597 (2d Cir. 1995), *cert. denied,* 517 U.S. 1229, 116 S.Ct. 1869 (1996).

ually abused at the age of 3 by men she believed to be Masons and drugged and forced to drink blood at a ritual involving a dead pig, "erodes our confidence in the allegations."[13] The panel also noted her hypnotist's lack of qualifications and his failure to keep records of his procedures and said that without such records a court cannot determine if the therapist was inadvertently suggestive or used suspect techniques in conducting the hypnosis. The court proposed that trial courts should consider the following (nonexclusive) factors at a pretrial evidentiary hearing before deciding whether to admit posthypnotic testimony: the aim or subject of the hypnosis session, possible suggestions from the hypnotist, whether a permanent record of the hypnosis session is available, and the existence of corroborating evidence. The burden of persuading the trial court that the balance tips in favor of admissibility should be on the party that seeks to admit the testimony, the appeals court added.

A different memory-recovery technique was used in the case of Holly Ramona, a 21-year-old woman who sued her father in 1992 for childhood sexual abuse based on recovered memories. As reported in the decision of the California court of appeals that heard the case,[14] Holly originally entered treatment for help with bulimia and depression. During the first session, her therapist told her that 60 to 80 percent of her patients had experienced abuse of some kind, including sexual abuse, and asked her whether she had been sexually abused. At that time Holly had no memories of abuse, but four months later she began to experience "flashbacks" of abuse occurring when she was 5 to 8 years old. Uncertain whether these flashbacks were true memories, she agreed to undergo a sodium amytal interview, after being assured by her therapist that a person cannot lie under the drug's influence unless trained to do so. Following the sodium amytal interview, Holly was told that she had just described sexual abuse and was again assured that she had not lied during the interview. Holly then confronted her father with her allegation that he had sexually abused her. As a result of the abuse allegations, Holly's parents were divorced and her father lost his job. Two years after the sodium amytal interview, Holly experienced new flashbacks of additional sexual abuse, including rape, that she believed her father had committed from the time she was 12 to 16 years old. It was then that Holly sued her father. Her father responded by suing Holly's therapists, saying they had caused his daughter to believe, mistakenly, that she had been molested as a child.[15]

---

13. Borawick v. Shay, 68 F.3d 597, 609 (2d Cir. 1995), *cert denied,* 517 U.S. 1229, 116 S.Ct. 1869 (1996).

14. Ramona v. Superior Court, 66 Cal. Rptr.2d 766 (Cal. App. 1997).

15. That case, Ramona v. Ramona, Super. Ct. Napa County, Cal., No. 61898, was resolved in 1994 when a jury awarded Mr. Ramona a $500,000 judgment. Holly did not appeal the jury verdict.

In 1997, a California appellate court dismissed Holly's claim against her father, holding that Holly had not met her burden of demonstrating the reliability of her postsodium amytal memories—the "memories" recovered both during and two years after the sodium amytal session. California courts had long held the results of sodium amytal interviews to be unreliable because sodium amytal, despite being called a "truth serum," does not guarantee the truthfulness of what is said; it merely lessens inhibitions and enhances a subject's willingness to talk. The court therefore held that Holly was barred from testifying because her memory was tainted by the therapeutic administration of sodium amytal.[16]

A significant number of cases, both civil and criminal, were dismissed or withdrawn when it was disclosed that the complainant had undergone hypnosis or other memory recovery techniques. In a case that is being appealed at the time of this writing, a Utah District Court judge reversed a jury verdict in favor of the plaintiff and dismissed the claim because of evidence introduced at the trial that a variety of techniques or methods were utilized to retrieve what the plaintiff came to view as "memories," including guided imagery, writing with the nondominant hand, trance-work, relaxation, communicating with metaphorical "inner children," and journal writing.[17] The judge found these techniques to be, like hypnosis, inherently unreliable for recovering memories, and there was no other evidence to corroborate the plaintiff's claims that she had been abused.

How Do the Complaints Explain the Alleged Memory Loss?

Although the majority of claimants alleging a temporary memory loss and subsequent "recovery" use the term "repression" to describe that phenomenon, some recent complaints have also spoken of "dissociation" and "traumatic" or "psychogenic amnesia."[18, 19] Regardless of the specific terminology used, documents filed in the 803 repressed memory cases (which include civil and criminal suits and restraining orders) fail to explain how years of repeated intrusive sexual abuse by a trusted individual could subsequently become lost to memory. The Maryland Court of Appeals (the state's highest court) described two possible models for the claimed memory loss:

---

16. For additional background on the Ramona case, see Johnson, M., *Spectral Evidence: The Ramona Case: Incest, Memory, and Truth on Trial in Napa Valley.* New York: Houghton Mifflin.

17. Franklin v. Stevenson, Third Judicial Dist. Ct., Salt Lake Co., Utah, No. 94-0901779PI, 1996.

18. See, e.g., Olsen v. Hooley, 865 P.2d 1345 (Utah 1993); Williford v. Bieske, 534 N.W.2d 695 (Mich. 1995), *reh. den.* 539 N.W.2d 504 (Mich. 1995); and Barrett v. Hyldburg, Superior Court, Buncombe Co., North Carolina, No. 94 CVS 793, affirmed and remanded in part, 487 S.E.2d 803 (1997).

19. See, e.g., Hearndon v. Graham, 710 So.2d 87 (Fla. App. 1998); Nuccio v. Nuccio, 673 A.2d 1331 (Me. 1996); and Guerra v. Garratt, 564 N.W.2d 121 (Mich. App. 1997).

1. The serial repression model, in which a victim of sexual assaults or other traumatic events could repress the memory of each event immediately after it occurred.

2. The collective repression model, in which a person remains aware of the events for a length of time, even over the course of multiple events, and then at some later date "represses" all the memories in a block.[20]

Either model poses a difficult problem for a court that must decide when the claimant reasonably should have known of the alleged abuse in order to decide when the statute of limitations began to run on the plaintiff's claim.

In order to toll (extend) the statute of limitations under the so-called "discovery rule," most claimants have alleged that their memory loss was involuntary and unconscious.[21] The implication is that the claimant was "blamelessly ignorant" of her cause of action until the memories were recovered into conscious memory and she was able to "discover" her cause of action or until her psychological injury manifested itself.[22] A few claimants describe the process of memory loss as a conscious one in which they actively pushed away images of abusive events.[23] Some courts, employing a case-by-case review, found a plaintiff's claim that she was prevented from timely filing by "dissociation" or "repression" to be contradicted by undisputed facts later presented to the court.[24]

The majority of claims state that it was the severity, or traumatic nature, of the alleged abuse that led to the memory loss. One early appellate court decision seemed to suggest, however, that repression might not be particularly difficult if the victim is not sufficiently traumatized or impressed with the wrongfulness of the acts.[25] The court did not draw a clear distinction between repression and forgetting, an issue that has received much attention in the years since that opinion.[26] Some claimants state that they repressed and subsequently recovered memories of the most profound abuse, while they never forgot other abusive incidents.[27] A number of complainants alleged that they continue to have flashbacks of new incidents even after filing their complaint.[28]

---

20. *Doe v. Maskell,* 679 A.2d 1087, 1088 (Md. 1996), cert. denied, 519 U.S. 1093 (1997).

21. See, e.g., Logerquist v. Danforth, 932 P.2d 281 (Ariz. App. 1996); Hehner v. Hehner, 918 S.W.2d 283 (Mo. App. 1996); and K.G. v. R.T.R., 918 S.W.2d 795 (Mo. banc 1996) (affirmed dismissal).

22. This phrase appears in *Urie v. Thompson,* 337 U.S. 163, 170 (1949).

23. See, e.g., *Lent v. Doe,* 47 Cal.Rptr.2d 389 (Cal. App. 1995); and *Guilbault v. DesRosiers,* 678 A.2d 873 (R.I. 1996).

24. See, e.g., *Hogle v. Harvey,* 1995 Ohio App. LEXIS 4351, No. 94A005 (unreported); *Casey v. Casey,* 673 N.E.2d 210 (Ohio App. 1996), cert. den. 669 N.E.2d 859 (Ohio 1996); *Moore v. Schiano,* 690 N.E.2d 597 (Ohio App. 1996), cert. den. 678 N.E.2d 1230 (1997).

25. *Petersen v. Bruen,* 792 P.2d 18 (Nev. 1990).

26. See, e.g., *Doe v. Maskell,* 679 A.2d 1087 (Md. 1996), cert denied, 519 U.S. 1093 (1997).

27. See, e.g., *Sellery v. Cressey,* 55 Cal.Rptr.2d 706 (Cal. App. 1996); *Taylor v. Taylor,* 1996 WL 490718 (N.D.Ill.); and M.E.H. v. L.H., 685 N.E.2d 335 (Ill. 1997).

28. See, e.g., Rezac v. Tolly, Supreme Ct. South Dakota, Nos. 18973/18974.

A significant number of claimants have argued that the statute of limitations should be tolled because they were under a legal disability (due to either repression, dissociation, "denial," post traumatic stress disorder (PTSD), multiple personality disorder (MPD), or psychogenic amnesia), that prevented them from managing their affairs and/or understanding their legal rights, but most courts have rejected this argument (see below).[29]

THE RISE AND FALL OF "REPRESSED MEMORY" LITIGATION

When Were Repressed Memory Claims Filed?

The epidemic of repressed memory claims emerged in the mid-1980's in a climate of national remorse for past failure to acknowledge the problem of child abuse and incest. Statistics on the prevalence of sexual abuse varied widely, with some stating that as many as one in every four women had been victimized. The political dynamics at the time led to an uncritical embracing of naive models of psychological constructs such as repression. Emotion-laden "survivor" stories became a staple of television talk shows. Popular books that oversimplified terms such as repression and dissociation and touted the curative power of unearthing memories filled shelves in the "recovery" sections of bookstores. Many newspapers and magazines contained advertisements placed by practitioners who claimed to specialize in recovering memories of abuse or treating abuse victims. Many who empathized with abuse victims were persuaded that memories of horrible abuse could be hidden away from consciousness for decades, only to come flooding back in adulthood. Consequently, in the mid-1980's half the states changed their statutes of limitations for victims of childhood abuse, making it easier for women and men who believed they had recovered memories of long-ago abuse to sue the alleged "perpetrators."

Data from the FMSF Legal Survey show that the number of new filings of repressed memory claims increased dramatically from 1989 to 1992, reached a peak during the period of 1992-1994, and declined sharply since 1994. Even if one takes into account a time lag between the filing of a claim and its identification by the FMSF survey effort, the decline in new filings appears to be significant. The filing dates of 589 repressed memory lawsuits in the U.S. are shown in the accompanying graph.

---

29. See, e.g., Lovelace v. Keohane, 831 P.2d 624 (Okla. 1992).

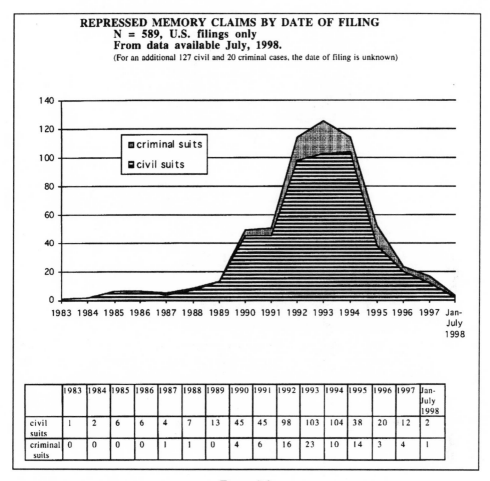

	1983	1984	1985	1986	1987	1988	1989	1990	1991	1992	1993	1994	1995	1996	1997	Jan-July 1998
civil suits	1	2	6	6	4	7	13	45	45	98	103	104	38	20	12	2
criminal suits	0	0	0	0	1	1	0	4	6	16	23	10	14	3	4	1

Figure 7-2

Regional Differences in the Number of Claims

Although repressed memory claims have been filed in every state, 72 percent (531/736) of the claims were filed in less than one-third of the states. Among the factors influencing the numbers of claims filed per state are the state's population, its statute of limitations on repressed memory claims, and the judicial actions taken in response to such claims in that state's courts. Other regional factors may be at play and constitute a topic for further research. Some of the states with the highest percentage of lawsuits per capita, such as Washington, Massachusetts, and Minnesota, are among those that passed statutes of limitations that specifically allow for delayed filing of sexual abuse claims.

REPRESSED MEMORY LAWSUITS BY STATE
N = 736, U.S. filings only
From data available July, 1998.

State	Civil Claims	Criminal Claims	Total	1990 Census Population
California	97	6	103	29.8 million
Michigan	38	8	46	9.3 million
Washington	39	5	44	4.8 million
Ohio	34	6	40	10.8 million
Illinois	32	1	33	11.4 million
Massachusetts	27	6	33	6.0 million
Texas	27	6	33	17.0 million
Pennsylvania	23	6	29	11.9 million
Minnesota	26	0	26	4.4 million
New York	22	1	23	17.9 million
Florida	15	8	23	6.4 million
New Jersey	19	3	22	1.5 million
Wisconsin	17	4	21	4.9 million
Arizona	17	3	20	3.6 million
Louisiana	18	0	18	4.2 million
Missouri	15	2	17	5.1 million
remaining states and District of Columbia	167	38	205	100 million

Figure 7-3

Statutes of Limitations: the "Discovery Rule"

By the early 1990's, approximately half the states had enacted a statute that specifically extended the time allowed for filing childhood sexual abuse claims. Washington and California, two states that were among the first to change their statute of limitations, are now among the states with the largest number of filings. Other states that also experienced a rapid increase in the number of filings after changing their statutes of limitations include: Minnesota (enacted MSA §541.073 in 1989), Wisconsin (enacted WSA §893.587 in 1989), Missouri (enacted MSA §537.046 in 1990), Illinois (enacted IRS§735.5/13-202.2 in 1991, and amended it effective Jan. 1, 1994), and New Jersey (enacted NJSA §37-1-30 in 1992).

Significant numbers of repressed memory lawsuits have also been filed in Michigan, Ohio, Pennsylvania, Texas, and New York, states that do not have statutes specifically extending the time for filing claims based on childhood abuse but that do allow a claimant to allege "delayed discovery" of assault and battery or a similar cause of action.

The statutes that extended the time for filing childhood sexual abuse lawsuits that were enacted between 1989 and 1994, which the Texas Supreme Court has called "first generation" statutes, generally allow claimants to file within 2-4 years after they discover that they have a cause of action. All but five of those statutes also contain a requirement that the plaintiff has acted with diligence or due care. Some states enacted statutes, known as statutes of repose, that extended the time for filing for only a limited period of time after the minor reached majority. In applying all of these statutes, courts have generally held that the statute of limitations begins to run when the plaintiff recovers her first memory.

Statutes, and amendments to existing statutes, enacted after 1994 and 1995 (the "second generation" statutes) are more complex and give greater weight to avoiding the danger of possibly fraudulent claims. For example, California's amendment (CCC § 340.1(d)(e), effective in 1995) to the discovery rule for childhood sexual abuse that it passed in 1986 requires that "certificates of merit" be executed by the plaintiff's attorney and a licensed mental health practitioner. The attorney must state that he or she has reviewed the facts of the case with at least one licensed mental health practitioner who is not a party to the litigation and has concluded that there is reasonable and meritorious cause to file the action. Colorado's statute (CRS 13-80-103.7), amended in 1993, requires that persons who claim psychological inability to acknowledge the abuse must prove both the disability and the occurrence of the abuse. The New Mexico statute (NMS § 37-1-30), effective July 1993, states that the claim must be corroborated by competent medical or psychological testimony. The Oklahoma statute (12 Okl. St. § 95-6), effective September 1994, requires objective, verifiable evidence both that the victim had psychologically repressed the memory of the facts upon which that claim was predicated and that the alleged sexual abuse actually occurred. According to the Texas Supreme Court, "The second generation of statutes shows that legislatures do not uniformly see simple adoption of the discovery rule in such cases as viable. Legislatures have begun to strike a more complex balance between the risk of cutting off meritorious claims and the dangers of fraudulent claims."[30] No state has enacted legislation to extend the time available to file a repressed memory claim since early in 1995.

Statutes of Limitations: The "Disability" Exception

In many states, a statute of limitations may be tolled if the claimant was unable to file earlier because of a disability or because the individual was of

---

30. S.V. v. R.V., 933 S.W.2d 1, 22 (Tex. 1996).

"unsound mind."[31] Plaintiffs in some repressed memory cases have claimed that past abuse led to psychological problems, such as memory repression, dissociation, psychogenic amnesia, depression, PTSD, or MPD, that rendered them unable to assert their legal rights. Appellate courts in 30 states have considered whether these conditions constitute the kind of legal disability that is contemplated by these statutes. Most have held that repression, per se, does not qualify as a statutory disability.

OUTCOMES OF "REPRESSED MEMORY" CASES

Outcomes of Civil Repressed Memory Cases

Civil lawsuits represent 86 percent (633/736) of all repressed memory cases filed in this country. Of the civil suits that have been resolved, approximately 13 percent (47/351) have gone to trial. Early in the history of repressed memory litigation, the outcomes were very different. In 1992, for example, 41 percent (12/29) of the civil repressed memory cases resolved that year went to trial, with almost twice as many ending in a verdict in favor of the plaintiff as ended in a verdict for the defendant.[32]

A decreasing proportion of civil repressed memory cases have gone to trial in recent years. Since the beginning of 1995, only 8 percent (14/177) of civil cases have been resolved at trial (10 in favor of plaintiffs and 4 in favor of defendants). During that same period, 70 percent (124/177) of the repressed memory lawsuits were either dropped by the complainant or dismissed by the court. Less than one-fourth were settled out of court. In some cases, the complainant subsequently retracted the allegations. Some cases were dropped after a motion was filed to restrict the admissibility of repressed memory testimony, but before the court ruled on the motion. Many cases that were filed years ago are still open. In a significant number of these cases, defense attorneys have told the FMSF, the plaintiffs have taken no action to pursue their claims in recent years.

---

31. The statutory definitions of "disability" and "unsound mind" vary from state to state but usually require an individual to demonstrate that he was unable to manage his daily affairs and/or assert his legal rights.

32. In an early repressed memory trial that was reported in a series of articles by S. Efron published in the Los Angeles Times between March 22 and April 23, 1991, two adult daughters, ages 48 and 35, had sued their mother for $7 million, claiming a childhood history of rape, incest, torture, druggings, ritual murders, cannibalism, and child prostitution. After hearing 13 days of testimony in which no physical evidence was offered, the jury was unable to agree on whether the abuse had actually occurred. They found the elderly mother negligent but declined to award the daughters any damages.

OUTCOMES OF CIVIL REPRESSED MEMORY LAWSUITS BY YEAR
N = 351. U.S. filings only.
Data available July, 1998.
(For an additional 282 cases, either the status is still pending.
or the outcome or date of resolution is unknown.)

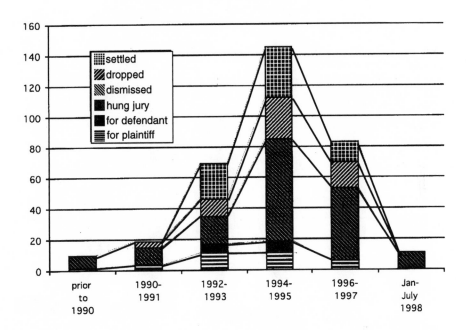

	for plaintiff	for defendant	hung jury	dismissed by court	dropped by plaintiff	settled out of court
prior to 1990	1	0	0	9	0	0
1990-1991	3	1	0	11	4	0
1992-1993	11	6	0	18	11	23
1994-1995	11	7	1	66	27	47
1996-1997	6	0	0	47	17	13
Jan-July 1998	0	0	0	11	0	0

Figure 7-4

Outcomes of Criminal "Repressed Memory" Cases

The FMSF Legal Survey contains records of 103 repressed memory criminal cases that were filed in 25 states. As is true of the civil repressed memory lawsuits, most criminal charges based on "recovered memories" were filed during 1992 and 1993. Overall, trends in outcomes of criminal cases are similar to those seen in the civil cases. The majority of criminal repressed memory cases on record were resolved during 1992-1994. Prior to 1994, the majority of cases went to trial; very few cases were dismissed. This tendency changed abruptly in mid-1994, after which over half of such criminal

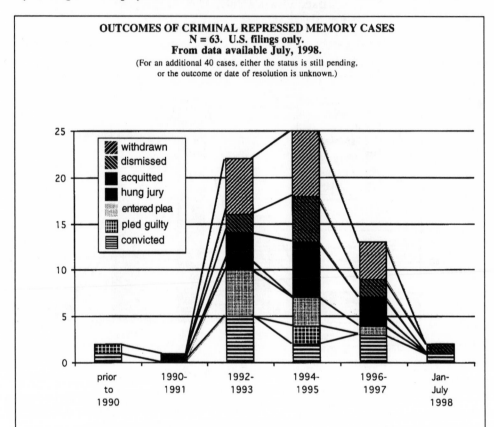

	convicted	pled guilty	entered plea to misde-meanor charge	hung jury	acquitted	dismissed	withdrawn
prior to 1990	1	1***	0	0	0	0	0
1990-1991	0	0	0	0	1	0	0
1992-1993	5	0	5	1	3	2*	6*,*
1994-1995	2**	2	3	0	6	6	6*
1996-1997	3**	0	1	1	2	2	4
Jan-July 1998	1****	0	0	0	0	1	0
Total:	12	1	9	2	12	11	16

*Complainant retracted the claims.

**One of these convictions was overturned on appeal and a new trial ordered.

***The defendant, Paul Ingram, in this widely publicized case pled guilty after he underwent what many have described as suggestive questioning. Ingram is still incarcerated and his efforts to reverse his plea have been turned down. This case is discussed below.

****State of Texas v. Kos, Criminal Dist. Ct. #1, Dallas Co., Tex., No. F-97-3222-32, April 1, 1998. Former priest found guilty of 7 counts of aggravated sexual assault of 4 former altar boys. Some accusers claimed alcohol and drugs given by the defendant hurt their memories; others claimed they "dissociated" from the most injurious of the alleged abuse while it was occurring.

Figure 7-5

charges were either withdrawn by the state or dismissed by the court, either on the merits or because the charges were filed after the statute of limitations had expired.

FMSF records indicate that 6 criminal repressed memory cases went to trial in the United States in 1993. Of those, 5 ended in a conviction and 1 ended in a hung jury. There were no acquittals. A few years later, during the two-year period, 1995-1996, 7 criminal cases went to trial. Two defendants were convicted and the remaining five were acquitted. The proportion of criminal cases that were withdrawn or dismissed increased significantly.

In a 1989 criminal case, the defendant, Paul Ingram, received a 20-year prison sentence after he pled guilty to the sexual and ritual abuse of two of his daughters.[33] The sisters asserted that years earlier they had been repeatedly raped and that at least 25 human babies, some born to them, had been sacrificed in rituals in the Ingram's back yard. Police dug up the Ingram's yard, but failed to locate the burial grounds for the alleged ritual sacrifices. Medical examination of the daughters failed to yield any evidence of sexual activity or of childbearing in either one. Yet Paul Ingram, the father of four children, a deputy sheriff, and a member of a born-again Pentecostal church, agreed that if his daughters said he had done these things, it must be true. Dr. Richard Ofshe, a social psychologist, interviewed Mr. Ingram at length and was able to show how he had been persuaded, by the use of long interrogations using visualization exercises and suggestion, to accept that he must have done the things he couldn't remember doing.[34] Dr. Ofshe performed an experiment using the same visualization techniques and got Mr. Ingram to confess to an incident that even the accusing daughters agreed had never happened. Mr. Ingram has since tried without success to withdraw his guilty plea and remains in prison.

Sentences in criminal repressed memory cases have ranged from 2 life terms plus 25 years, following a 1993 Florida conviction, to one year of house arrest on an assault and battery charge, in a 1993 Maryland case (after the other sexual abuse charges were dropped when a medical exam showed one of the claimants to be a virgin).

Because the burden of proof in a criminal case is higher than in a civil case (beyond a reasonable doubt, as opposed to a preponderance of the evidence), and because a criminal defendant who is found guilty may face many years in prison, one might expect the state to evaluate a claim carefully before bringing an indictment. In a significant number of criminal repressed memory cases, however, the state proceeded against the defendant only to

---

33. State of Washington v. Ingram, No. 88-100752-1, Superior Ct., Olympia, Washington. The case became the subject of a magazine article: Wright, R. (1993, May 17, May 24). "Remembering Satan." *New Yorker*, Part I, May 17, 1993, pp. 60-81, Part II, May 24, 1993, pp. 54-76.

34. Ofshe, R.J. (1992), "Inadvertent hypnosis during interrogation: False confession due to dissociative state," *International Journal of Clinical and Experimental Hypnosis*, XL:3:125-156.

discover later that there was evidence that clearly contradicted the claim,[35] or that the allegations were developed under hypnosis or other suggestive circumstances.[36] Several cases were withdrawn after the complainant's therapy records were reviewed or following the granting of a motion for an independent psychological evaluation of the complainant. Some criminal charges were withdrawn when the complainant retracted her claims.[37]

Criminal charges in a New Hampshire case were withdrawn after that state's Supreme Court ruled that repressed memory testimony is insufficiently reliable to be admitted at trial.[38]

Murder Charges Based on Repressed Memory Claims

Murder charges have been brought in a number of cases where an individual came forward claiming to have only recently recovered memories of witnessing a murder years earlier. A review of these cases demonstrates that while the "witness" may have explained his delay in coming forward as due to repression, the facts often suggested other compelling reasons why the individual may not have reported the alleged crime earlier. In one case, for example, the witness testified that he had repressed memories of what he had witnessed but also stated he did not come forward at the time because he was afraid the police might blame him for the murder because he was often in trouble with the law.[39]

In several murder cases, the defense presented evidence that the witness who claimed that he had recovered repressed memories had been hypnotized shortly before coming forward. In jurisdictions that prohibit the use of posthypnotic testimony, this may result in withdrawal or dismissal of the murder charges.[40]

George Franklin, whose case was heavily publicized, spent almost 7 years in prison for the murder of his daughter's childhood friend before his conviction was overturned in 1995.[41] Franklin's daughter, Eileen Franklin-Lipsker, had testified against him at trial, drawing on supposedly recovered repressed memories of the day of the killing 20 years earlier. Many of the details she claimed to have witnessed had been published in the media years earlier, but Franklin's lawyers had not been permitted to introduce that fact into evidence at the trial. The exclusion of this evidence and the lack of any

---

35. See, e.g., State of Ohio v. Castor, No. 95CR00205, Portage Co., Ohio.

36. See, e.g., State of Nevada v. Dorsey, No. 31163, Ninth Judicial District Ct., Douglas Co., Nevada, 1995.

37. See, e.g., Commonwealth of Pennsylvania v. Althaus, No. CC9115657/CC9115654, Ct. of Common Pleas, Allegheny Co., Pa., 1992.

38. State v. Hungerford, 697 A.2d 916 (N.H. 1997). See also State v. Walters, 698 A.2d 1244 (N.H. 1997).

39. Commonwealth v. Crawford, 682 A.2d 323 (Pa. Super. 1996), *rev'd,* 718 A.2d 768 (Pa. 1998).

40. See, e.g., State of Illinois v. Stegman, Circuit Ct., Massac Co., Illinois, No. 93-CF-82.

41. Franklin v. Duncan, 884 F.Supp. 1435 (N.D. Cal. 1995), *aff'd,* 70 F.3d 75 (9th Cir. 1995).

physical evidence implicating Franklin in the murder were among the grounds for reversal of Franklin's conviction. A year after Franklin's conviction was overturned, as prosecutors planned to retry him, it was disclosed that Eileen had been hypnotized by a therapist before the first trial. Posthypnotic testimony is barred in California because it is seen as unreliable.[42] In July 1996, the prosecutors announced that they would not retry Franklin.

George Franklin has sued the county prosecutors and the state's experts associated with his murder trial for wrongful prosecution and violation of his civil rights. Franklin claims that sheriff's investigators and state prosecutors conspired to suppress the fact that his daughter underwent hypnosis before she recovered the memory of her playmate's murder 20 years earlier. In 1998, a U.S. District Court refused to dismiss the wrongful prosecution charges and agreed that certain of the state agents' actions are not protected by absolute immunity.[43] One of the issues that will be addressed at the trial of this case is whether the state has any responsibility in such cases to determine whether the complainant underwent hypnosis, and if so, to inform the court.

APPELLATE REVIEW OF REPRESSED MEMORY CLAIMS

When Did Delay-filed Claims Reach the Appellate Courts?

The Washington State Supreme Court was the first state supreme court to consider a repressed memory claim, in *Tyson v. Tyson*, in 1986. Most of the troublesome evidentiary issues presented in *Tyson* continue to lie at the heart of repressed memory litigation. Indeed, courts continue to cite *Tyson* today, despite the fact that the decision was superseded by a later-enacted Washington statute (RCW § 4.16.340, effective 1988).

The Washington Supreme Court expressed concern about the length of time that had elapsed since the alleged abusive events and declined to apply the discovery rule in the absence of objective evidence that the alleged abuse had in fact occurred. In other categories of cases where the discovery rule is applied, the incident that gave rise to the litigation (for example, that a sponge was left inside a patient who underwent surgery, or that an individual was exposed to a toxin) can be objectively verified. The court's task in

---

42. In 1990, Eileen also told investigators that she remembered her father committing three more murders. Two of the murders could not be linked to any unsolved crime and DNA tests and other records proved that Franklin could not have committed the third.

43. Franklin v. Terr, 1998 WL 230983 (N.D.Cal. 1998).

those cases is to determine whether there is evidence that the incident in fact *caused* the subsequent injury. In repressed memory cases, however, as the *Tyson* court pointed out, there is usually no means of independently verifying the plaintiff's allegations, and proof of the event, the injury, and the discovery of the event and the injury all rest on the complainant's subjective statements.

The *Tyson* court noted that there was no proof that the memory recovery process is reliable; indeed, there were studies that showed the opposite is true. The court said the testimony of treating psychologists or psychiatrists would not alter the subjectivity of plaintiff's claim and warned that there is a great potential for spurious claims in repressed memory cases and an unreasonably low probability of determining the truth. Even today, after years of intense debate, numerous studies, and hundreds of lawsuits, these same problems remain. For these reasons, a significant number of appellate courts have concluded either that the statute of limitations cannot be extended for such claims or that testimony based on recovered repressed memory is inadmissible.

As noted above, new filings of repressed memory claims peaked during 1993-1994. After a 2-3 year delay, many of those lawsuits began to reach the appellate courts. By October of 1998, the FMSF Legal Survey had identified 305 delay-filed cases that reached the appellate courts since the 1986 *Tyson* decision. Over half of the appellate decisions in these cases were rendered in the three-year period from mid-1995 to mid-1998.

How Have Appellate Courts Decided "Delay-filed" Claims?

Most appellate courts have affirmed trial court decisions to dismiss delay-filed cases on motions for summary judgment based on the statute of limitations issue even though the party who moves for summary judgment has a heavy burden of proof: he must convince the court that there is no genuine issue of material fact to be decided. In deciding this question, the court is required to draw all reasonable inferences in favor of the party opposing the motion. Over two-thirds (102/145) of those dismissals were made after an appellate court determined that the facts of the particular case before it would not justify extending the statute of limitations. Approximately half of the remaining cases were remanded back to the trial court with instruction to determine, using objective standards, the date of discovery or the status of plaintiff's mental state before issuing a new decision on the summary judgment motion.[44, 45]

Figures 7-7 and 7-8 show that most appellate courts that considered a

---

44. Farris v. Compton, 652 A.2d 49 (D.C. 1994); Clay v. Kuhl, 696 N.E.2d 1245 (Ill. App. 1998), *cert. den.* 705 N.E.2d 435 (1998); Sheehan v. Sheehan, 901 S.W.2d 57 (Mo. 1995); Peterson v. Huso, 552 N.W.2d 83 (N.D. 1996).

45. Jones v. Jones, 576 A.2d 316 (N.J. Super. A.D.), *cert. denied,* 585 A.2d 412 (N.J. Super. 1990); Dattoli v. Yannelli, 911 F.Supp. 143 (D.N.J. 1995), applying New Jersey law; Anonymous v. Anonymous, 154 Misc.2d 46, 584 N.Y.S.2d 713 (N.Y. Sup. Ct. 1992).

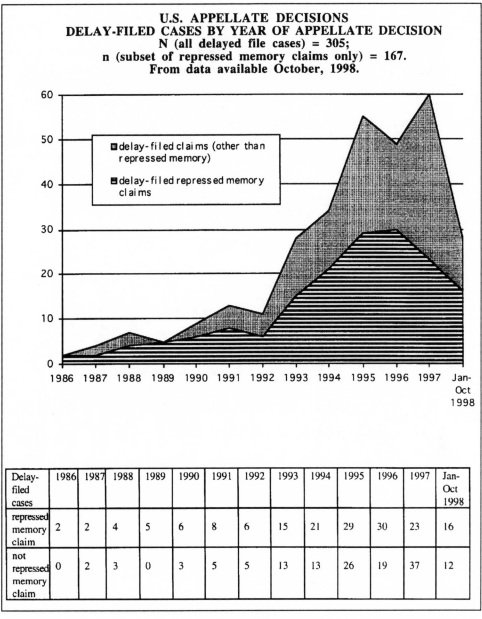

U.S. APPELLATE DECISIONS
DELAY-FILED CASES BY YEAR OF APPELLATE DECISION
N (all delayed file cases) = 305;
n (subset of repressed memory claims only) = 167.
From data available October, 1998.

Delay-filed cases	1986	1987	1988	1989	1990	1991	1992	1993	1994	1995	1996	1997	Jan-Oct 1998
repressed memory claim	2	2	4	5	6	8	6	15	21	29	30	23	16
not repressed memory claim	0	2	3	0	3	5	5	13	13	26	19	37	12

Figure 7-6

statute of limitations issue in either a delay-filed or a repressed memory case either affirmed the trial court's dismissal of the claim or reversed a trial court ruling that had denied a motion to dismiss or a motion for summary judgment. For delay-filed cases, the percentage is over 70 percent (171/242) and for the subset of repressed memory cases the percentage is similar.

Appellate rulings on questions other than the application of a statute of limitations have recently increased in number. Among the issues that have been considered are the reliability of the proposed repressed memory testimony, the exclusion of posthypnotic testimony, a defendant's right to access to the plaintiff's psychotherapy records, the liability of insurance companies for these claims, and the liability of agencies or individuals that employed or supervised the person accused of committing the abuse (for example, a diocese's liability, under the principle of respondeat superior, for a priest found

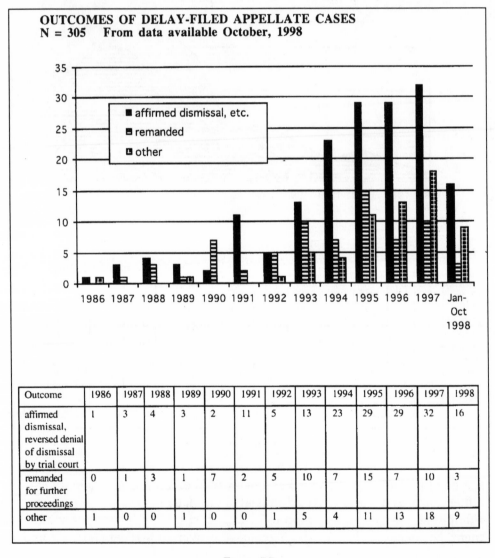

OUTCOMES OF DELAY-FILED APPELLATE CASES
N = 305   From data available October, 1998

Outcome	1986	1987	1988	1989	1990	1991	1992	1993	1994	1995	1996	1997	1998
affirmed dismissal, reversed denial of dismissal by trial court	1	3	4	3	2	11	5	13	23	29	29	32	16
remanded for further proceedings	0	1	3	1	7	2	5	10	7	15	7	10	3
other	1	0	0	1	0	0	1	5	4	11	13	18	9

Figure 7-7

to have committed abuse).

Application of the Discovery Rule

The issue that most frequently faces appellate courts in repressed memory cases is whether to apply the discovery rule. Nearly 70 percent (96/140) of appellate courts that were asked to decide that question either affirmed dis-

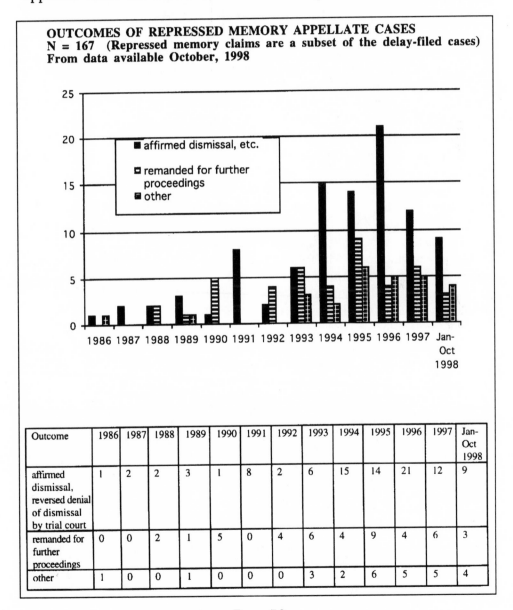

OUTCOMES OF REPRESSED MEMORY APPELLATE CASES
N = 167 (Repressed memory claims are a subset of the delay-filed cases)
From data available October, 1998

Outcome	1986	1987	1988	1989	1990	1991	1992	1993	1994	1995	1996	1997	Jan-Oct 1998
affirmed dismissal, reversed denial of dismissal by trial court	1	2	2	3	1	8	2	6	15	14	21	12	9
remanded for further proceedings	0	0	2	1	5	0	4	6	4	9	4	6	3
other	1	0	0	1	0	0	0	3	2	6	5	5	4

Figure 7-8

missal or reversed a lower court ruling that denied a motion for summary judgment or for dismissal of the case.

In nine jurisdictions, the highest court to consider the question of whether to apply the discovery rule to repressed memory claims has refused to do so. The courts that rendered these decisions include the state supreme courts of Maryland, Michigan, Minnesota, Pennsylvania, South Dakota, West Virginia and Wisconsin, and intermediate appellate courts in Florida and New York, two states whose supreme courts have not yet ruled on the issue.[46, 47]

The Maryland Court of Appeals (the state's highest court) noted, in *Doe v. Maskell*, that "[T]he studies purporting to validate repression theory are justly criticized as unscientific, unrepresentative and biased."[48] The Court determined, based on expert testimony presented at a lengthy evidentiary hearing before the trial court, that science had not progressed to the point that "repression" could be distinguished from simple "forgetting," and that the two should therefore be treated the same under the law, i.e., neither should activate the discovery rule.[49]

In seven other jurisdictions, the highest court to consider the question declined to apply the discovery rule to the specific repressed memory allegations presented and declined to either adopt or reject application of the discovery rule to repressed memory claims in general.[50] In 1997, the Supreme Court of Maine declined to adopt a judicially crafted discovery rule in repressed memory cases but did not close the door to a future reexamination of the question.[51] The Oklahoma Supreme Court held in 1992 that the discovery rule did not apply to the specific repressed memory claim before it and declined to formulate any specific rule governing the application (or nonapplication) of the discovery rule to sexual abuse cases.[52] Soon after, the Oklahoma legislature enacted a statute mandating that actions for child sexual abuse be supported by objective, verifiable evidence of both the abuse and the suppression of memory of abuse (12 Okla. St. § 95-6, effective

---

46. See Doe v. Maskell, 679 A.2d 1087 (Md. 1996), *cert denied* 519 U.S. 1093 (1997); Lemmerman v. Fealk, 534 N.W.2d 695 (Mich. 1995); Blackowiak v. Kemp, 546 N.W.2d 1 (Minn. 1996); Dalrymple v. Brown, 1997 WL 499945 (Pa. 1997); Shippen v. Parrott, 506 N.W.2d 82 (S.D. 1993); Albright v. White, 503 S.E.2d 860 (W.Va. 1998); Doe v. Archdiocese, 565 N.W.2d 94 (Wis. 1997).

47. See Lindabury v. Lindabury, 552 So.2d 1117 (Fla. App. 1989), *cert. den.* 560 So.2d 233 (1990); Burpee v. Burpee, 578 N.Y.S.2d 359 (N.Y. Sup. Ct. 1991).

48. Doe v. Maskell, 679 A.2d 1087, 1091 (Md. 1996), *cert. denied,* 519 U.S. 1093 (1997); citing Pope, H.G. and Hudson, J.I. (1995). "Can memories of childhood sexual abuse be repressed?" Psychological Medicine 25, 121-126.

49. Doe v. Maskell, 679 A.2d 1087, 1092 (Md. 1996), *cert denied* 519 U.S. 1093 (1997).

50. See M.E.H. v. L.H., 685 N.E.2d 335 (Ill. 1997); Wolford v. Mollett, 1995 WL 258258 (Ky.App.), unpublished opinion; Doe v. Roman Catholic Church, 656 So.2d 5 (La.App.) *cert. denied,* 662 So.2d 478 (La. 1995); Doe v. R.D., 417 S.E.2d 541 (S.C. 1992); Hunter v. Brown, 1996 WL 57944 (Tenn.App. 1996), aff'd, 955 S.W.2d 49 (Tenn. 1997); Dovey v. Sorrow, 1993 WL 41165 (Tenn. App.); Roe v. Doe, 28 F.3d 404, 407 (4th Cir. 1994).

51. Harkness v. Fitzgerald, 701 A.2d 370 (Me. 1997).

52. Lovelace v. Keohane, 831 P.2d 624 (Okla. 1992).

September 1994).

Some courts have held that if a plaintiff's cause of action was time-barred before a new statute of limitations was passed that would have allowed the action to be brought, the new statute of limitations will not be applied retroactively to revive the plaintiff's claim.[53] Several courts have held that once the statute of limitations starts to run, no later-commencing disability will cause it to stop running.[54]

Repressed memory claims present special challenges when a court must determine the date on which plaintiff discovered the abuse. Some plaintiffs describe the process of discovery as lasting several months, or even years. Some have testified that they feel additional abusive acts must have happened even though they cannot remember them and cannot name them in their complaint. Several have testified that new images of abuse continued to emerge after depositions were taken, or even during the trial. A number of courts have rejected the argument that the limitations period begins anew with each emerging memory. The Iowa Supreme Court said, in *Woodroffe v. Hasenclever*, 540 N.W.2d 45, 47 (Iowa 1995), that to allow such a "rolling statute of limitations" would, in effect, eliminate the statute of limitations altogether.

In general, courts will apply the discovery rule where there is objective proof of both the event and the injury alleged.[55] In repressed memory cases, however, such proof is often lacking. Many courts have questioned whether expert testimony can overcome the subjective nature of a repressed memory claim or create a question of fact for a jury to hear.[56, 57] A number of courts, including the 4th Circuit Court of Appeals, have cautioned that application of the objective person standard is especially important where the potential for serious harm is great. As one Justice noted:

> [a]llowing such lawsuits to proceed absent any evidence other than the alleged victim's testimony based wholly upon newly recovered memories - the reliability of which is yet to be proven - can, in light of the stigma associated with even the accusation that an adult has sexually abused a child, be disastrous."
> (*Roe v. Doe*, 28 F.3d 404, 409 (4th Cir. 1994), Hall, J., concurring.)

---

53. Boyce v.Cluett, 672 So.2d 858 (Fla. App. 1996); M.E.H. v. L.H., 669 N.E.2d 1228 (Ill.App. 1996), aff'd 685 N.E.2d 335 (Ill. 1997); Frideres v. Schiltz, 540 N.W.2d 261 (Iowa 1995); Sarafolean v. Kauffman, 547 N.W.2d 417 (Minn. App. 1996), review denied (Minn. July 10, 1996); Rezac v. Tolly, South Dakota Supreme Ct., Nos. 18973/18974; Roark v. Crabtree, 893 P.2d 1058 (Utah 1995).

54. See, e.g., Swackhammer v. Widnall, 119 F.3d 7 (9th Cir. 1997), unpublished.

55. See Hunter v. Brown, 1996 WL 57944 (Tenn.App.), *aff'd,* 955 S.W.2d 49 (Tenn. 1997); S.V. v. R.V., 933 S.W.2d 1 (Tex. 1996); Pritzlaff v. Archdiocese of Milwaukee, 533 N.W.2d 780 (Wis. 1995), *cert. den,* 516 U.S. 1116 (1996).

56. See, e.g., Anonymous v. Anonymous, 584 N.Y.S.2d 713 (N.Y. Sup. Ct. 1992); and Moore v. Schiano, 690 N.E.2d 597 (Ohio App. 1996), cert. den. 678 N.E.2d 1230 (Ohio 1997).

57. See, e.g., Johnson v. Johnson, 766 F.Supp. 662 (N.D.Ill. 1991); J.M. v. Merkl, 1998 WL 100598 (Minn. App.), unpublished.

The majority of jurisdictions have applied an objective reasonable person standard to the discovery question.[58] To do otherwise, most courts agree, would be contrary to public policy and would undermine the protections intended by the statute of limitations. Some courts have also recognized the potential for fraudulent claims in these cases.[59] Several courts have commented on the hazards of allowing the emotional content of the allegations to influence a decision on the statute of limitations rather than relying on sound judicial policy.[60]

Recent appellate decisions in Arizona and California, in which the courts applied the discovery rule to the date plaintiff said she discovered the causal connection between the alleged abuse and the resulting psychological injury, represent exceptions to the objective approach.[61] Despite these appellate rulings, trial courts in both states have declared repressed memory testimony to be unreliable and therefore inadmissible based on their findings at an evidentiary hearing.[62]

A growing number of courts have concluded that the potential unreliability of some recovered memories requires courts to employ reasonable safeguards to ensure the proper use of such memories.[63] The Texas Supreme Court ruled that in order to apply the discovery rule, the wrongful event and injury must be objectively verifiable. After reviewing both the case law applying the discovery rule and the scientific literature on memory and repression, the Court concluded that the requirement of objective verification could not be satisfied by expert testimony on a subject on which there

58. See, e.g, Lemmerman v. Fealk, 534 N.W.2d 695, 702 (Mich. 1995); Blackowiak v. Kemp, 546 N.W.2d 1, 3 (Minn. 1996); W.J.L. v. Bugge, 573 N.W.2d 677 (Minn. 1998); K.B. v. Evangelical Lutheran Church in America, 538 N.W.2d 152, 157-58 (Minn. App. 1995); Lovelace v. Keohane, 831 P.2d 624, 630 (Okla. 1992); Dalrymple v. Brown, 701 A.2d 164, 170 (Pa. 1997); Baily v. Lewis, 763 F. Supp. 802 (E.D.Pa. 1991), *aff'd*, 950 F.2d 721 (3d Cir. 1991); Ernstes v. Warner, 860 F.Supp. 1338, 1341 (S.D. Ind. 1994); Tyson v. Tyson, 727 P.2d 226 (Wash. 1986); John BBB Doe v. Archdiocese of Milwaukee, 565 N.W.2d 94 (Wis. 1997); Pritzlaff v. Archdiocese of Milwaukee, 533 N.W.2d 780 (Wis. 1995), *cert. den.* 516 U.S. 1116 (1996).

59. See, e.g., Pritzlaff v. Archdiocese of Milwaukee, 533 N.W.2d 780, 788 (Wis. 1995), *cert. den.* 116 S.Ct. 920 (U.S. 1996).

60. See, e.g., Baily v. Lewis, 763 F.Supp. 802, 803 (E.D. Pa. 1991); Burpee v. Burpee, 152 Misc.2d 466, 578 N.Y.S.2d 359 (N.Y. Sup. Ct. 1991).

61. See, e.g., Doe v. Roe, 955 P.2d 951 (Ariz. 1998); Sellery v. Cressey, 55 Cal.Rptr.2d 706 (Cal.App. 1996); Lent v. Doe, 47 Cal.Rptr.2d 389 (Cal.App. 1995). For cases that refused to take this approach, see Marsha V. v. Gardner, 281 Cal.Rptr. 473, 477 (Cal.Ct.App. 1991); Schwestka v. Hocevar, 1994 WL 224390 (N.D.Cal.).

62. See, e.g., Engstrom v. Engstrom, Superior Ct., Los Angeles Co., Calif., No. VC016157, Oct. 11, 1995, *aff'd* Engstrom v. Engstrom, No. B098146 (2nd App.Dist. Cal., June 18, 1997) unpublished; Logerquist v. Danforth, Superior Ct., Maricopa Co., Arizona, No. CV92-16309, June 11, 1998, following Logerquist v. Danforth, 932 P.2d 281 (Ariz.App. 1996).

63. See, e.g., Peterson v. Huso, 552 N.W.2d 83 (N.D. 1996); Petersen v. Bruen, 792 P.2d 18 (Nev. 1990); Olsen v. Hooley, 865 P.2d 1345 (Utah 1993); Fager v. Hundt, 610 N.E.2d 246 (Ind. 1993); *Clay v. Kuhl*, 704 N.E.2d 875 (Ill.App. 1998), cert. den. 705 N.E.2d 435 (1998); K.B. v. Evangelical Lutheran Church in America, 538 N.W.2d 152 (Minn. App. 1995); U.S. v. Bighead, 128 F.3d 1329 (9th Cir. 1997).

is no settled scientific view.[64]

The Utah Supreme Court placed the the burden of proving repression on the plaintiff because it was concerned about both the reliability of memory in general for events that occurred long ago and the difficulty of defending against claims of revived memories of sexual abuse.[65]

The Rhode Island Supreme Court held that a court must determine the reliability of the repressed memory theory before extending the statute of limitations.[66] If the trial court finds that the theory of repression is scientifically valid, it must then determine whether the evidence shows that plaintiff actually repressed the memory or was of unsound mind during the period the memory was repressed. Soon after this ruling, the Rhode Island Supreme Court overturned a criminal conviction based on recovered repressed memories of sexual abuse, holding that the trial court had committed reversible error in failing to hold a preliminary hearing to determine whether the accuser's flashbacks of abuse were reliable.[67] The Court was not convinced that cross-examination can effectively expose any unreliable elements or assumptions of expert testimony and remarked that in such cases ". . . the expert's conclusions are as impenetrable as they are unverifiable."[68]

The Reliability of "Repressed Memory" Testimony

A growing number of courts have held, after reviewing the available evidence, that the theory of "repression" is not yet generally accepted and that there is no reliable method at present of determining the accuracy of a repressed memory claim. Many of these courts have noted the lack of consensus and scientific support for the theory of repressed memory, even in recent peer reviewed articles on the subject.[69]

Trends in this area of the law have paralleled a general trend towards increasing reliance on scientific expert testimony in deciding certain questions of liability. (See Introduction to this volume by Sheila Taub, J.D.) A growing number of courts have held pretrial hearings to determine the admissibility of testimony of either expert or lay witnesses on the phenome-

---

64. S.V. v. R.V., 933 S.W.2d 1 (Tex. 1996).

65. Olsen v. Hooley, 865 P.2d 1345 (Utah 1993).

66. Kelly v. Marcantonio, 678 A.2d 873 (R.I. 1996).

67. State v. Quattrocchi, 681 A.2d 879 (R.I. 1996).

68. Id at 882.

69. See, e.g., State v. Hungerford, 697 A.2d 916 (N.H. 1997); Clay v. Kuhl, 696 N.E.2d 1245 (Ill.App. 1998), *cert. den,* 705 N.E.2d 435 (1998); Doe v. Maskell, 679 A.2d 1087 (Md. 1996), *cert. denied,* 519 U.S. 1093 (1997); Lemmerman v. Fealk, 534 N.W.2d 695 (Mich. 1995); Ault v. Jasko, 70 Ohio St. 3d 114, 637 N.E.2d 870, 875-76 (Ohio 1994); Dalrymple v. Brown, 701 A.2d 164 (Pa. 1997); Commonwealth v. Crawford, 682 A.2d 323 (Pa. Super. 1996); Kelly v. Marcantonio, 678 A.2d 873 (R.I. 1996); Hunter v. Brown, 1996 WL 57944 (Tenn.App.); S.V. v. R.V., 933 S.W.2d 1, 17-18 (Tex. 1996); John BBB Doe v. Archdiocese of Milwaukee, 565 N.W.2d 94 (Wis. 1997).

non of repression. Of the ten trial courts to consider this question to date, all but three concluded that the repressed memory testimony in question had not been demonstrated to be reliable and was therefore inadmissible.[70] One of the three rulings that admitted repressed memory testimony was overturned by the New Hampshire Supreme Court, which held that the proponent of testimony comprised of recovered memories must demonstrate that the testimony is reliable and that the trial court had improperly shifted the burden of proof to the party opposing its admissibility.[71] A second case, *Isely v. Capuchin Province,* 877 F.Supp. 1055 (E.D. Mich. 1995), which considered motions to restrict repressed memory testimony after the trial had begun, is generally believed to have applied the scientific standard of admissibility incorrectly.[72] The third ruling, *Shahzade v. Gregory,* 923 F.Supp. 286 (D.Mass. 1996), overly restricted the "relevant scientific community" to include only those therapists who specialize in trauma, ignoring memory researchers and professional organizations that have contributed to the scientific debate over the validity of recovered memories.

A California Court of Appeal upheld a trial court's ruling that precluded the plaintiff from testifying to any recovered repressed memories, saying that the California standard for admissibility of scientific evidence had not been met.[73]

In 1997, the New Hampshire Supreme Court, after carefully analyzing the underlying science, held that recovered repressed memories had not yet been established as sufficiently reliable to be admissible.[74] The Court affirmed a Superior Court ruling that followed a two-week pretrial admissibility hearing during which the trial court heard testimony from seven professionals and the two complainants. Over the State's objection, Superior Court Justice J. Groff held that the prosecution would bear the burden of demonstrating that the phenomenon of memory repression and recovery are reliable and have gained general acceptance in the psychological communi-

---

70. Repressed memory testimony was ruled inadmissible in: Barrett v. Hyldburg, Superior Ct., Buncombe Co., NC, No. 94-CVS-793, ruling dated October 20, 1998 following Barrett v. Hyldburg, 487 S.E.2d 803 (N.C. 1997); Carlson v. Humenansky, 2nd Dist., Ramsey Co., Minn., No. CX-93-7260, Dec. 29, 1995; Doe v. Maskell, Circuit Ct., Baltimore City, MD, No. 9423601/CL18756, May 5, 1995, *aff'd* Doe v. Maskell, 679 A.2d 1087 (Md. 1996), *cert. denied* 519 U.S. 1093 (1997); Engstrom v. Engstrom, Superior Ct., Los Angeles Co, Calif., No. VC016157, Oct. 11, 1995, *aff'd* Engstrom v. Engstrom, No. B098146 (Cal.App.2nd App. Dist., June 18, 1997) unpublished, *cert. denied;* Logerquist v. Danforth, Superior Ct., Maricopa Co., Arizona, No. CV 92-16309, June 11, 1998 following Logerquist v. Danforth, 932 P.2d 281 (Ariz. App. 1996); Mensch v. Pollard, Superior Ct., Whatcom Co., Washington, No. 93-2-01427-5, oral decision dated Sept. 9, 1998; State of New Hampshire v. Hungerford, 1995 WL 378571 (N.H.Super.), *aff'd* State v. Hungerford, 697 A.2d 916 (N.H. 1997).

71. State v. Walters, 698 A.2d 1244, 1246 (N.H. 1997).

72. See Faigman, D.L., et al (ed.) (1999) "Repressed Memories," Chapter 13 in Modern Scientific Evidence; The Law and Science of Expert Testimony. Volume 1. St. Paul, MN: West Group, pp. 112-155.

73. Engstrom v. Engstrom, No. B098146, Court of Appeal, 2nd App. Dist., California, June 18, 1997, unpublished opinion.

74. State v. Hungerford, 697 A.2d 916 (N.H. 1997).

ty. Following the hearing, the Superior Court held that the victims' testimony based on their recovered memories of the alleged assaults would not be admitted because neither the phenomenon of memory repression nor the techniques used to recover repressed memories had gained general acceptance in the field of psychology. The Court stated that "[T]estimony that is dependent upon recovery of repressed memory through therapy cannot be logically dissociated from the underlying scientific concept or technique of recovery."[75]

The New Hampshire Supreme Court affirmed, holding that the State's proposed expert testimony did not rise to a threshold level of reliability. The Court held that the lay testimony (of the complainants, describing their repressed memories) was inadmissible as well because the reliability of that testimony could not be separated from the validity of the phenomenon of repression.

The Court, drawing on comprehensive literature reviews by Drs. Harrison Pope and James Hudson, concluded that the studies cited in support of the theory of repression contained serious methodological problems that negate their conclusions.[76] The Court specified a stringent set of factors that would have to be met before testimony based on recovered repressed memories could be found reliable enough to be admissible, including the presence or absence of objective, verifiable evidence and the circumstances of the retrieval process.

Several appellate courts have held that a witness may not present her story based on recovered memories unless that testimony is accompanied by expert testimony.[77] Other appellate courts have ruled that the reliability and admissibility of the expert testimony is an issue that must be resolved at trial.[78] Many courts have determined, however, that the theoretical basis of the proposed expert opinion on recovered repressed memory renders it inadmissible.[79]

---

75. Id at 919.

76. Pope, H.G. and Hudson, J.I. (1995). Can memories of childhood sexual abuse be repressed? Psychological Medicine, 25:121-126. See also, Pope, H.G., Oliva, P.S. and Hudson, J.I. (1999). The scientific status of research on repressed memories. In Faigman, D.L., et al (Eds.) Modern Scientific Evidence; The Law and Science of Expert Testimony, Vol. 1, pp. 115-155; Pope, H.G., Hudson, J.I., Bodkin, J.A. & Oliva, P. (1998). Questionable validity of "dissociative amnesia" in trauma victims. British Journal of Psychiatry, 172:210-215.

77. See, e.g., State v. Hungerford, 697 A.2d 916 (N.H. 1997), in which the court said "The very concept of a "repressed" memory, that is, that a person can experience a traumatic event, and have no memory of it whatsoever for several years, transcends human experience...To argue that a jury could consider such a phenomenon, evaluate it and draw conclusions as to its accuracy or credibility, without the aid of expert testimony is disingenuous to say the least." See also Barrett v. Hyldburg, 487 S.E.2d 803 (N.C. App. 1997).

78. Olsen v. Hooley, 865 P.2d 1345 (Utah 1993); K.B. v. Evangelical Lutheran Church in America, 538 N.W.2d 152 (Minn. App. 1995).

79. See, e.g., Logerquist v. Danforth, Superior Ct., Maricopa Co., Arizona, No. CV 92-16309, June 11, 1998; Mensch v. Pollard, Superior Ct., Whatcom Co., Washington, No. 93-2-01427-5, oral decision dated Sept. 9, 1998.

Application of the Disability Exception

Historically, courts have permitted plaintiffs who alleged memory repression to employ the disability exception to the running of a statute of limitations only under very limited circumstances, such as where the plaintiff suffered from a legally recognized mental incompetency or insanity that rendered the plaintiff unable to manage her business affairs or to comprehend her legal rights. Nearly every one of the 91 appellate courts to consider the applicability of the disability exception to recovered memory cases has rejected it. The primary question, in cases where this issue was considered, was whether the alleged psychological condition reached the level of mental disability or incompetence sufficient to utilize this exception. A few appellate courts remanded the matter back to the trial court for a determination of whether the plaintiff could demonstrate that she was so disabled as to be unable to manage her business affairs at the time in question. As a general rule, the burden falls to the plaintiff to show legal disability sufficient to toll the statute of limitations, especially where plaintiff's claim of disability is challenged by defendant.[80]

Several courts have concluded that to permit unsupported allegations of memory repression to constitute legal disability or to allow a plaintiff to determine subjectively the point at which his or her emotional distress became disabling would have unacceptable ramifications.[81]

Some courts have held that neither an expert's affidavit "based on mere conjecture" nor Plaintiff's "self-diagnosis" are sufficient to meet that burden of proof, especially when the psychologically disabling symptoms are alleged to have developed years earlier.[82] In this regard, claims of having suffered from PTSD, depression, guilt, anxiety and other forms of emotional distress and of being incapable, as a result, of managing one's own affairs have generally been found insufficient to toll the statute of limitations.[83] Nor has a claim of psychological trauma, repression, suppression or denial, absent evidence of overall disability, generally been found sufficient to apply relevant

---

80. See, e.g., Anonymous v. Anonymous, 584 N.Y.S.2d 713 (N.Y. Sup. Ct. 1992); Casey v. Casey, 673 N.E.2d 210 (Ohio App. 1996); Hogle v. Harvey, 1995 Ohio App. LEXIS 4351, No. 94A0053, unreported; Horn v. Reese, 1995 WL 596065 (Ohio App. 1 Dist.); Peters v. Medaglia, 1989 WL 36709 (Ohio App. 8 Dist.), jurisdictional motion overruled by 545 N.E.2d 905 (Ohio 1989); Smith v. O'Connell, 997 F.Supp. 226 (D.R.I. 1998); Florez v. Sargeant, 917 P.2d 250 (Ariz. 1996); Teater v. State of Nebraska, 559 N.W.2d 758 (Neb. 1997).

81. See, for example, Travis v. Ziter, 681 So.2d 1348, 1355 (Ala. 1996).

82. See, e.g., Florez v. Sargeant, 917 P.2d 250 (Ariz. 1996); Moore v. Schiano, 690 N.E.2d 597 (Ohio App. 1996), *cert. denied* 678 N.E.2d 1230 (1997); Doe v. Rupp, 1998 WL 32774 (Ohio App. 8 Dist.), *cert. denied*, 694 N.E.2d 75 (1998); Detweiler v. Slavic, 1994 WL 706151 (Ohio App. 8 Dist. 1994), *cert. denied*, 649 N.E.2d 280 (Ohio 1995).

state disability clauses.[84]

MALPRACTICE LAWSUITS

Third Party Suits Brought By Families Who Say They Have Been Falsely Accused

Records show that suggestive therapy practices are involved in the development of most repressed memory claims. What recourse does an accused person have when he believes that false allegations are the result of suggestive intervention by a mental health professional? The FMSF is currently tracking over 150 malpractice claims against therapists in which this issue has been raised. While most of these third-party lawsuits allege malpractice or negligence, some allege other legal causes of action, including: defamation (libel or slander), intentional or negligent infliction of emotional distress, nuisance, breach of contract, abuse of process, invasion of privacy, and fraudulent misrepresentation.

Recovered memory therapy creates a special relationship between the therapist and the accused third party, who not only finds himself accused of a heinous crime, but may also face public denunciation, inside or outside of a courtroom, often undertaken for its supposed "therapeutic" value. The patient is typically encouraged to break off all communication with the accused third party, thus making it difficult, if not impossible, for the accused to address the true facts. The frequency with which therapists working in this area use certain suggestive techniques and recommend confronting the accused, "detaching" from family members and others who disbelieve the

---

83. See, e.g., Rigazio v. Archdiocese of Louisville, 853 S.W.2d 295 (Ky. App. 1993); Anonymous v. Anonymous, 584 N.Y.S.2d 713 (N.Y. Sup. Ct. 1992); Bassile v. Covenant House, 575 N.Y.S.2d 233 (N.Y. Sup. Ct. 1991), aff'd, 594 N.Y.S.2d 192 (N.Y.A.D. 1 Dept. 1993), *cert. denied*, 624 N.E.2d 177 (N.Y. 1993); Detweiler v. Slavic, 1994 WL 706151 (Ohio App. 8 Dist. 1994), *cert. denied*, 649 N.E.2d 280 (Ohio 1995); Florez v. Sargeant, 917 P.2d 250 (Ariz. 1996); Hildebrand v. Hildebrand, 736 F.Supp. 1512 (S.D. Ind. 1990); Hogle v. Harvey, 1995 Ohio App. LEXIS 4351, No. 94A0055, unreported; Lemmerman v. Fealk, 534 N.W.2d 695 (Mich. 1995); Meiers-Post v. Schafer, 427 N.W.2d 606 (Mich. App. 1988); Moore v. Schiano, 690 N.E.2d 597 (Ohio App. 1996), *cert. denied* 678 N.E.2d 1230 (1997); Overall v. Klotz, 846 F.Supp. 297 (1994), aff'd 52 F.3d 398 (2d Cir. 1995); Smith v. Smith, 830 F.2d 11 (2nd Cir. 1987); Travis v. Ziter, 681 So.2d 1348 (Ala. 1996).

84. See, e.g., Bock v. Harmon, 526 So.2d 292 (La. App. 1988), *cert. denied*, 531 So.2d 275 (La. 1988); Burpee v. Burpee, 578 N.Y.S.2d 359 (N.Y. Sup. Ct. 1991); Doe v Roe, 931 P.2d 1115 (Ariz. App. 1997), rev'd, 955 P.2d 951 (Ariz. 1998); E.W. v. D.C.H., 754 P.2d 817 (Mont. 1988), superseded by statute; Horn v. Reese, 1995 WL 596065 (Ohio App. 1 Dist.); McAfee v. Cole, 637 A.2d 463 (Me. 1994); Nicolette v. Carey, 751 F.Supp. 695 (W.D. Mich. 1990); Olsen v. Hooley, 865 P.2d 1345 (Utah 1993); Whatcott v. Whatcott, 790 P.2d 578 (Utah App. 1990); Swackhammer v. Widnall, 119 F.3d 7 (9th Cir.(Wash.) 1997); Gilp v. Neville, 681 N.E.2d 1173 (Ind. App. 1997); Doe v. Maskell, 679 A.2d 1087 (Md. App. 1996), *cert denied*, Roe v. Maskell, 519 U.S. 1093 (1997).

accusations, and suing the "perpetrator" has led many professional organizations, ethics panels, and clinicians to recommend new safeguards and standards of practice in therapeutic work with alleged trauma victims.[85] These groups agree that therapists who work in this sensitive area should have special training and knowledge and should take care to avoid the inappropriate use of leading questions, hypnosis, narcoanalysis, or other memory enhancement techniques directed at the production of hypothesized hidden or lost material. They also caution therapists that recovered memories, however emotionally intense and significant to the individual, do not necessarily reflect factual events and they encourage therapists to discuss this fact with their patients, especially if the patient intends to take action outside the therapeutic situation. Following these prudent safeguards should not make the therapy less effective or impose too great a burden on the therapist.

Clearly, a false allegation of criminal sexual molestation will directly and foreseeably endanger the accused person's reputation and cause him to suffer serious injury and damage. Given the potentially grave injury to a falsely accused individual, does the therapist have a duty to that person to avoid the use of suggestive techniques known to create false memories, to consider available information that contradicts the developing memories, and to avoid accepting the resulting images as true without external corroboration? Should the therapist who fails to do these things be held liable if a patient acts on false memories by filing civil or criminal charges? Should the therapist be held accountable to the accused if she "validates" allegations she knows to be of questionable truth to others or in court? These are among the questions raised in third-party suits. At the time of this writing, this area of law is still in its infancy. Nearly half of the third-party cases identified by the FMSF have not yet been resolved. In at least seven malpractice cases that are currently on appeal, the issue of whether a mental health professional owes a duty to the third party rests squarely before the court. The courts are expected to consider whether the foreseeability of the harm to the accused and the fact that the accused person was directly injured by the allegations that developed during therapy are sufficient to generate a duty. The courts will no doubt also consider such public policy issues as the need to balance the rights of abuse victims to seek legal redress with the rights of citizens to be protected from false criminal charges.

As of September 1998, the FMSF Legal Survey had identified 152 malpractice claims brought by a third party against a mental health care provider. Of these, 56 were brought by the parents of adult patients who, the parents allege, were led to believe, through negligent therapy practices, that they had been abused as children. The remaining 96 lawsuits were brought

---

85. See Freyd, this volume.

by accused parents of minor children. In many of these lawsuits, the parent claims that the child was led, through suggestive interview techniques, to make false allegations that resulted in criminal charges against the parent. In addition to these third-party suits, the FMSF Legal Survey contains records of over 50 related actions taken by the accused person. These include wrongful death lawsuits brought by accused family members after an adult child committed suicide while under the care of a therapist providing treatment for recovered memories, defamation actions against the accuser and/or her therapists, and other miscellaneous lawsuits.

Of the few third-party lawsuits that have gone to trial, nearly three-quarters ended in a jury verdict in favor of the injured third party. Some higher courts have held that under certain circumstances a therapist may owe a duty to a third party.[86] Other courts have dismissed these claims, holding that no duty is owed a third party or that the third-party claim was time-barred.[87, 88] A number of third-party claims filed by an accused parent of a minor child were dismissed when the court held that the therapist's actions were protected from liability by statutes that mandate the reporting of suspected child abuse. Other appellate courts have allowed such cases to go forward, holding that defendants' actions went beyond those protected by reporting in good faith.[89] These courts rejected a policy of blanket immunity for all therapists' actions and held that negligent or reckless actions that are independent of the reporting are subject to the same standards that apply to other members of society.

In the first third-party repressed memory lawsuit to go to trial, Gary Ramona successfully sued his daughter's therapists for implanting false memories of sexual abuse. (See discussion of Holly Ramona case, supra.) Following his daughter's accusations of sexual abuse, Mr. Ramona had suffered the breakdown of his marriage and family and the loss of his job. He also faced civil charges of child sexual abuse. The trial court recognized that, as a matter of public policy, the defendant therapists owed a legal duty of care not only to the patient but also to the patient's immediate family. In May 1994, the jury awarded Mr. Ramona a half million dollars and specifi-

---

86. See, e.g., Althaus v. Cohen, 710 A.2d 1147 (Pa. Super. 1998), cert. granted Oct. 27, 1998; Sawyer v. Midelfort, 579 N.W.2d 268 (Wis. App. 1998), cert. granted, 584 N.W.2d 122 (Wis. 1998); Tuman v. Genesis Assoc., 894 F.Supp. 183 (E.D. Pa. 1995); Sullivan v. Cheshier, 846 F.Supp. 654 (N.D. Ill. 1994).

87. See, e.g., Doe v. McKay, 700 N.E.2d 1018 (Ill. 1998); Flanders v. Cooper, 706 A.2d 589 (Me. 1998); Strom v. C.C., 1997 WL 118253 (Minn.App.), unpublished.

88. See, e.g., Glasspool v. Seltzer, Superior Court, Appellate Div., New Jersey, No. A-1662-95T5, unpublished; Lundgren v. Eastern Montana Community Mental Health Center, 1998 WL 208152 (Mont.).

89. See, e.g., James W. v. Superior Court (Goodfriend), 21 Cal. Rptr.2d 169 (Cal. App. 4th Dist. 1993); Wilkinson v. Balsam, 885 F.Supp. 651 (D. Vt. 1995); Montoya v. Bebensee, 761 P.2d 285 (Colo. App. 1988); Peterson v. Walentiny, 1995 U.S. Dist. LEXIS 4290, No. 93-C-399-K, unpublished; Caryl S. v. Child & Adolescent Treatment Services, Inc., 614 N.Y.S.2d 661 (N.Y. Sup. Ct. 1994); Byrnes v. Haynes-Seman, No. 93-CV-3125, Court of Appeals, Colo.

cally found that the defendants were negligent in providing health care to Holly Ramona and had implanted or reinforced false memories that her father had molested her as a child.[90]

A third-party claim against a Pennsylvania psychiatrist led ultimately to a jury award in 1994 of $272,232 in favor of the Althaus family against their daughter's therapist, Judith Cohen. The parents had claimed that Dr. Cohen, a psychiatrist, had encouraged their daughter to believe that she had been the victim of criminal acts. They also charged that Dr. Cohen had failed to challenge bizarre beliefs that their daughter developed as a result of dreams and of being in a trance-like state, and had failed to consider information that contradicted those developing beliefs. In April 1998, a Pennsylvania appellate court upheld the jury award and held that a duty was owed to the parents as well as the daughter.[91] The court noted that the psychiatrist had treated the daughter specifically for parental sexual abuse, that the parents were directly affected by the psychiatrist's negligent misdiagnosis and treatment when the daughter filed criminal charges against them, and that it was foreseeable that the parents would be harmed by the psychiatrist's negligence. The court said that the psychiatrist knew that at least some of the girl's allegations were untrue, but she nevertheless "validated...unwittingly false testimony" during and before the criminal proceedings. "Dr. Cohen became deeply enmeshed in the legal proceedings against the Althauses and, in doing so, placed herself in a role that extended well beyond the therapeutic treatment context," the majority wrote. "However, because she chose to take this active role, the Althauses, as alleged child abusers, had a reasonable expectation that Dr. Cohen's diagnosis of [their daughter] affecting them as it did, would be carefully made and would not be reached in a negligent manner."[92] The appellate decision has been appealed to the Pennsylvania Supreme Court.

Attorneys who defend these third-party claims often argue that any extension of a therapist's duty beyond the patient to a third party would be unreasonably burdensome because it would cause therapists to be overly concerned about the possible impact on some third party of their interactions with their patients. In addition, they argue that imposing a duty to a third party would have a chilling effect on the treatment and reporting of child abuse. The *Althaus* court disagreed, saying: "While we recognize that great social utility arises from allowing therapists to diagnose sexual abuse, no social utility can be derived from shielding therapists who make cavalier diagnoses that have profound detrimental effects on the lives of the accused and their family."[93] Other courts have been persuaded by these arguments,

---

90. *Ramona v. Isabella*, No. C61898, Superior Court, Napa Co., Calif.

91. *Althaus v. Cohen*, 710 A.2d 1147 (Pa. Super. 1998), cert. granted October 27, 1998.

92. Id at 1156.

however. The Illinois Supreme Court, in June 1998, dismissed a third-party malpractice claim brought by an accused father against his adult daughter's psychologist.[94] The majority expressed concern that to allow the action would improperly enlarge a therapist's duty of care and would be inconsistent with the duty of confidentiality to the patient. A strongly worded dissent noted that the plaintiff was a relative of the patient who accused him of sexual abuse and that the therapist had specifically arranged to have him join the patient's therapy sessions, which he did with the patient's consent. Under these circumstances, the dissent felt, divulging the patients records would not compromise confidentiality. The dissent foresaw no adverse consequences from placing a duty on the therapist in a case such as this, where the damage to the accused father was foreseeable, the likelihood of injury was great, and the burden of guarding against that injury was slight.

One common hurdle that faces plaintiffs in third-party lawsuits is the problem of gaining access to the patient's therapy records. In some cases, therapy records were disclosed as part of a lawsuit filed by the patient against the person(s) she accused of abuse. A few third-party claims have been filed as cross-complaints; if the original repressed memory lawsuit was dropped,the cross-complaint was generally dropped or dismissed at the same time.

In a case filed in Wisconsin, the parents of a young woman discovered the role that therapy had played in the development of their adult daughter's false allegations of sexual abuse only after the daughter died and the mother, who became administrator of the daughter's estate, was able to obtain the daughter's therapy records. In March 1998, a Wisconsin appeals court refused to dismiss the parents' claim against the therapist, saying that the injury was both direct and foreseeable and that to allow recovery by a third party for psychological harm due to negligence would not put too great a burden on the therapist.[95] The defendant therapist argued that she had no duty to determine the truth of what her patient was saying, but the court held that the therapist did have a duty to ensure that her therapy did not cause foreseeable harm to others. This ruling has been appealed to the Wisconsin Supreme Court.

---

93. *Id.* at 1157.

94. Doe v. McKay, 700 N.E.2d 1018 (Ill. 1998).

95. Sawyer v. Midelfort, 579 N.W.2d 268 (Wis. App. 1998), *cert. granted,* 584 N.W.2d 122 (Wis. 1998).

Malpractice Suits Against Therapists Brought by Their Former Patients

The FMS Foundation has also collected information on malpractice lawsuits filed by former patients who claim that suggestive techniques used by their mental health care providers led to the development of false memories. Court records from these cases show that serious, long-lasting injury resulted from improper therapy that led patients to believe, erroneously, in a horrifying personal history of sexual abuse. The complaints in these cases detail a potent combination of therapist suggestion, exposure to "survivor" books and films, use of questionable techniques such as hypnosis and guided imagery, isolation from family and friends, and a heavy reliance on medications, all of which may work together to increase the risk of suggestibility in an already vulnerable patient.

The facts of these cases seem to fall into a relatively uniform pattern of events. Typically, the individual seeks help for a relatively benign condition such as depression, an eating disorder, or difficulty in a relationship. Often the individual has no memory of any sexual abuse in her past, although in some cases she has a memory of isolated abusive incidents. The therapist may voice suspicions that the individual's symptoms suggest a history of child sexual abuse. Through the use of symptom "checklists," nonpathological aspects of a normal personality may become distorted and be seen as symptoms of something deeper. The therapist may tell the patient that her symptoms are too severe to be attributed only to the patient's current life difficulties, and that the patient should explore her past. After being led to imagine horrifying acts of rape and incest, the patient, not unexpectedly, is overcome by feelings of revulsion and degradation. Many patients are encouraged to view these feelings as a response to real memories of actual events–not just imaginings. Any doubts the patient may voice are often treated as an indication that the patient is "in denial" and is not yet ready to accept the images as truth or is still under the control of the alleged abuser.

If, in addition, the therapy includes sessions of hypnosis and hypnosis-like procedures, both of which are known to increase a person's susceptibility to suggestion, the stage is set for the development of false memories. Many court records describe, in addition to the use of hypnosis, the administration of high levels of antidepressants and other drugs to the patient. Most patients were encouraged to cut off contact with family members. Some were hospitalized for long periods in units for patients with dissociative disorders. Some were instructed to "detach" from all contacts outside the therapy group.

The techniques cited in many complaints are quite similar to the practices described in a recent U.S. Grand Jury Indictment as those commonly associated with mind control and brainwashing.[96] Several professional organizations have warned that hypnosis and related techniques, such as guided imagery, meditation, visualization, trance work, relaxation techniques, age regression, sodium amytal interviews, journaling, and "inner child" work, may lead to increased suggestibility and confabulation, memory hardening, source amnesia, and a loss of critical judgment. It has long been understood that these techniques do not enhance the accuracy of recall; instead they may render a person overconfident of the memories retrieved, whether or not they are accurate. Most professional organizations, ethics panels, and clinicians have called on therapists to recognize the dangers in certain suggestive techniques and to avoid using them.

Despite the fact that obtaining informed consent has long been an accepted part of rendering proper care, nearly every complaint charges the defendant therapist with failing to inform the patient that the techniques used are capable of generating false memories or that the diagnosis of MPD is controversial. The patient therefore lacks information necessary to give an informed consent to the treatment or to consider an alternative form of therapy.

As in most malpractice cases, the complaint usually states that the defendant therapist failed to meet the appropriate standard of care. The specific allegation may be that the therapist failed to treat the patient's presenting problem, failed to accurately diagnose or develop and document an appropriate treatment plan, and/or failed to correct the treatment program despite clear evidence of the patient's deteriorating clinical status. Evidence of just such tragic circumstances was documented in a malpractice suit filed by Laura Deck against her former therapist in January 1994, King County Superior Court, Washington State and settled in April, 1995.[97] Pretherapy personality testing (MMPI) showed all scales to be within normal limits, with nothing to suggest that Ms. Deck had been the victim of childhood sexual abuse. When the test was administered after Ms. Deck underwent the therapy that led her to believe she had been horribly sexually abused by trusted family members, the scales were elevated beyond normal limits, suggesting that Ms. Deck had undergone severe trauma since the first test was administered. According to experts who evaluated the test results, if the therapist induced Ms. Deck to believe that she had been violently raped by a family member and had been a victim of satanic ritual abuse, even if these things had not actually happened, the trauma of believing that they had occurred would probably be sufficient to produce the changes observed in Ms. Deck's

---

96. United States of America v. Peterson, et al., U.S. Dist. Ct., Southern Dist., Texas, No. H-97-237.

97. The FMS Foundation has been asked not to publish additional identifying information about this case in order to protect Ms. Deck from being accused of breaching the confidentiality clause of the settlement agreement with her former therapist. Court filings with the defendants' names deleted are available from the Foundation, however.

MMPI profile.

Psychiatric malpractice claims in which patients allege that therapists negligently implanted or encouraged the development of false memories of childhood abuse are a recent phenomenon. The first such lawsuit was resolved in 1993.[98] At that time, no state professional ethical review board had yet investigated a claim involving the improper use of memory recovery techniques. Since 1993 the number of new claims has grown steadily. As of October 1998, the FMSF Legal Survey contained information on 139 malpractice suits brought by former patients. Of these 139 claims, eleven have gone to trial. Nine of the eleven ended in a verdict in favor of the plaintiff. In the remaining two cases, the jury found in favor of the defendant therapist. Additional cases were resolved when two lawsuits were dismissed, two were voluntarily dropped by the plaintiff, and fifty-six were settled out of court. Sixty-seven lawsuits are still ongoing. More lawsuits of this kind may be filed as the standard of care in this area becomes more widely known through the publication of statements by professional organizations, the results of investigations by state regulatory agencies, and the outcomes of malpractice litigation.[99]

The overwhelming majority of these malpractice lawsuits were resolved by being settled out of court, many on the eve of a scheduled trial. A few settled during trial after the plaintiff presented her case. The settlements and awards in these cases have been for staggering amounts. One recent case ended when a $10.6 million settlement was finalized on the very day trial was scheduled to begin.[100] Most agreements stipulated that the amount of the settlement must be kept confidential, but a partial list of recent cases for which the amount was published is given below.

The majority of malpractice claimants in this survey (84/139) were diagnosed as having multiple personality disorder (MPD) caused by supposed sexual or ritual abuse. Records confirm that nearly 80 percent (66/84) of those diagnosed with MPD were treated with hypnosis or sodium amytal. The MPD patients were often given strong medications, particularly benzodiazepines, such as Valium, Halcion, and Xanax. Most stated they were told to read highly disturbing books, including *Sybil* and *The Courage to Heal*.

---

98. As part of the settlement agreement, the plaintiff, Laura Pasley, agreed not to disclose the name of the defendant therapist. The complaint is available from the FMS Foundation.

99. At the time of this writing, an additional 70 individuals had informed the FMSF that they were consulting attorneys about a possible cause of action against their former therapists for improperly using suggestive techniques, resulting in the implantation of false memories. FMSF surveys of affected families show that the number of reconciliations within families is increasing, which suggests that more and more former accusers are coming to believe that their recovered memories are false.

100. Burgus v. Braun, Circuit Ct., Cook Co., Ill. No. 91L08493.

Althaus v. Cohen, Court. of Common Pleas, Allegheny Co., Penn., No. GD92020893.
In 1994, jury awarded $272,232 to 17 year old girl and her parents. In 12/96 trial judge affirmed jury decision in strongly worded ruling, noting that as girl's charges became "progressively more outlandish," the stories were never challenged, in fact, the therapist refused input from parents. "Expert testimony demonstrates overwhelmingly that Cohen deviated from that standard [of care]." The girl entered therapy when her mother became seriously ill. Criminal charges of childhood sexual and ritual abuse against parents were filed, but later dropped. Affirmed, *Althaus v. Cohen,* 1998 Pa. Super. LEXIS 63 1.

Hamanne v. Humenansky, U.S. Dist. Ct., 2nd Dist., Minn., No. C4-94-203.
In 1995, jury awarded over $2.46 million to woman after finding psychiatrist negligently failed to meet recognized standards and directly caused injury. Woman sought treatment for anxiety after a move, but was diagnosed MPD, childhood sexual and ritual abuse despite contrary evaluations and lack of memories of abuse. Treatment included hypnosis, guided imagery, sodium amytal, anti-depressants, lengthy hospitalizations. No informed consent. Also awarded $200,000 to husband for loss of consortium.

Halbrooks v. Moore, Dist. Ct., Dallas Co., Tex., No. 92-11849.
In 1995, jury found therapist guilty of negligence and that his actions were proximate cause of damage to his former client. Awarded $105,000 and attributed 60% negligence to defendant therapist. Woman had sought treatment for recurring depression and familial conflicts, but claims therapy caused her to have false memories of childhood sexual and ritual abuse and to be mis-diagnosed MPD. The treating hospital settled prior to trial for nearly $50,000.

Carlson v. Humenansky, Dist. Ct., 2nd Dist., Minn., No. CX-93-7260.
In 1996, unanimous jury verdict found that psychiatrist failed to meet recognized medical standards and directly caused injury. Awarded $2.5 million. Woman had entered therapy for depression and marital problems, but claims therapy caused her to develop false memories of childhood sexual and ritual abuse. Treatment included sodium amytal, guided imagery, hypnosis.

Carl v. Keraga, U.S. Federal Ct., Southern Dist., Tex., Case No. H-95-66 1.
In 1997, jury found remaining defendant 24% liable (individually and through her corporation) for injury to patient. Awarded $5.8 million. Several jurors said they were concerned about failure to warn of the risks of treatment. Woman claims she was mis-diagnosed MPD and told she had over 500 personalities to cope with childhood abuse, ritual murder, cannibalism and torture. She was instructed to report herself to the police as a child molester, even though she had no memory of ever abusing her own children. Her teenage children were also hypnotized and told they were victims of a cult. All but 2 of other 25 defendants settled out of court prior to trial.

Figure 7-9. TRIAL OUTCOMES

Mark v. Zulli, et. al., Superior Ct., San Luis Obispo Co., Cal., No. CV075386.
In 1995, a settlement was reached with the primary therapist who treated a woman who suffered from unexplained chest pains after witnessing a serious accident. The therapist told her the chest pains were body memories of childhood sexual and ritual abuse. The therapy included hypnosis and relied on *The Courage to Heal.* Eventually the woman was diagnosed with MPD with 400 personalities. The primary therapist had no insurance and settled for $157,000.

Fultz v. Carr and Walker, Circuit Ct., Multnomah Co., Oregon, No. 9506-04080.
In 1996, two treating therapists settled out of court, one for $ 1.57 million, the other for a confidential amount. Patient had sought help for mild depression and weight problems, but she claims the therapists misdiagnosed childhood sexual and ritual abuse and MPD. Her preschool children were also treated and persuaded they were abused by a cult. The treating therapist assisted in obtaining a restraining order against patient's parents and siblings.

Rutherford v. Strand, et al, Circuit Ct., Green Co. Missouri, No. 1960C2745.
In 1996, a church in Missouri agreed to pay $1 million to a woman and her family who said that under the guidance of a church counselor, the woman came to believe that her father had raped her, got her pregnant and performed a coat-hanger abortion – when in fact, she was still a virgin and her father had had a vasectomy.

Cool v. Olson, Circuit Ct., Outagamie Co., Wisc. No. 94CV707.
In 1997, after 15 days of courtroom testimony, defendant agreed to settle for $2.4 million. Testimony described how psychiatrist induced horrific false memories of childhood sexual and ritual abuse, including demonic possession and misdiagnosed MPD. Therapy techniques included hypnosis, age regression, exorcism and drugs which caused hallucinations. The patient had originally entered therapy for bulimia and help after a traumatic event had befallen family.

Burgus v. Braun, Rush Presbyterian, Circuit Ct., Cook Co., Ill., No. 9 1 L08493/93L 14050.
In 1997, on the day scheduled for trial, a $10.6 million settlement was finalized. The patient originally sought treatment for post-parturm depression but was diagnosed MPD as result of supposed childhood sexual and ritual abuse including cannibalism, torture. She claims psychiatrist utilized suggestive techniques, but failed to obtain informed consent. Her preschool age children were also hospitalized, diagnosed MPD and treated for SRA.

Figure 7-10. SETTLEMENT OUTCOMES.

Although Multiple Personality Disorder is found in the standard psychiatric diagnostic manual, the DSM-IV, under the heading "dissociative identity disorder," many critics of the diagnosis believe that it is primarily a condition created by therapy. Several reviews have shown that until the mid-1980's the condition was very rare, with only about 200 cases appearing in the medical literature prior to that time. During the past decade, however, tens of thousands of people–almost exclusively women, and almost all of them in the United States–have been declared to be suffering from MPD.

Few studies examining the effectiveness of MPD treatments have appeared in peer-reviewed journals. A review of the MPD cases in the FMS Legal Survey shows that most plaintiffs had no psychiatric history prior to the repressed memory therapy. After beginning the course of treatment, many were hospitalized in psychiatric wards, some for as long as two years at a time. Nearly half (40/84) sued the hospital where they had been hospitalized during their treatment program. Nearly half (36/84) indicated that they had either attempted suicide or had cut or mutilated their bodies because of their horror at the emerging images of abuse. Of the complaints that recorded the number of years in therapy, most indicated treatment lasting between 3 and 7 years. Several plaintiffs had been in therapy for 10 or more years. Some individuals were even encouraged to hospitalize their young children. They were made to fear that the children were at risk from a ritualistic cult and that they might show signs of MPD.

Despite suffering serious psychological injury, many plaintiffs did not file lawsuits until some time after they left therapy or changed therapists. They say they were unaware of the source of their injury at the time it occurred. In addition to being advised by their therapist that they "must get worse before they can get better," many were instructed to relive the abusive images again and again. The plaintiff may assert that the negligent treatment rendered her temporarily unable to understand the harm done, thus placing her under a legal disability, or the plaintiff may state that she quite naturally relied on the therapist, but that the therapist fraudulently concealed information that the treatment was in fact improper.

There are few published opinions on the statute of limitations question as it pertains to these claims. A U.S. District Court in Pennsylvania has twice rejected defense motions to dismiss a malpractice claim as time-barred, saying that the nature of the injury could render the patient unable to distinguish between true and false memories, so that the patient "may have assumed her psychiatrist was providing proper treatment and may not have become suspicious" until some time after the treatment ended.[101] A U.S. District Court in Illinois refused to dismiss a malpractice suit as time-barred, saying the defendants' arguments were contradictory: "On one hand, [defendants] assert that [their patient] was mentally competent and able to understand her rights and her cause of action, while on the other, they maintain that [their patient's] mental condition was serious enough that it required that she be hospitalized, medicated and psychologically treated for four years of her

---

101. Lujan v. Mansmann, et al, 956 F. Supp. 1218, 1226 (E.D. Pa. 1997); Lujan v. Mansmann, et al, 1997 WL 634499 (E.D.Pa.).

life."[102]

In 1998, a Georgia appellate panel refused to allow a psychiatric malpractice claim any extension of the statute of limitations.[103] The panel did not consider the special factors that may block a patient's ability to think critically about her treatment or to challenge a therapist about the treatment rationale and approach. They found that the plaintiff's injury occurred at the time of the misdiagnosis and said the clock should begin to run at that time. They said that "plaintiff knew the facts of her past," but chose to believe her therapists' opinion and allow treatment to continue. Though plaintiff later came to believe their opinion was wrong, both of her views "were based upon the same knowledge in her possession, but were interpreted in different ways."[104]

Although most of the primary care providers in these cases appear to be therapists with a masters degree or less, the defendants range from psychiatrists to therapists with no more than a high school diploma and include psychologists, social workers, marriage and family counselors, nurses, physician assistants, Christian counselors, and miscellaneous therapists. Some therapists worked in private practice, but others were affiliated with an institution. Two universities were sued for improper supervision of university-run student health clinics where two undergraduate students say therapists led them to falsely accuse their parents of childhood sexual abuse.

In addition to raising the statute of limitations defense, some defendants have argued that their treatment simply responded to what their patients reported to them; they were doing the best they could with a patient who was already disturbed. Malpractice attorneys have pointed out that all mental health patients enter therapy for a reason, whether it is depression, marital problems, or something else. They argue that because individuals enter therapy in a vulnerable state, ready to rely on the advice and treatment given by their therapists, therapists must be held to a high standard of care.

Some defendants have testified that they did not know whether abuse of the type described by their patients existed; they say they are not detectives and have no responsibility to check the accuracy of the emerging images. This approach has been rightly criticized. At best, failing to model critical thinking or reality checking to a patient can delay a patient's improvement. At worst, encouraging a patient to act on a false and injurious history leads directly and foreseeably to injury to the patient and the patient's family.

Some courts may attribute a degree of contributory negligence to the

---

102. Shanley v. Braun, 1997 WL 779112 (N.D.Ill.), Memorandum Opinion and Order dated Dec. 10, 1997 at 24.

103. Charter Peachford Behavioral Health System, Inc. v. Kohout, 504 S.E.2d 514 (Ga. App. 1998), cert. denied November 20, 1998.

104. Charter Peachford Behavioral Health System, Inc. v. Kohout, 504 S.E.2d 514, 521 (Ga. App. 1998), cert. denied November 20, 1998.

patient, but other courts have rejected that notion. For example, a Pennsylvania trial court judge in a detailed posttrial ruling, affirmed a jury verdict and specifically rejected defense claims that the patient or her parents had significantly contributed to her injuries.[105] The judge concluded that it is precisely because of the patient's presenting psychological problems that her representations to her treating therapist cannot be seen as contributory negligence.

In addition to a medical malpractice or negligence cause of action, many claimants have also alleged breach of contract, fraud, deceptive trade practice, intentional or negligent infliction of emotional distress, and in some cases, where the therapist engaged in inappropriate contact, assault and battery. When other family members joined the former patient's lawsuit, additional charges of loss of consortium or defamation were often added. The charges of fraud made in 11 of the malpractice suits that have been resolved involved charges of improper billing and/or misstating the immediacy or severity of the patient's symptoms in order to continue receiving insurance payments. These claimants also allege the defendant therapist deliberately concealed the controversial nature of the treatment and its potential hazards.

In October 1997, a federal grand jury brought what are believed to be the first criminal charges in a case involving the negligent development of false memories.[106] The 61-count criminal indictment charged that a hospital administrator and four therapists conspired to collect millions of dollars in fraudulent insurance payments by exaggerating patients' diagnoses and inducing false memories of being part of a satanic cult. The criminal trial began in September 1998. A mistrial was declared early in January, 1999, after five members of the jury panel had been dismissed for various reasons, leaving only eleven jurors to hear the case. Defense attorneys objected to proceeding with less than twelve jurors.[107] As of this writing several psychiatrists in other states are facing disciplinary actions, including the loss of their licenses to practice, for engaging in negligent practices that allegedly caused patients to develop false memories of terrible abuse.

SUMMARY

A little over a decade ago, repressed memory lawsuits first appeared in the courts. Initially, legislatures in many states opened the courthouse doors to these claims by extending the statutes of limitations, but courts soon came to

---

105. Althaus v. Cohen, Ct. of Common Pleas, Allegheny Co., PA, No. GD92020893.

106. United States of America v. Judith A. Peterson, et al, Crim. No. H-97-237, U.S. Dist. Ct. So. Dist. Texas, Houston Div.

107. Personal communication, Peter Freyd, February 10, 1999.

recognize the significant evidentiary problems inherent in these cases. As of this writing, the number of new filings has declined sharply and most recovered memory lawsuits are being dismissed. Courts have become increasingly skeptical of repressed memory claims and increasingly cautious in dealing with the troublesome evidentiary issues that these claims present. In recent years, responsible professionals have urged caution in the use of suggestive therapy techniques. Former patients and their families have begun to file malpractice suits against therapists, charging them with creating false memories of abuse by the misuse of such techniques. More and more courts are recognizing that a therapist owes a duty, not only to the patient, but to a third party who has been wrongfully accused of abuse on the basis of false memories implanted in a patient during suggestive therapy. As this chapter was being completed, the New Hampshire Supreme Court recognized just such a duty in *Hungerford v. Jones.*[108] The duty, said the Court, arises from the foreseeable injury that the false memories will inflict on the person accused and on society's efforts to identify and eradicate true sexual abuse.

As courts apply increasingly stringent standards to evidence offered in support of claims of abuse based on memories recovered in therapy, one may expect that the more implausible and bizarre claims will be dismissed and only meritorious claims will be brought to trial or settled. Greater judicial scrutiny of these claims will, one hopes, inspire the mental health professions to adopt higher standards of education and training and more explicit ethical guidelines that will reduce to a minimum the questionable therapy practices that gave rise to these claims.

---

108. Hungerford v. Jones 722 A.2d 478 (N.H. 1998).

INDEX